Tales From A Briefcase

Robert James

Swanstone Wynot

Tales From A Briefcase
Robert James

Copyright © 2005 Robert James

All rights reserved. No part of this publication may be reproduced, stored in a retrieval system or transmitted in any form or by any means, electronic, mechanical, audio, visual or otherwise, without prior written permission of the copyright owner. Nor can it be circulated in any form of binding or cover other than that in which it is published and without similar conditions including this condition being imposed on the subsequent purchaser.

The events described in this book actually occurred, although the identities of the individuals and companies involved have been disguised. Any resemblance to actual persons, living or dead, or to actual business establishments, is therefore entirely coincidental.

ISBN 0-9768447-6-1

Cover by Tin Racer Design

Book design and typesetting by Robinson Associates

Published by
WYNOT BOOKS
A Division of Swanstone Wynot
Suite 1009, 4607 Cypresswood Drive,
Spring, Texas, 77379, USA
www.swanstonewynot.com

PROLOGUE

Six years after entering the army, including three years spent fighting in the Korean War and the Malayan Emergency, Robert James narrowly missed gaining a services place at Cambridge University; he had simply been too long away from the academic scene and too much had happened in the military campaigns to destabilise his emotional makeup. He decided on a change of career.

On hearing of his son's intention to leave the army, go to London, work in a factory and study at night school, Robert's father, an ex-regular soldier, banished him from the family. "You'll never make it in Civvy Street. You were born and bred for a career as an officer in the army. You'll never make it in industry – and what do you want a degree for anyway? I didn't need one! Get out of my house and my sight."

Stung by such harsh words, Robert resolved to show his father how wrong he was: he would rise to the top of the industrial ladder and progress further in civilian life than he would have done in the army. Proving his father wrong would be his sole motivation for the immediate future. It would be a tough journey, starting again from the bottom in another career. His army experience would count for little in civilian life, and he would miss the comradeship of the army, the comforts of the officers' mess and the clearly-mapped path of soldiering.

A farmer friend needed some summer help and Robert took a job as a farmhand until something suitable in London appeared. Working on the land, tending the animals and enjoying the open-air life, would help him to take a first step on his new journey. It would give him some clues as to how he should fit into this new environment as an 'ordinary, normal person', because, somehow, he felt different to the others about him. Even now, the army still haunted him with a dream: the one where he was face-to-face with the Chinese soldier, clutching a jammed rifle, waiting for the enemy's bullet to finish it all. And some nights he would wake with a high temperature as the malaria, caught in the Malayan jungle, revisited him and emphasised his nightmares.

Robert at first viewed going to work in the capital, without family support and completely alone, with some misgiving. However, he would never let feeling lonely and being a little afraid swamp his determination to prove his father wrong. In London, he found a job in a factory in Hammersmith, digs in Fulham and a night school in Islington, and set about fulfilling the destiny that he had appointed for himself.

Throughout his business life, a briefcase was constantly at Robert James' side. Initially it carried sandwiches, a newspaper and university books and papers. More latterly, it contained briefings and notes on meetings, itineraries, passports, airline tickets, and a calculator. It became his civilian equivalent of his old army kitbag. Like his much-travelled kitbag, by the time he retired his briefcase had a wealth of stories to tell.*

* See *Tales From A Kitbag,* Robert James, 2004

CONTENTS

BOOK 1   BECOMING A CIVILIAN

Chapter	*Page*
1 To Be A Farmer's boy	2
2 Mushrooms And Wet Knickers	6
3 A Verbal Warning	12
4 Starting Up The Ladder	21
5 Horticulture In Sussex	25
6 Which Foot Do You Dig With?	30

BOOK 2   MOVING INTO MANAGEMENT

Chapter	*Page*
7 Aggie	36
8 The Factory Nurse	49
9 She Never Came Back!	53
10 Diamond John	58
11 The Commissar	66
12 A Fine Old English Company	71
13 An East African Adventure	77

Continued...

CONTENTS...

Chapter		Page
14	The Sunset Scavengers	90
15	Hot Air & Cutting Grass	95
16	I Left My Heart In …	101
17	A Factory In Slough	113

BOOK 3   AT THE CHAIRMAN'S BEHEST

Chapter		Page
18	The Chairman	122
19	A Saharan Emergency	127
20	I've No Bloody Legs!	149
21	A Nigerian Adventure	154
22	A Swim In The Caribbean	163
23	Shut Down Our Japanese Operation	175
24	A Day At The Races	181
25	Escape From Iran	188
26	Contrasts Of India	194
27	A World Of Printing	199
28	The Cancelled Order	204

CONTENTS...

Chapter	*Page*
29 City Of Steel	214
30 A Lancashire Interlude	219
31 Up A Welsh Valley	224

BOOK 4   TALES FROM CONSULTANCY

Chapter	*Page*
32 Bull's Sperm & Harbourmasters	238
33 The Bikers Café In Brighton	244
34 Hats, Wrapping & Vending Machines	252
35 Free Newspapers & Concrete Plans	261
36 Welsh Matters	266
37 Videos, Data Processing & Jumbo Jets	275
38 Business Adventures With Peter	291
Epilogue	295

BOOK 1
BECOMING A CIVILIAN

CHAPTER 1

TO BE A FARMER'S BOY

Malvern, Autumn 1955

She turned her head to look me straight in the eye. Her big brown eyes were open wide and a large expanse of white eyeball signalled she was afraid of me. I was probably more frightened of her but I gathered up my courage and stroked her face.

"It's alright, Lulu. I won't hurt you. You know more about this than I do. You'll have to help me."

She responded with another baleful look of those eyes. I couldn't tell if she was contemptuous of what I was doing to her or just impatient to get the business over.

Lulu was one of Farmer Tom's herd of Herefords who were milked twice a day. Some were milked by hand but most stood quietly in a stall whilst the machine noisily sucked the milk away to the collecting vats.

Apparently Lulu was an older cow who needed to be started with hand-milking before being coupled up to the machine.

"Just talk to her like a lady," Tom had said, "but don't get behind her. She has a fierce kick!"

I took his advice but my voice quavered with fear as I approached her very gingerly with my stool and two pails, one containing lukewarm water to wash down her under-parts and the other to collect the milk.

Tom had shown me the drill. "Keep talking to her. Place your stool by her flank so that, when you sit down, you can rest your head on her back quarter. Using clean water, wash her udder and teats. Then clean down her backside, back legs and tail. Then grab a teat in each hand between first finger and thumb and pull down, right hand then left. The milk should squirt out with each pull. Keep going until the udder is partially emptied, like this."

Tales From A Briefcase

He had prodded the udder to make it wobble and show that it was not as distended as before.

It had sounded simple when he had explained the process, but Lulu was a cow weighing nearly half a ton and I was not at all certain that she was friendly. She knew Tom, but I was a newcomer and inexperienced in touching her intimate parts. I had been a farmer's boy for just one week.

Tom, having lost two of his farm hands to national service, had asked me if I could help out on his farm in the summer. I took the job, feeling that going back to the land would be a good place to start my new life. The farm sat at the foot of the Malvern Hills. Later, I walked those hills, looking down over the town of Malvern with its Georgian buildings, the nearby village of Hanley Swan and the distant River Severn, and marvelled at the countryside. With the hill wind in my hair, I could close my eyes and almost hear music from the festival choirs of the three cities of the area – the glorious music of Elgar.

Sitting on the stool and having done the washing bit, I blew on my hands to warm them. Lulu stamped her feet, probably, I thought, displaying impatience. I grabbed two of her teats and pulled. The warm milk flowed into the empty bucket with a tinny sound. Lulu settled down to munch feed from the trough in front of her. I poked her udder, got the right amount of wobble and connected the four suckers to her teats and switched on the milking machine. The suckers danced crazily as they extracted milk in gulps which were carried in clear, flexible, plastic pipes to the vat at the end of the milking shed. Her udder eventually drastically reduced in size and it was clear that there was little more milk to come.

"Have you finished, old girl?" I asked timorously, patting her neck.

She responded by mooing. I disconnected the machine and, of her own accord, she backed out of the stall and trundled down the yard to where the other cows were gathering to walk back to the pasture.

My life was now structured around the cows: the walk to and from the pastures; the twice-daily milking and machine cleaning routines. The day started at six in the morning with hastily gulped tea in the farmhouse kitchen. After morning milking, there would be a big fried breakfast cooked by the farmer's wife, Jane.

There always seemed to be jobs to be done on the farm: hedging and ditching, repairing the farm buildings. At midday, Jane would bring doorstep sandwiches and a thermos of tea and a bottle of brown ale to the place where we were working.

As July turned into August, the wheat ripened to that familiar golden hue and we brought the machines out of store and greased them for the long days of harvesting ahead. I learned to drive a tractor and to be patient with the walking pace needed for most of the farm jobs. Cutting and binding a field of wheat required more concentration than I expected. The cutting lines had to be straight and the turning circle, at the end of the swathe, planned and precise.

From time to time the machine got blocked and had to be cleared. Twine balls had to be replaced and a wary eye kept for untied sheaves. Whilst absolutely humdrum, wheat cutting never became monotonous. Rabbits and grouse often suddenly appeared, and sometimes Tom would be ready for them with his shotgun. There was no time to moon about the past, my lost career, my unfaithful fiancée and my father's rejection of my leaving the army.

After this, I planned to go to London, to start again at the bottom and work my way up. I'd show my father that I could succeed in civilian life. But right now, I was content to be 'a farmer's boy'.

After the wheat cutting came the stooking, normally a job for two, each grabbing a pair of sheaves and thrusting them together with his partner's into a near-vertical stack. Some days later, hopefully after a dry, windy spell, the sheaves were collected with a tractor and cart and taken to the farmyard. The threshing machine was coupled up to the pulley of a tractor and the sheaves were thrown onto its conveyor where they were consumed by the noisy, shaking mechanism, separating out grain from the straw. The wheat grain was bagged and the straw re-bundled into sheaves. Using pitchforks, we placed each bundle carefully and systematically on the rick, which grew sturdily upwards until it reached its prescribed height and was then tied down and thatched.

Tales From A Briefcase

September came and I was despatched to the orchards with ladder and a sack to pick apples and pears and, later, to the fields to dig potatoes and root crops.

I was now fit and strong and enjoying my outdoor life. The autumn dusk came earlier and I spent the longer dark evenings eating Jane's wonderful suppers, reading books in front of big log fires and going to bed thoroughly tired but happy. Tom and I had become great friends, despite our different backgrounds. He and Jane had not been able to have children but they loved their animals and accepted farm hands as their extended family.

The expected letter eventually came, enquiring if I was still interested in the factory job in London and asking when would I be able to start. Talking it over with Tom and Jane, I decided to leave the farm at the end of October. When the time came, I said my goodbyes to Lulu with a last milking.

Tom and Jane had friends who had rooms to let in Fulham, not far from the factory in Hammersmith, so now I had both a job and digs. Expressing my grateful thanks for my hosts' hospitality and the chance to metamorphose in their farm environment, I trudged down the muddy farm lane with my large suitcase to the bus stop on the main road, on the first stage of my journey to London. With much misgiving, I looked back along the lane to the farmhouse which had been my home and refuge for the past three months, the place where I had turned my back on the army, and then I squared my shoulders to the thought of living in London. I took the bus to Malvern station and caught the train to Paddington. From there, a tube train took me to Baron's Court and a short walk led me to Normand Gardens and the terraced house which was to be my home for the next two years.

CHAPTER 2

MUSHROOMS AND WET KNICKERS

Fulham W14

A short, black-haired, Jewish-looking lady answered my knock on the door. I introduced myself.

"Hello, we meet at last. I'm Anita and this is my husband, Jan. I'm South African and Jan is Polish." Jan, a rather nondescript, taciturn man, was standing in the kitchen doorway. We shook hands.

Anita asked, "How are Tom and Jane? They said some nice things about you."

"I left them in good health, but very short-handed on the farm."

"Let me show you to you room," invited Anita, and we climbed the stairs to the front bedroom.

"This is our nicest room. It has a lovely view of the houses and trees on the other side of the street. It's only five pounds a week with supper thrown in."

I looked at her and thought she must be a typical West London landlady – foreign and out to maximise the rent. True, the room was newly decorated and bright with light streaming in through the large bay window. And, after all, the digs were just down the road from the factory where I was going to work.

"I have two other nice young gentlemen living here, on this floor. Hugh is a trainee hairdresser with that TV chappie. Charlie, the other, is an apprentice engineer on the underground. You'll like them. This is your bathroom and toilet, but at night you'll have to share it with them because my husband and I can't have them using our facilities downstairs. By the way, no visitors after ten o'clock."

I opened my mouth to protest. Her letter had clearly stated 'bed-sit with own bathroom and toilet', but on reflection I decided not to complain and to accept the room.

Anita continued, "Supper is at seven o'clock, down in our dining room. Behind this curtain are a gas ring and a small sink where you can make yourself a snack."

I responded, "I'm afraid that I'll not be able to get to supper at that time. My night school, over in Islington, starts at half past six and I can't get back here before ten o'clock."

"Well," replied Anita, "I'll have to leave something warming on the stove for your return. Is there anything particular you fancy?"

"Now you ask, I adore mushrooms and gravy in which I can dip some bread."

"Well, then that's what you shall have!"

The next morning, I awoke to the alarm at six, washed, made breakfast of tea and cereals, and set off for the factory a mile away. My route took me back past Baron's Court, up Edith Road to Hammersmith Road, past the J. Lyon's factory, into Brook Green, and to Shepherd's Bush Road on which the factory stood.

Large wrought iron gates led into a courtyard surrounded by factory buildings several stories high. A throng of people were passing through the gates past two uniformed security men.

"Stop!" came from a uniformed commissionaire. "I don't know you."

I wondered how he recognised a new face from the hundreds now passing through the gates, but handed him my joining papers.

"Right, sonny, you need Personnel but they don't open until eight o'clock, being management. You can wait in their reception room, through that door."

My eyes followed his arm pointing to a door. "Right, thank you. My name is Robert James and I wear three of the campaign ribbons you are wearing, so I'll thank you not to call me sonny," I said irritably.

His surprise lasted a few seconds before he brought his heels together and saluted me. "Delighted to make the acquaintance of a military man, sir."

Tales From A Briefcase

"I was commissioned, Sergeant, but here I am to be a trainee manager. That does not warrant a salute and a 'sir' but we'll enjoy talking together about the Imjin, won't we?"

"That we will, and good luck to you in your new job."

Later, a young female personnel officer, not much older than myself, told me about my induction programme as a management trainee. This involved progressively visiting all parts of the factory and learning how to do all the various jobs in making lamps and electronic valves.

"I've booked you on an electronics degree course at Northampton College in Islington. It's a bit of a journey across London but the course is precisely what the company needs. There are three parts, each taking two years and with lessons four nights a week. You will start your working day here at 7.30 am sharp and finish at 5.30 pm in time to get to Islington by tube for 6.30 pm. The lessons finish at 9.30 pm. You'll have an hour for lunch here, when you can get a subsidised canteen meal, and you can get a snack at college during the evening break. We have a two-week shutdown in the summer and various bank holidays throughout the year. Any questions?"

I shook my head, totally confused by the dense flow of information pouring out at me.

"Thursday is pay day, when you will get a brown pay packet with cash inside. You should count this and sign the sheet to say that it is correct." This sounded rather demeaning to me because, in the army, Cox and King's Bank had made my salary available on a monthly basis and drawable by cheque.

"I'll take you up to your department – Department N, managed by Peter Thompson. Here are two white coats, one on and one in the wash. Come along!"

I followed her trim figure, with its intentional mannequin sway, up several flights of stairs to a floor with its own entrance doors, and on to an office where a competent looking man in a dark suit sat behind a battered desk. She smiled and left.

"Ah, Robert, welcome. I'm Peter Thompson." We shook hands. I guessed he was in his thirties and very good at his job.

He continued, "We employ about one hundred and twenty people here making lamp bulbs, from start to finish. In the three months you will be here, we would like you to have a go at all the jobs, including glass blowing. I am putting you with a senior supervisor, John Fuller, who will look after you on a day-to-day basis and you will have the title Technical Assistant. Good luck." He held out his hand just as a tall middle-aged man entered the office, exactly on cue.

"Oh hello, John. This is your new assistant, Robert James. He's just out of the regular army and should know something about man management – but maybe not so much about woman management!" I noticed the merest flicker of a wink being exchanged between them.

"Come along Robert, I'll show you around the department and the main operations in light bulb manufacture."

I followed him into a section where girls were winding filament coils and bending bits of metal. "This is a metal component section where all the non-glass bits are made. The work is very repetitive but these young ladies don't seem to mind. They warble away to the piped music and chatter away amongst themselves. They're paid piecework, which means that the more they produce, the more they earn."

As we walked through the section I noticed I had become a focus of attention. Some girls said 'Good morning' with a broad smile, and some even winked at me. I felt myself blushing but said 'Good morning' to everyone. At twenty-four, I was deeply conscious of the attentions of the opposite sex of about my own age, a group with whom I rarely made contact in the army.

John continued, "In this section we fix the wires into the glass formers. The seals do not have to be airtight but they must hold the wires firmly. The girls take the moulded glass former, put it into a metal jig, which can be spun, insert the wire elements into the holes in the former, present the gas jet to the jig, blow air through the mouth tube to get the right gas-air mixture and melt the glass on to the wires. You'll be having a go yourself and you'll find that it takes some skill to control the glass at temperature. The girls acquire semi-skilled status after about six months and earn more money."

We moved on to another section where the operator sealed the sub assembly into a glass envelope. "This is like glass blowing. The operator has to bring the envelope to the right temperatures before sealing in the innards. It's easy to produce a lop-sided bulb. These girls are our most skilled and highest paid. It takes them about a year to reach this level of skill."

In the next section, a number of complicated machines with circular tracks were clattering away, the sealing-in process being effectively automatic. Operators loaded and unloaded the machines, in which rotating jigs moved from station to station in a circle, each station being a discreet operation replacing each of the manual operations of the operators. The key process was sealing the bulb on to a vacuum pump, exhausting the air, filling it with an inert gas and sealing the bulb off the vacuum line. The maker's product code, power output and production batch number were stencilled on to the bulb as a finishing process.

By now the bulbs were beginning to look light electric lamps but a further and final operation was needed, fitting the metal base. The bases were either of the bayonet or 'screw in' type.

A welding process connected the wires in the bulb to the base, and the base was then filled with a hardening compound which was later baked in an oven to fix the base and bulb together.

The final section was testing and packaging, where the finished lamps were lit, had their light intensity measured, and were then packed into individual boxes.

The glass sealing machines and ovens heated the department to a point where, even with ventilation, light clothes were advisable and people could be seen sweating. Many of the girls wore no brassieres and opened their blouse-buttons to reveal large expanses of bosom, so much so that I found it difficult to look into their faces when talking to them.

The lunch-hour break arrived. Some people had brought sandwiches and thermos flasks; others went up to Hammersmith to shop, but most went to the canteen for the good quality meals served at subsidised prices. Tea trolleys with biscuits and cakes circulated the department at the ten-minute morning and afternoon breaks.

The factory was regulated by warning bells and by clocking in and out. Not being at your workplace by the second starting bell, or having put your coat on by the first finishing bell, were grievous crimes penalised by losing a quarter of an hour's pay and, if repeated, by the sack.

Tales From A Briefcase

By 5.30 pm I was exhausted and joined the noisy masses surging through the factory gates to walk the short distance down Shepherd's Bush Road to Hammersmith Tube Station.

The Piccadilly Line took me straight through to The Angel Islington in about forty minutes, and then a short walk down John Street brought me to the college. Most of the students on the night school degree course were mature and worked in factories during the day. Each evening was divided into four forty-minute lectures and a twenty-minute meal break.

I met another mature student, Ian McDonald. He was about my own age and working in a factory at Southgate, and was on the same degree course as me – Electrical Engineering. During the six years of the course we would become staunch friends.

I was desperately tired on my tube ride home to Fulham, but looking forward to the mushroom supper awaiting me. Falling in through the front door of my digs at ten-thirty, I found there were no lights on and no noise from anywhere. I went to the kitchen where I could see the small blue light of a gas burner under a saucepan and some slices of bread ready for toasting under the grill. I switched on the kitchen light to confront the gas cooker. Above the gas rings was a plate rack on which were draped a pair of black and white frilly knickers drying from their evening wash, immediately above the saucepan of mushrooms! I decided to give supper a miss and flopped into bed, exhausted.

CHAPTER 3

A VERBAL WARNING

Hammersmith

In the year that followed, I continued my training in the manufacturing departments. Some were making light bulbs, of all sizes for domestic and commercial use, others electronic valves for domestic radios and televisions, while yet others were making special devices for radar and guided missile systems.

About a third of the workforce were West Indians; women represented about eighty per cent of the employees. The men were largely skilled workers or electronic technicians. Each departmental manager had several section supervisors, and each supervisor several technical foremen responsible for small groups of operators. The technical foremen were young and, like me, taking professional qualifications on day release or at night school.

The factory had a two-week summer closure when maintenance was undertaken. At Christmas, the shutdown normally lasted several days, and in the preceding days the departments were decorated with paper-chains and bunting. On the last day before the break, food and drink were brought in and the employees were allowed to stop work at the morning break and party until lunchtime, when they could go home for the rest of the day.

Apart from these breaks from routine, factory life became monotonous. The environment was airless and hot, and my nose was regularly assailed by chemical smells from the cleaning and plating processes. The days were punctuated by warning signals, and I joined the clock-watching fraternity who lived for the time to escape.

The tube journey to the college seemed to be endless and my fitness was eroded as I took virtually no exercise. My leisure

Tales From A Briefcase

time was spent in the Odeon in Kensington High Street, or in pubs in Earls Court where mostly I drank alone, occasionally meeting up with itinerant Australians or Irish. I bought a broken television set and repaired it, thereafter spending many an hour on a Saturday watching 'Dr Who and the Daleks' and 'That Was The Week That Was'.

At college I met a rugby player who had joined the Rosslyn Park club at Barnes. Having played rugby through my school days and in the army, I decided to go along for a trial. The observers rated me quite highly and I was soon appointed to hooker of the second fifteen. We trained on Friday, my only free evening. Rugby introduced a new social dimension to my life, with home and away games and Saturday evening parties with the team after the match.

Every month or so my mother came to London from Portsmouth on a Saturday, and always brought a food basket. My father would not be associated with her visit and maintained his vow never to speak to me again.

On the first anniversary of my engagement at the factory, I was called to the works manager's office in the suite of executive offices on the top floor.

The works manager welcomed me. "Come in Mr James and take a seat," indicating a chair which had been strategically placed in front of his desk. Unlike the factory, the office was light and airy. Potted plants were scattered around the room and a silver framed photograph stood on his desk; I guessed it contained a photograph of his family. Framed certificates on the wall trumpeted his education and professional qualifications.

I took a closer look at the man who had climbed to the highest rung on the factory's ladder and was now in charge of a site employing eight hundred people. I guessed he was about forty-five, immaculately dressed in a blue suit, institute tie, highly polished shoes, smart conventional haircut, and with a polished accent which barely gave away his northern birthplace.

"Over the past year, we have been reviewing your progress around the departments. Everyone seems happy with the way you have applied yourself to civilian life and we think you are ready to take the first step into management as technical foreman. You will be on six months' probation and, if your performance is up to scratch, you will go on to monthly-paid staff and get a pay increase to £600 a year. Well done and good morning." His hand was held out to be shaken.

I left the office, stunned by the shortness of the interview and full of unanswered questions.

John Fuller came up to me as I arrived back in the factory. "Peter Thompson wants to see you now. Come back to me when you've finished."

Peter was waiting for me. "Good morning, Robert. Good news, I hear, from the boss. Well done! I am giving you a small section of six operators which is making a new design of X-band magnetron for airfield ground control approach radar. The assemblies are very precise and the products need checking at every stage of manufacture. The women are amongst our best operators but they are 'old soldiers' and can be difficult at times. The job will require strict operator supervision and a high level of technical control. John Fuller will show you the ropes."

John had a supervisor's desk on the shop floor and I could see that he had imported several chairs for a meeting in which I was to be introduced to my charges. "Don't worry about it," he told me. "They're all dragons and have eaten up young technical foremen before this. Let me tell you about them. Firstly, they are all skilled operators and know their jobs. They also know the company's rules backwards and the union handbook by heart. They'll argue with you if you let them and you'll probably come off worst."

He went on, "Lil, the blonde, is in her late forties and dresses like a twenty-year-old. She is very chirpy – outspoken, I mean – and will be the ringleader in any trouble. Bertha, approaching her sixties, a spinster, has worked here for over thirty years. She has the company at heart but can be led by Lil. Constance is Jamaican, about forty, came to England about five years ago and has only worked here; she'll follow Lil. Mary is unmarried about thirty-five; she's Irish and has her own mind. She won't follow Lil but will not side with management either. Rita is about forty-five, married but a man-eater, no hanky panky with her or she'll blackmail you. Finally, Miranda from Barbados; younger then the rest, chats up the men and cheeks the other

Tales From A Briefcase

women. They should prove quite a handful for your first civvy job – and good luck."

I looked at John. He was a bit of an old soldier himself, walking the thin line between workers and management, showing no favouritism and remaining calm during the frequent outbursts and the occasional emergencies. I felt that he would be a good role model. John had a wiseness forged over many years of working on the shop floor.

"Let's have the girls in," suggested John, disappearing down the factory and returning with them. They sat on the chairs arranged in a semi-circle around John's desk. For a few minutes, there was much chatter, hair preening and skirt adjusting.

"Well, here is your new foreman, Robert James. He was in the army and has just finished a year's training around the departments. He knows nothing about magnetron production and it's up to you to show him the ropes. Treat him gently. Most of you are old enough to be his mum. I'm sure, in return, he'll not throw his weight around. Any questions?"

Lil was straight in, "Is he to give us our instructions instead of you?"

"Yes, as far as you're concerned he's in charge."

"Will he start at 7.30 like we do?"

"If he's sensible he'll be in earlier to note which of you are the late-comers."

"Does he know about unions and meetings and things?"

"He will after I give him the low-down, official and unofficial."

It went on for nearly an hour before they became bored and started to fidget. "Right," said John, "off you go and Robert will greet you nice and early at clocking-in tomorrow morning." He said this with a smile and a wink.

John took me by the arm, "I'll walk you down to the Technical Department where they'll tell you all about magnetrons. Stay down there for the rest of the day and meet me here tomorrow morning at 7.20."

The next morning, John Fuller took me to the clocking-in machine, positioned at the doors of the department, where we awaited my six operators. By 7.25, two had clocked on, three

Tales From A Briefcase

came in with a rush just before 7.30 – and Lil had not appeared at all. At 7.45 she came to John's desk and said, breathlessly, "The buses were terrible this morning."

"No excuse," replied John, "I'm docking you a quarter of an hour's attendance. This is the third time you've been late this month. Next time it will be a verbal warning. And, today, I don't want to see you leave your workplace and go to the cloakroom until the first finishing bell. I've instructed Robert to watch out for these things. OK?"

"Yeah, OK. But you know that I won't stand for being picked on – that's victimisation and the union will have something to say about that!"

She flounced down the corridor to her workstation, conscious that everyone in the department had heard the exchange.

"That's what you'll have to contend with – the two finger treatment. She's a good operator but there is only so much management can take of someone deliberately flouting the rules. Be careful about the union position, though. Talk it over with me before you formally reprimand anybody. Go down to your section now. Here's the production programme for this week; check how they are progressing against it and see me at the end of each day."

I spent the next few days watching the girls assemble the magnetrons; it was precise work and called for their complete attention most of the time. The glass-to-metal seals had to be blown so that the wires were central within the glass envelopes. Copper components had to be brazed together accurately in radio frequency heaters. In the final assembly, all the components had to be totally airtight otherwise the magnetrons could not be exhausted to a state of near vacuum.

Although the operators were trained to do all the production jobs, Bertha and Mary did most of the glasswork and Lil and Rita did the vacuuming and testing.

The test machines were heavily screened. Lil complained, "I've told the management and union about them machines. They give off dangerous rays that'll penetrate our wombs and make us incapable of having children! Our periods are all over

Tales From A Briefcase

the place. You should watch out too – you could become sterile; maybe it'll affect you getting horny." I pondered on this and resolved to take it up with the engineers.

Being a new section working on a new product, it appeared quite acceptable for about a half of the output not to perform on test. I decided to analyse the faulty products and see which parts of the process were likely to be causing the defects. In the Development Department, good results had been achieved with technicians making the products, but on transfer to the factory the operators proved less skilled, particularly in judging positioning of parts by eye. I enlisted the support of some of the engineers, who produced jigs to hold the components more accurately. Slowly the yield of good products climbed.

Unfortunately, in parallel to this, the discipline of my section fell away. Absenteeism, lateness and disobeying the rules increased. I gathered the team around my table and appealed to them to improve their ways but Lil piped up, "What more do you bloody want? We've got the yield up and the company must be making a fortune on these products. There's no extra money for us so we're going to take things a bit easy!"

I talked this over with John Fuller and he agreed I was in a difficult position. "You'll have to get a grip on the discipline. The personnel records are already reflecting the absenteeism and lateness and it won't be long before the departmental manager will be visiting to see for himself."

The last day of work before the Christmas break arrived. The departmental manager had sent a written note to all staff explaining the arrangements. Emphasis was placed on the instruction that work had to continue until the morning break, after which food and booze could be put out on spare tables in the department but not on the workbenches. Employees could clock out at 12.30, when their holidays could start.

I arrived early to switch on the equipment. My six ladies straggled in, as usual, after 7.30. Out of their carrier bags came bottles of beer, gin and port.

I felt I had to intervene: "Look here ladies, you've read the instruction and also I've told you about it. Clear those bottles and glasses away until break."

Tales From A Briefcase

"You're just a spoil-sport. We do this every year," complained Lil, and to reinforce her position she took an enormous gulp of neat gin.

I scooted up the department to ask John's advice.

"Oh, Lord, have they started already? The rest of the department will follow them. I'll come down right away and see if I can stop them."

It was to no avail. By then, other sections were bringing out their bottles. The arrival of the departmental manager only hastened the tippling and management beat a swift retreat to their offices to avert the riot which strong intervention would cause. When the bell rang for the break period, drinking, eating and dancing were well underway and couples were sliding away to find a quiet spot to canoodle – except in my section, where all but Lil were snoring peacefully, heads on arms, unconscious to the world. As ever Lil was ready with the last word: "It's their only chance to have a bit of fun in this dreary place. They're management's responsibility now – unless they're sent home in taxis they could get electrocuted with all this equipment around."

I rushed up to John again, "They want management to send them home in taxis before they get electrocuted!"

"Too bad, laddie. You received this week's pay this morning. You'll have to find the fares yourself. Here's the number of a local taxi firm."

So that was how six taxis arrived at the factory to collect six wobbly old ladies from Hammersmith.

* * *

It was after the Christmas break that the departmental manager sent for me. "You know what this about. I have seen your team flouting the rules and you obviously cannot control them. The debacle before Christmas put the lid on it. I'll have to give you a verbal warning to improve this situation over the next four weeks. If you don't improve I'll give you a written warning, and if you then don't improve you will be sacked. Do you understand? It is down to you and only you. I would have thought your military experience in handling people would have helped you enforce discipline over the people that you control."

Tales From A Briefcase

I replied somewhat ruefully: "My soldiers were men, disciplined from the day that they joined the army. We had regulations and soldiers who broke them were penalised – hard. They did not have a union to appeal to. This lot here were difficult workers before I got them. If my job is on the line, I will resort to disciplinary action and look to you to back me against the union."

"So be it, but you had better understand the union culture. We can't have you starting a factory-wide strike. Good afternoon."

I didn't sleep that night but resolved to appeal to the girls' one more time.

The next day I invited them to tea and biscuits at my table during the morning break. They all turned up.

"Well, ladies, I've been called up before the big boss and been given a warning. I have to get you under control in short order or get the sack. You know my personal circumstances – I need the job and the money while I study at night school. You have the power to keep me here or see me off. To see me off all you have to do is to keep on misbehaving as usual. If you don't want to get me the sack you'll have to toe the line as far as regulations go. For my part, I will make a plea on your behalf for increased money on grounds of efficiency. I want you to discuss this amongst yourselves and let me know your decision tomorrow. I cannot survive unless we work as a team. It's down to you. Thank you for listening."

During break time the following morning, Mary came up to my table. "We want you to know that we have no beef about you and we wouldn't like to be the cause of your dismissal. From now on we'll do everything to get you off the hook."

"Well, Mary, that's a relief for me. Does that offer stand for everyone, including Lil?"

"Yes, she's in after a lot of moaning. She'll go along, with the rest of us making sure that she does."

"Fine. I'll start making a case for more money for the team."

And it happened just like a dream, and they got their pay rise.

Three months later I was in Peter Thompson's office to hear my annual review. "What the hell did you do to those girls to make them conform like that?"

"I played the little boy lost and appealed to their motherly instincts. I can't believe that I did it; it's in nobody's training manual."

"Well you did it, and we are going to promote you and give you a pay rise. Well done!"

John Fuller came up to me and offered his hand. "Let me be the first to tell you. You are promoted to supervisor in the Microwave Department. It's taken you under two years to get there where it took me over twenty. No hard feelings and I wish you luck."

And that marked my first step on the management ladder, on which I would take a further step to departmental manager over the next three years.

Also, I had passed the first of three parts of my degree. I now felt that I could relax a little and step up my social life. At rugby that week, the team lists showed that I had been promoted to hooker of the first team.

To add spice to my life, the female occupant of a flat across the road started to undress in front of her window with the curtain open and the light on. Many a hard day was brightened at its end by her strip show! As much as I tried, I never saw her in the street or got to know her name or telephone number.

CHAPTER 4

STARTING UP THE LADDER

On Saturday evenings, I started going to dances at the Varsity Club at Chelsea Town Hall and Kensington Town Hall. I was not a good dancer but could jive well enough to interest the girls.

Here I met Katie, a well-built Irish girl from Cork City. After a few dates, she informed me that she was a good Catholic and she didn't participate in shenanigans. She lived in a flat near Gloucester Road tube station with three other Irish girls.

With Saturdays taken up with rugby, Sundays were free to take Katie out; sometimes the other two girls came as well. Katie had her own room and I was able to persuade her to let me stay over on Saturday nights and even share her bed. The strain on me to avoid 'shenanigans' was enormous. She would pile out of bed at eight o'clock on a Sunday morning and leave me there while she attended nine o'clock mass at Brompton Oratory.

Eventually, one Sunday I went with her and was amazed at what I witnessed. Accustomed as I was to the poorly-attended Church of England services and dwindling congregations, the Oratory appeared to me to be packed to overflowing for each mass, which ran hourly on the hour. The congregation prayed fervently and crossed themselves energetically, reacting to the tinkling bells which signalled a significant part of the service. Nearly all went up to the altar to take communion, served by a flock of priests and altar boys. The congregation left the church like children leaving school at the end of lessons, laughing and chattering.

Throughout the next week I thought about what I had seen. Had these Roman Catholics got a compelling creed by which they lived their lives, just as I had done with the army and its rules and regulations? Was this something I was now missing in civilian life – a meaning for life, a spiritual path, a disciplined structure, a sense of community?

I talked this over with Katie, who could sense my loneliness and lack of direction. She saw that she had a potential convert on her hands and introduced me to a priest who was a brother in one of the sects based at the Oratory. I agreed to attend a conversion course. As the weekend sessions with the priest progressed, I realised that it would take almost blind faith on my part to take the final step to conversion. It was too much, and I discontinued taking the lessons. Katie gave me up for Lent!

The fourth anniversary of my leaving the army soon passed and I settled into a new flat in West Kensington. By then I had achieved management status in the Microwave Department with a hundred and twenty people under my control.

Now I had my own office, and four supervisors reporting to me. One supervisor controlled a section working in an ultra clean room with the staff dressed up in gowns, hats and overshoes. Apart from being intricate work and requiring a clean environment, the work was classified 'secret' and special security arrangements were in force. The Cold War had produced a great demand for missile control systems and for sophisticated tracking devices in early warning systems. The company was one of only two British manufacturers producing devices for this market. Thus, my department grew and grew and I became more senior and better paid.

My social life became even more active, with rugby and entertaining the opposite sex still being its dominant features. My transport also improved in style and reliability; the station wagon I'd bought became impossible to maintain and I acquired a smart Riley drop-head coupe in British Racing Green. Theatre became my new interest, and I saw most of the new plays and musicals which were beginning to hit London in the late Fifties. London social life was beginning to change; coffee bars flooded Kensington and Earls Court, and Indian and Chinese restaurants proliferated. Italian bistros went up-market and served a richer clientele.

I now reported to the director who controlled the Hammersmith site. He sent for me as I entered my last year of

Tales From A Briefcase

night-school. "I know you are still attending evening classes and that you take your finals next summer," he began. "However, we have tied up with an American manufacturer and there will be a two-way flow of products for manufacturing in each country. We want you to head this project for the next year with the title of Project Executive. There'll be more money for you, but it will disrupt your academic studies and your social life. You're only twenty-seven and there'll be time for marriage and a family later. We've spoken to your college and we are prepared to offer you a scholarship so that you can attend college full-time on full pay for the next academic year. You'll then be placed to move into a general manager's position. What do you say?"

It was an offer I couldn't refuse and I was soon shuttling backwards and forwards across the Atlantic to Newark and Rochester. Transfer teams were appointed on either side of "the pond" who took instructions from me and did the detailed work. I found I quite liked the American engineers; they took their jobs seriously and they had an air of professionalism not shown by their British counterparts. I found myself working on the Distant Early Warning Line, a chain of tracking stations stretched across Canada. It used the British products made in Hammersmith. During my time off, I skied in the Rockies and visited Vancouver.

Life back in London became very disjointed. My visits to Rosslyn Park for training and playing rugby became spasmodic and I lost my place in the first team. However, I enjoyed playing in the fifths where the game was taken less seriously and social activity was dominant.

A few of my female acquaintances were prepared to associate with an itinerant chap and to accept dates made at the very last moment. Being reasonably well paid, I could afford to entertain my partners to the latest theatre shows, the best concerts, and good restaurants. At twenty-seven and with a very busy lifestyle, thoughts of marriage and family rarely entered my head. The next year went by quickly, during which I became international in my outlook and a worldly businessman.

On one of my trips across the Atlantic, I sat next to Zabaleta, an internationally acclaimed Spanish harpist, and we became friends. He sent me tickets to his solo performances at the Queen

Tales From A Briefcase

Elizabeth Hall. I was overawed by his professionalism and charmed by his playing.

During one of my fleeting visits to the factory at Hammersmith, I was asked to visit the director. "Ah, Robert," he greeted me, "I see that you are doing famously on both sides of the Atlantic." He went on to discuss the various projects for which I was responsible, and then got to the point. "I had promised you a scholarship to take the final part of your degree full-time at college after a year at this job, but I'm afraid you've become too valuable and we would like you to go on for yet another year. We'll give you an increase in status and salary. What do you think?"

I thought it over. I'd be twenty-nine before I'd finished with college. Could I wait that long before I started to settle down? Was the degree that important for my future? Were there any strings to hold me in the company after I had taken my degree?

"I have one reservation," I told him. "I want eventually to be a managing director, and if the company can meet that ambition within a year of me leaving college, fine. But if not, I want to be free to leave. What do you think?"

"Well, we have invested a lot of time training you and it will cost us some more to release you for your final year at college."

I interrupted him with: "True and I'm grateful for that. But I've given this company five years of my life. It doesn't own me and I have a programme for my own life. I need your undertaking or I'll hand in my notice now and attend college under my own steam."

He smiled and said, "You drive a hard bargain. You'll make a good chief executive one day. Do another year on the transatlantic run and we'll fund your year at college full-time and on full pay without strings. OK?"

"OK!"

So, in September 1958 I went back to school as a mature student.

Tales From A Briefcase

CHAPTER 5

HORTICULTURE IN SUSSEX

Worthing

The advertisement in the *Daily Telegraph* read:

Become a Business Consultant.

If you are a graduate, aged 25-35, with at least five years business experience and have a lively, enquiring mind, you may have what it takes to become a business consultant. You must be prepared to work away from home.

Send your curriculum vitae and a handwritten page about yourself to us at the address below. Successful applicants will be given training, an attractive salary, and interesting assignments across Southern England.

The address given was in Windsor.

It was 1960; I was twenty-nine, a graduate and had worked at the factory for five years. I was still unmarried and living in a rented flat in Barnes. Consultancy, I thought, would broaden my knowledge and experience of business, taking me further into commercial life than I had been before. My application was sent in, and after two interviews I was selected for training.

Considering the small size of the consultancy practice, the training was thorough. I found particularly interesting the subjects like structure of business, accounting and marketing, which I had barely encountered in my factory work.

Another trainee consultant, Denis, and I were allocated to a horticulture nursery located just outside Worthing, where they grew chrysanthemums. This was almost factory farming. Young shoots were planted in large wheeled trays which, over an

Tales From A Briefcase

eight-week cycle, passed through different environments as they grew to full maturity. Fed and watered all the way through the cycle, the plants were subjected to varying exposures of light, by shading in daylight or being lit by light bulbs at night, creating the "autumn" conditions that are the plant's natural growing period. The chrysanthemums, known as 'mums' in the trade, were sold as single large heads or as sprays, the type of debudding creating one or the other. Denis and I spent long days with notebooks and stopwatches studying the working methods of the horticultural workers and deciding how they could apply themselves more efficiently. As they were mostly young girls with a healthy interest in sex, we were subjected to plenty of suggestive remarks and even rough handling in the crotch area.

After our first day at the nursery, we checked in at a hotel in Worthing. Arriving at about six thirty, we found a crowd of aged people, mostly female, crowding the foyer. As if on some signal, the doors of the dining room, leading off the foyer, were flung open and the crowd elbowed their way in, grumbling and shouting.

The lady receptionist who handled our check-in apologised for the scrum in the foyer: "They are our winter guests, staying from October to just before Christmas and again from January to Easter. They think they own the place and are terribly badly behaved!"

After settling into our rooms, we decided to get some drinks from the bar and watch the early evening news on television. We found the TV room whose set was tuned to ITV, switched it over to BBC news and settled into comfortable high-backed chairs, sipping our drinks. Suddenly, we became aware of a commotion at the door. Advancing towards us was a grey-haired old lady, her wrinkled face livid with anger and her fists shaking vigorously in our faces.

"This is the ITV room. We watch Coronation Street every evening at seven. That is my chair you are sitting in," she said to Denis, "and that," pointing to mine, "is Major Ponsonby-Smith's. We have been coming here for the last twenty years and never had invaders before. Please remove yourselves."

Denis and I took ourselves off to the dining room, where the head waiter, very dishevelled and obviously at the end of his tether, told us: "They're like bloody gannets – impatient, bad tempered, eat everything in sight."

Then he smiled as his mood changed and he patted down his tails. "It's a change to have civilised diners who appreciate the delicacies which we present for them. Gentlemen, what can I get you from our extensive menu?" He waved a large leather bound multi-page menu at us. "Or will you have the Plat du Jour, like the other lot?" his lip curling at the thought.

"I think we'll have chef's lobster bisque followed by fillet steak, rare, and a nice bottle of claret," I said, winking at Denis, on whom it was dawning that we had just blown about three days' hotel allowance on our first evening meal.

"Cheer up, Denis," I jollied, "we'll get superb service in future, even if we only have the Plat du Jour!"

It was two evenings later that we decided to have a night out in Brighton, about half an hour's drive from Worthing. We ate fresh fish and went dancing at the Palais. We accepted an invitation to have a nightcap with two friendly girls at their flat, and it was two in the morning before we arrived back at the hotel in Worthing.

At the door of the hotel, we found a bell-push marked 'Night Porter'. Repeated pressings produced no result, even though we could hear the bell ringing within. "Look," I said, "there's a telephone box just across the road. You keep ringing this bell and I'll telephone the hotel's number."

Someone answered the telephone and agreed to open the door to us after we had declared our room numbers. Back at the door we could hear bolts being drawn and a great jangling of keys as the locks were freed.

The door opened and we could hardly believe our eyes. There stood an old man with a white beard, his striped pyjamas covered with a heavy dressing gown and his feet kept warm by slippers decorated with pom-poms. The apparition was completed by a nightcap with a single tassel dangling from its top. He looked like 'Grumpy' from 'Snow White'.

"You young gentlemen should know that this hotel closes at eleven," said the apparition. "In fact, most our residents are in bed by nine. It's my job to see them tucked up with their cocoa and clean the shoes they leave outside their doors. After that I go to bed."

Tales From A Briefcase

"Is it too much to ask for two large scotches?"

The porter's mouth dropped open. He looked as though he would explode but thought better of it. We followed him into a lounge where there was again much jangling of keys as he opened a drinks cabinet and poured the drinks.

"I hope that you young gentlemen don't feel that you can get me out of bed at this hour every night," he said, "or we shall have to make special arrangements with the management for you to have keys. There's the bloody bottle. I'm going back to bed!"

We stayed at the hotel for several more months, through that winter, the next spring and to Easter, when all the winter residents left and a new set of residents, younger and livelier, occupied the hotel. The old porter was replaced by a young Italian who was happy to be up all night serving drinks and chatting with the customers.

After a brief period with mushroom and cress growers, Denis and I went our separate ways, him to get married and work in the Thames Valley and me to the Hayward's Heath area to work at a well-known grower of carnations. At the turn of the century three brothers, seedsmen, had come to Sussex to start their horticultural nursery and produce varieties of carnations which would make them world famous.

Only one brother had survived, Mr George who was now eighty-two, and the fortunes of the company had begun to change for the worse. Competition from Holland and Israel had increased, leaving prices on the floor at the main market, Covent Garden. True, the competitor's carnations were not as beautiful, did not smell as beautiful, nor displayed such quality, but the horticultural world was beginning to run on price, not quality.

As for most markets, when there is a glut of supply, prices drop. Mr George had to sell his carnations at rock bottom prices. However, old-fashioned production methods and rising costs of heating during the winter season drove up his costs and made him unprofitable. Eventually, the bank started to worry about its loan and told his directors that Mr George must change his management or the bank would withdraw their lending facilities.

The directors approached the Windsor consultancy and I was appointed chief executive. Corrective measures had to be taken urgently, but those proposed were fiercely contested by Mr George. To increase the return on our products, we cut out Covent Garden and sold directly to the flower shops in southern England, delivering in the early morning with pretty uniformed girls and branded vans. We stopped the practice of throwing away 'shorts', broken or weak stemmed flowers, and got pensioners making buttonholes for weddings and city gentlemen; British Overseas Airways had a daily delivery for their first class passengers on long haul flights. Previously, the Friday crop could not be sold because Covent Garden was shut at the weekend and the flowers had to be committed to the rubbish dump. They were now harvested and distributed amongst employees with cars, for sale at the local industrial estates and to visitors driving down the Brighton Road.

We advertised on local television, promoting our gift vouchers for spring bedding plants and collecting the money before they were despatched to customers in the spring. We promoted our gift box service for birthdays and anniversaries. Other growers approached us to deliver their goods to the shops, and our catalogue was expanded to include fencing and wrought iron gates. As the company started to recover, Mr George became angrier and angrier, raging that the world had changed and not for the better. However, he still had his annual week of glory at the Chelsea Flower Show, where the company regularly won prizes and he rubbed shoulders with the royal family.

I was offered the permanent job of managing director, but my contract with the consultancy did not permit me to join a client. I handed over to another consultant. Still, the job had given me a taste of the power of a chief executive and I decided that it was time for me to return to management.

Tales From A Briefcase

CHAPTER 6

WHICH FOOT DO YOU DIG WITH?

Lurgan, Northern Ireland

It was my last day at 'the Optical'. I sat at my desk in the office, now stripped of those personal items which made it mine. On the desk were my briefcase, a box of text books, and my other personal possessions, which I would shortly take home. I had been sacked!

Stupid bugger! Fancy sticking my neck out for a principle, for justice, fighting the establishment, protesting against the religious bigotry which would last at least another forty years. It would leave a trail of dead and maimed and of broken hearts; for this was 1962 and Northern Ireland was entering another phase of its Protestant-Catholic struggles, started, as the Protestants would have it, with King Billy, William of Orange, at the Battle of the Boyne in 1690.

I had come with my new wife to Lurgan in Northern Ireland, about twenty miles southwest of Belfast, to be technical director of a factory making ophthalmic lenses. She was a Protestant but was one of the few who didn't carry the hate of the opposite persuasion. It was a chance for us to live in the beautiful countryside and make babies.

My selection for the job had started with an interview in London by the British directors of the American subsidiary of a large international optical engineering firm in New York State, to be followed by an interview in America. My degree in engineering and my work in manufacturing and sales with the factory in Hammersmith eminently qualified me for the job. I would now have to learn the magic of lens-making: putting curves on to glass surfaces, designing tools which would rough-grind, smooth and then polish glass to the finished product, and cutting plastics to form spectacle frames.

Tales From A Briefcase

I found a large farmhouse to rent, set in two acres of grounds. At the front were sweeping lawns, a miniature village made out of stone – a centre of attraction for tourists, and a running stream in which trout flashed by. At the rear of the house was a vegetable garden tended by Hugh, a retired farm worker who lived in a cottage across the road. Not only did he supply vegetables but acted as maintenance man and a gateman too. He would wait at the five-bar gate at the start of the drive and would see the approach of my car several hundred yards away. As I neared, he would swing open the gate, stand back, doff his hat and shut the gate after me. His wife, Mary, was a gem, helping my young wife with cleaning, washing and ironing and 'redding up' the large Victorian house.

Hugh's Northern Ireland brogue was very broad, difficult for me to understand and made more complicated by the substitution of old Irish words for modern English ones; for example, a garden fork was a 'grape'.

The job went well at first with me learning the technology of the industry and spending time on the shop floor getting to know the workers. My tutor was the local English director, the only person with the technical knowledge but who was imminently to retire. The senior managers, I noticed, were all Ulstermen and were bound into a tight-knit group, into which neither the director nor I were accepted. To me they appeared to be an Irish power group intent on maintaining Protestant control over and above the routine management role. It also appeared to me that they were manoeuvring one of their own into the role of understudy to the English director and saw me as a potential usurper.

In the managers' dining room I was asked one day, "Which foot do you dig with?"

I looked up from eating. "I don't understand you."

The others had laughed. One leant forward to put his face close to mine. "Are ye Protestant or a Fenian?" The words carried all the hatred he could muster for the word 'Fenian', which I had not heard before.

"I was brought up Church of England. Is that the right answer? And you? Aren't you Church of Ireland or Presbyterian? Do you think that all Roman Catholics are the Fenians, the enemy?"

Tales From A Briefcase

"You watch your step, young man. We'll not have Fenian lovers in our management team." I decided that watching my step was good advice.

The demand for spectacles under the National Health Service increased dramatically and there was pressure to expand factory capacity. The American parent had recently developed a high-speed processing line which they proposed should be adopted by the factory in Lurgan. I was sent to Rochester in New York State to learn the technology and transfer it to Northern Ireland. It became obvious that I would need a team of both Americans and Irish to effect the transfer and I would need to select a supervisor to control the Lurgan end.

I searched the employment records and interviewed several potential candidates for the job of Supervisor – Fast Processing Line. James Donovan appeared to stand head and shoulders above the rest. Not only was he a competent technician, but a good people-manager and a first-class administrator.

I conveyed my findings to the English director. "There'll be trouble, you know," he warned. "Although Donovan is well qualified to do the job, he's a Catholic. The Ulster management will not stand for it!" I noted the word 'Ulster'. It really meant Protestant and anti-Catholic.

I found this pathetic. "When you ran the factory in London, did you note down the religious persuasions of your workers and promote only the Protestants?"

"No, it didn't matter what religion they were," came his expected reply.

"Then why do you use different standards here? You are the Director; you control the site on behalf of both the Americans and the English. Why not employ their standards?"

"It's different here. Local culture and politics come into play."

"So you believe this forces you into continuing the Protestant culture of suppressing the Catholics within this factory, letting yourself be brow-beaten by the Protestant management, and not being just and fair?"

He looked at me through his spectacles, obviously taken somewhat aback by my criticism. He was over sixty, near retirement, technology was more his interest than people. He was for the quiet life and left it to his bigoted management to impose their culture in the factory.

"How are you going to handle this?" I asked. "I'll stick to my guns and promote Donovan."

"Will Donovan accept the job? Will he take up a company house bang in the middle of a Protestant area in Lurgan? Will he face the personal aggravation that the Protestants will heap upon him?"

"He says he will. His living conditions can't be much worse than they are now. He lives with his parents and his wife with hers. They have been married for two years and want children. All the council houses are allocated to Protestants by the Protestant council. They have no chance of finding a house for themselves. For God's sake man, we have a chance to break this mould, introduce conditions which we operate elsewhere and stand up for fairness and justice. What are you frightened about – starting a civil war? If someone doesn't stand up, it will be civil war."

He said quietly, "You are young and have energy to fight for a changed world. I'm too old to fight for such radical changes. Are you going to stand by your decision?"

"Yes, I bloody am. I want to go to the parent company in America and discuss this. Will you at least support my visit?"

"I will, but I will not be associated with your mission."

The American Vice President responded to my request with almost undue haste, I thought. He greeted me with rather false jollity and chatted about my domestic scene. In the boardroom we were joined by the Director of Human Relations.

"Right," he said, "shoot. You called the meeting."

"Are you aware of the Protestant-Catholic divide operating in Northern Ireland?"

"Yes, we detected it when we did our evaluation about setting up a factory there four years ago."

"Do you understand that the government at all levels is Protestant and that positions of power, management and infrastructure are controlled by Protestants who have but one ambition – keeping Catholics out of power?" They just looked at me, so I continued: "In population and voting terms,

Tales From A Briefcase

Protestants out-number Catholics but the latter are breeding so fast that the writing is on the wall. Catholics will be in power within a generation, two to three decades from now. But my guess is they won't wait that long and they'll turn to armed conflict. There are too many hotheads on both sides who are still fired up by the troubles of the early twenties. But the problem has already been solved by the Republic of Ireland where the Protestants are in the minority but hold a strong political power."

"We haven't come to listen to you lecture us about Irish politics," the Director of Human Relations said. "The British government will sort it out one day. Meanwhile we have a factory to run over there. We are not going to let you impose your high ideals of justice and fairness for the world and cause a schism in a factory which is stable and running well. You will return to Ireland and toe the present party line. You will take advice from the management, albeit Protestant, and you will get on with your job which is well defined. If you can't, I'll accept your resignation now and my colleague here will draw up you release papers. What do you want to do?"

I looked at him and saw a smug, rich, established person who appeared not to be interested in his employees across the pond. I thought of James Donovan and the many like him. True they had jobs shipped in by these Americans but at what cost to their dignity and hope for the future? I had been brought up as an English Protestant. I was not fanatical but my liberal outlook gave me a tolerance of others' callings. Still, why should I fight for these Irish Catholics and lose a good job?

"I resign."

"Very well Mr James. Sign your papers and be on your way. You can go into the factory once more to collect your personal things but no talking to the staff."

The journey home was long and lonely. How would I tell my wife? I needed a work permit to stay in Northern Ireland. I would have to go to England to get another job.

I waved at Hugh as I swept into the drive, wondering when we would have to leave our home.

My wife was at the front door, beaming. "Good news, darling. The doctor says I'm pregnant!"

BOOK 2

MOVING INTO MANAGEMENT

Tales From A Briefcase

CHAPTER 7
AGGIE

Leeds

"Did you see this?" I asked.

John Scott, the Personnel Manager replied, "Yes, Robert, I did. It will come as a blow to the old 'uns'."

I again read the instruction from group headquarters: "All employees who are past formal retirement age and still working are to have their employment terminated forthwith. Factory managers are required to deal with the matter – immediately." I knew that foreign competition, particularly Japanese, was forcing prices down in the markets and that British top management was cutting manning costs to preserve profits. Wasn't it ever thus? I thought – profits before people. It was my job to wield the knife at this factory in Leeds.

I looked out of the window for inspiration. I could see the city of Leeds sprawled across its seven hills, the centre with its new, tall office blocks dominating the skyline. Nearer to the factory were back-to-back terraced houses, some with small gardens. Here was where many factory workers lived. The factory dominated their domestic outlook, but living so close had the advantage that they could fall out of bed and be clocked on in five minutes.

As a southerner, I was always amused by the way these northerners were so friendly. They co-operated with their neighbours in many ways, which southerners would not – such as stringing a washing line between the houses across the back alleys, where the wind could dry off the week's laundry on Mondays. Yes, these Yorkshire people were a tight community and really looked after their own.

"John, get me a list of those past retirement age and those who will reach it within the next six months," I instructed.

Tales From A Briefcase

"Right – it will be on your desk tomorrow morning," and John left the office.

I returned to considering how to handle the retirements. Some workers had been at the factory all their working lives, since leaving school at fourteen years of age. Something special would have to be arranged, but what? A party, a big social event? No, they weren't going to be in that joyous a mood. Perhaps a small tea party in the factory manager's office? Despite their long service, most would have not been to the office block, never mind the manager's office.

I glanced around my office. Apart from large windows looking out over Leeds, it screamed of luxury – potted plants and bright flowers, deep-pile carpet, colour-matched decor, a large desk with upright chairs and a sofa with easy chairs encircling a low coffee table. Both the workers and I would feel out of place here.

I started to think about the people I would have to see. Were they victims of modern industrial life, which pronounced that at a certain age you were no longer useful to the community? Were they lambs to the slaughter? Those who had given all their lives to the company, which had extracted their last energies and would now release them into God knows what, exhausted, without focus for life, without hope for the future?

They would have joined the old family company as teenagers and taken lowly jobs to get a foot on the ladder towards learning a skill or becoming an apprentice. Their working conditions, over fifty years ago, would have been appalling by today's standards, which were now quite bearable – but not quite like my office. If I brought them up for tea, how would they react?

A wave of guilt swept over me. I, a southerner, had been recruited and appointed by the big boss in London. I had been with the group only a few years and with the factory at Leeds only a few months. And yet here I was, a newcomer, a virtual foreigner controlling the destinies of those staying and those about to leave.

My secretary popped her head around the door and asked, "Coffee, Mr James?" I looked at her: tall, blonde, slim, good figure and in her early twenties. Helen was bright and had the next stage of her life mapped out. Yorkshire did not feature much longer in her plans. She had decided that London was the place to be and the way to get there was by becoming qualified at the local college, finding a job as a top secretary at a local factory and then moving on to a London, where there was money, excitement and eventually a rich husband to be had.

"Yes, please, Helen. And come in with your notebook."

She came in with a tray, set it down on a side table, poured my coffee and brought it to my desk. She took one of the upright chairs opposite me and sat, crossing her legs with a swish of stocking on stocking, her skirt well above her knees. I looked up and noted that she was watching me closely, her pencil poised between her lips, in what she thought was an alluring stance. With her, sex always appeared close to the surface. I looked away, my eyes focusing on the headquarters instruction.

"Thanks for the coffee. I need your advice." She put down her pencil and notebook and shifted to a more relaxed position on the chair.

"Did you see this group communication about getting rid of people past retirement age?" I asked.

"Yes – I read it when I took it out of the envelope," she replied.

I looked at her straight in the eyes and asked with some seriousness, "You were born in Leeds, weren't you?"

She nodded her head, her blonde curls bouncing and flouncing. "Not far from this factory, actually."

"Do you know many of our workers?" I asked.

"I know most of the nine hundred by sight and several hundred by name. You're going to ask me how many of those I know are likely to affected – and what you should do about it."

"Yes, actually I was. What will they be thinking? Will many of them welcome retirement? How can we alleviate the blow?"

"My, my, Mr James!" she quipped, "there's a lot of questions for a mere secretary."

"Come on, Helen, stop teasing me," I said exasperatedly. "Help me. If not, help me to help them."

I knew some of the history of the company. It was a Leeds family business and had started just before World War One. It made box cameras for the growing domestic market in photography. Many of the people here today had joined the company when it opened. The working conditions were poor

Tales From A Briefcase

and wages were low by comparison with today. But the workers became close friends, and when necessary, ganged up together to fight the owners on what they considered to be unfair issues.

Most who lived in the local district either worked here themselves or had relatives in the factory – sometimes, whole families of them. Their family histories were inextricably tied up with the history of the company.

Helen nodded, then said, "Well, the group acquired the business a few years ago just after I'd joined the factory here. It introduced rules and regulations which were far tougher than anything the original owners could have dreamed up. Since then the staff have felt used, exploited and controlled from afar. They believe that the bosses in London couldn't care a damn about them. The southerners just use them to increase profits to make other people rich. Nothing is put back into Leeds to improve the lot of the workers here. There you have it – you'll have a hell of a job on your hands."

In desperation, I asked, "Perhaps a party on the shop floor and tea with me here on the day of retirement?"

"Fat reward for over fifty years of service!" she snorted "What has the group done for these people? Stopped the social club, stopped the factory outings to the seaside, given them pathetic wages and pensions. Do you expect them to respect the group which you represent? To be grateful?"

"Helen, I haven't set the working conditions or made this latest ruling. I am trying to be a human in my job of running the factory. I want to change things – make life better for the people. I need to do something!"

"You're on your own, Mr James," she responded flatly.

During the time I had been at the factory, I had walked round and chatted with some of the workers. One in particular had attracted my attention. She had called out to me from her workbench, where she was sitting and swinging the handle of a fly-press. I had walked over and watched her select a small metal disc from a box with her left hand, place it into the press tool and, with her right hand, swing the vertical handle vigorously from right to left, leaning back in her chair to avoid it hitting her in the face. The press tool banged into the flat disc, squashing it into a small cup shape which was later to be used as a part of an assembly. I could see that the muscles in her right arm were very developed from this swinging over the years: I wouldn't like to be on the end of her right hook when she got mad, I thought. I looked at her more closely – grey hair, round face, glasses perched on the end of her nose, plumpish and, as far as I could imagine from her posture on the chair, pear-shaped.

"Are you just up from London, lad?" she had asked. "Do you think you'll be staying long?"

I had met these old biddies elsewhere, trying to belittle managers, being over-familiar, even being disrespectful and certainly playing to the audience of their work mates. I could deal with this breed!

"Er – yes, I'm from London. What's your name?"

"Aggie – Agnes Featherstone. You can call me Aggie, everyone else does. What's yours?"

"Er – I'm Robert James, the new factory manager," I had said.

"Well, we'll just call you Robbie," she piped up. This was accompanied by a wry smile on her face, a twinkle in her eye and a turning of her head to her work mates before giving them a big wink.

I had to bring this conversation back to order – back to where I had re-established my authority. I ignored the insolence and tried another tack

"Well, Aggie, how long have you been here?"

"Ee, lad, a helluva long time – I shan't tell you how long 'cos it would give my age away and, being a gentleman, you wouldn't be interested in my age," this with a hearty chuckle and a circling of her head to catch the eyes of her 'mates'.

"How many time a day do you swing that handle?" I had asked, thinking about the repetitive boredom of the job and how long she had done it.

"Ee, lad, I wouldn't know. I've never counted. I don't think about it. Me and me mates occupy ourselves with long chats about last night's telly, local scandal and best of all – sex." The last bit had been said to make me blush.

"Er, well fine Aggie," I'd said, my face reddening. "I'm glad you enjoy it here. Keep up the good work!"

"That I will, lad, that I will. And we'll be watching you – seeing if you're tough enough to deal with us as well as the

Tales From A Briefcase

bosses in London. You can tell them from us that we're Yorkshire and we don't take to southerners, and particularly Londoners."

A final shot from me in redemption: "And I'll be watching you and your mates and expecting you to make sure that the Londoners have nothing to complain about our work in this factory. You know, my head's first on the line if this factory doesn't perform. You should remember that."

But she was going to have the last word, come what may. She had shouted at my departing back as I'd walked away: "Ay, Robbie, we'll remember that – but you remember we'll be looking after our own."

When Helen had gone back to her own office, I sat with my head in my hands. I just knew that Aggie was going to be on the list!

* * *

There was a knock on the door and John Scott walked in.

"Hello, Robert, I have that list for you."

"Thanks, John. How many?" I asked, taking several typed pages from him.

"Sixty-four now and another thirty-five within the next six months."

My God, I thought, that was ten percent of the work force – their leaving would cause chaos on the shop floor. It would take years to replace their skills.

"Any ideas how we might handle the enforced retirements, John?" I asked. "Could we interview them individually? Find out what personal problems might hit them, see if there is any financial compensation we can get them from the group or the DHSS?"

"Yes, Robert, we'll explore all of that, but I just cannot see a way of breaking it gently to them. It's a tough one. The unions are bound to weigh in on this."

I thought for a moment. "'ll prepare three documents – a personal letter to the individuals concerned, a statement for the factory and the unions, and a press release. It won't be long before the press gets wind of this anyway. After that, I'll see all those retiring individually, have a meeting with the unions and

Tales From A Briefcase

address the factory, department by department. Please set it up for me, John. Today is Wednesday; we'll start tomorrow and finish by Friday. That will give us two more weeks until the end of the month, which is the deadline I have been given by group to complete the exercise."

"I'd better get cracking," said John, leaving the office in a rush. Good man, I thought, but not quite human enough to be a personnel manager – not enough sensitivity and emotion to feel the desperateness of it all.

Looking down the list John had given me I found the name Agnes Featherstone, and alongside it: 'Age 63, spinster, no next of kin, joined 1914, press operator, press section'. I did the mental calculation in my head – my God, 49 years service – she would have got her gold service medal and an increased pension if she had stayed on one more year. This woman was beginning to haunt me.

In a funny way, I respected Aggie, understood what she stood for, could imagine her working in the factory over all those years. Whatever her own problems, she was strong, lifted the spirits of those around her, kept them going day after day through the hours of monotonous drudgery. It was people like her who had created the factory community. The company and its managers had little to do with that.

Yes, as the factory manager, I could live with the Aggies of this world – could take their backchat, even their piss taking. They were the real leaders of the shop floor and their support was essential if the factory was going to succeed. And how would the Press Section take the news of her retirement? Was there an up-and-coming Aggie, following along behind?

I switched back into my priorities of the day: afternoon factory tour at 2 pm. Could I face it, knowing what was to be announced the next day? What would the workers think of me? What *could* they think of me? I would be seen as the hatchet man of the bosses in London for the rest of my time in Leeds. I would never be able to show my true personal colours, my need to demonstrate the humanity of a middle manager, my concern for the workers and the well-being of their families. Was this all pie in the sky, my dreaming of creating an industrial community where there was at least some harmony between the needs of the

Tales From A Briefcase

workers and the needs of management? Had modern industry swept away such fine thoughts in its fight to create profits and compete in world markets?

I stood up, put on my coat and left the office. "Just going out for a breath of fresh air, Helen," I shouted as I passed her office.

She came into the corridor. "What?" she asked incredulously, "You have a full programme this afternoon!"

"Bloody cancel it. I'm going up to the moors to think," I snapped back.

"What shall I tell anyone who asks for you?" she queried.

"Tell them I've gone off to find myself!" I answered angrily, and left the building.

The Jaguar purred down the road, calming my jangled nerves. What's got into me? I thought. It's a factory manager's job to deal with these problems, coolly and calmly, without emotion, without showing feelings. Was I failing in my job? Did I not have enough guts to face what had to be done? Maybe I was just blowing off to myself; there was no one else I could share this with. I told myself that I'd be alright on the day, that I just needed to feel the wind in my hair, admire the beauty of the moors and adjust my sense of proportion. Thinking about it rationally, I decided that industry needed people like me – a conscience at the lower level, a humane interpreter of inhumane top decisions. Yes, that was my role. It was needed and I would do it.

The bleak and beautiful Yorkshire moors came into view. I drove on at a moderate pace, a classical tape playing Mozart's violin concerto – it was very soothing. There on the horizon was Otley, and now the drive down to Burley-in-Wharfedale. I parked the car near a park and found a path that went along the banks of the River Wharfe, tree lined at this point but shallow enough to flow fast over rocks and produce delightful gurglings.

This river kept popping up into my life. I had first seen it as a young soldier based at Richmond Barracks over fifteen years before, had courted along it and revisited it somewhere along its path from Bolton Abbey to Richmond many times since. Yes, it was a good place to recover a perspective on life.

I sat on the riverbank throwing stones into the water. Later, when I felt refreshed in mind and body, I returned to the car and

Tales From A Briefcase

drove back the way I had come. I felt thirsty and decided I would visit a very pleasant hotel down at Pool Bank. Parking the car in the hotel car park, I went in through the reception and into the bar. A grey haired, middle-aged barman appeared. "We've just opened the bar. What will you have, sir?"

"I'll have a pint of Tetley's, please."

I paid him, lifted my glass and started towards a cosy-looking fire further down the room.

"I was watching you as you drove in. Nice car – Jaguar – British Racing Green. Bet that cost you a packet," the barman commented.

"It's not mine. It's the company's."

"By heck, mister, you must have a grand job and cushy at that, drinking at six o'clock in the evening," he remarked casually.

I fixed my eyes on him, wondering if I should reply or leave it there. I couldn't.

"You don't get to drive company cars like that unless you've put in years of hard graft, clawed your way up the bloody ladder and got yourself into a position where someone still stands on your head and you still carry the shit."

The barman was visibly taken aback by my vehemence. "I'm sorry, mister – keep your hair on."

I walked away to the fire, sat and drank my beer, thinking, "That's how the real people view me – I have an easy life because I drive a big car and take a few hours out. But they don't know the other side of the coin." I finished the beer and left.

The drive back to Leeds was uneventful; rush hour was over. The factory was shut and no one was around except for the commissionaire. "Good evening, Mr James. Working late?"

I looked him over. Smart uniform, medals from many war campaigns, quietly confident and cheery. I'd met his kind in the army – the long service NCO on whom it depends for its backbone. I'd found out that we had both been in Korea at the same time, and I had often taken time to swap army stories with him. I felt at one with Charlie. "Nice sunset tonight, Charlie, and not too cold. Bit different from November on the Imjin in '52'."

"Too, bloody right, sir. You know, a bit of active service in a place like that would sort out some of our tearaways here in the factory," the commissionaire commented wistfully.

Tales From A Briefcase

"I'm not sure, Charlie. We wouldn't wish on them what we've been through, would we?"

"You're right, sir, they should take their fun when they can. The hard times will hit them soon enough."

I moved on, pondering Charlie's remark. Was he talking about the responsibilities of marriage and parenthood, which would come later in their lives, or did he have an insight on the future of work and jobs in Britain?

I climbed the stairs to my office and strode to the window. The lights were twinkling all over the city. I could look right into the nearby houses. Curtains were not pulled to shut out the world, as was the case in the wealthier areas of Leeds. Televisions flashed and the residents could be seen moving about the rooms, serving supper and playing with children. That is the real world, I told myself – not like mine, not like this.

I picked up the file on the impending retirements, left for me on the desk by Helen, and started to write the announcements for tomorrow.

* * *

The announcements and group meetings had gone as well as could be expected. The end of the month was fast approaching, when the last working day for many people would arrive.

"Helen, what is the programme for Friday?" I enquired.

"You have a stream of retiring long service people coming for tea with you. Some are bringing work mates – it will be quite a jamboree," she said with some levity. "There are parties and presentations in all the departments, organised by the workers."

"When is Agnes Featherstone coming to see me?"

"At 3.30 pm. You've been worrying about her, haven't you?"

"Yes, I suppose so. She seems to epitomise the spirit of the company. I'm afraid that losing her and others like her will damage the company, change its character, take morale down."

"Well the bloody group should have thought of that before issuing those bloody stupid instructions," she retorted and stomped out.

A knock on the door presaged the entrance of John Scott. "We're going to have trouble tomorrow, Robert. Just about every department is putting up the shutters after lunch break.

Tales From A Briefcase

Food and booze will be brought in and presentations are to be made to those retiring. That's against company rules – no booze, no food, no partying. It's a safety issue. The supervisors are looking to management for instructions."

I looked at him and could see that he was earnestly concerned.

"There are times in business life, just as in the real world, when events take over and you can do nothing about them. As much as you try to stop them or avoid them, they become inevitable. We have such a situation here. On Monday, those who have not retired will come into work and it will be management's job to see that they give us a fair day's work. If we stop them tomorrow, we may not be able to do that on Monday. It's a matter of judgement – which is the lesser evil. We'll let them go ahead. Management will be there to ensure there is no trouble but management will smile and watch benignly. I'll see the managers this evening after work and give them my instructions. Organise it, please, John."

"Right," came John's clipped reply. Clearly, he did not like the decision but was not sufficiently committed to his viewpoint to protest.

* * *

"It's 3.30 pm, Mr James. Are you ready for Agnes and her friends?"

"Yes, Helen. Please bring the tea things in first and ask them to come up."

Their arrival was heralded by much giggling and many "oohs" and "aahs".

"Ello, Robbie – we've come to see the lion in his den – or is it the lamb? What a lovely office," she continued, "look there's my house down there."

Her two friends, introduced as Dot and Beryl, crowded into the window area and started to point and chatter excitedly.

Rather uncomfortably I pointed to the sofa and easy chairs and said, "Please sit down, ladies, and we'll have some tea."

This was followed by more excited comments on the tea service and the array of cakes and biscuits on the coffee table.

"Ee, Robbie, you does yourself well up here!" said Aggie.

"It's not like this all the time," I protested. "This is special – er, just for you!"

Tales From A Briefcase

She turned and winked at her friends, who dissolved into another fit of the giggles.

"Well, Robbie," she said taking the lead, "what shall we talk about?"

"Well Aggie, I'd like to hear your story. You've been here the longest and you must have some tales to tell?"

"That's right, Robbie, and there's some I couldn't tell and some you would not wish to hear."

"Tell me about the day you joined, Aggie."

She frowned and became serious. "That was a long time ago – 1914 to be exact. My school friends and I saw the factory being built – it took over two years, although it's had many extensions since then. People came from miles around to get jobs and I and two friends came too."

"Were you living in that house there at the time?" I asked, nodding my head at the window.

"Yes, I lived there with my mother and two brothers. Dad had gone off to the war."

"What happened to your family, Aggie?" I asked gently.

"My father and my elder brother went off to the war and were killed. My younger brother emigrated to Australia and I haven't heard from him since he went. I then lived with my mother until she died of cancer about eight years ago. Now, I'm on my own," she explained resignedly.

I had to ask the next question. "Did you ever marry, Aggie?" I asked very quietly, looking straight into her eyes, which had started to become misty.

"No, I didn't." After a few seconds to regain her composure, she explained: "But I had a young man, though. He was a few years older than me. A lovely boy, handsome, big and generous. He was a gentleman and I loved him dearly."

I was too choked to ask any more questions but Aggie continued to talk, "He joined up in 1917 and went to France. He was killed too, in the summer of 1918. I really loved him, you know."

There was a stunned silence in the room. Aggie had obviously not told this story in public before; not even to her work colleagues.

Tales From A Briefcase

Helen broke the awkward silence and I was grateful for her intervention.

"Come on, ladies, let's have some tea and cakes."

The excited small chatter resumed – about the party on the shop floor, the presents and who said what. Eventually, Helen intervened again: "Come on, ladies, Mr James can't chat to you all day. He's other people to see."

They all stood up and Aggie went over to the window. In a quiet and serious voice she said, "You know, Robbie, on Monday I'll be staying at home and I'll be looking from my window down there up to this window and imagining you working here. I shall miss working in this factory and seeing my friends every day. I don't know what I shall do with my time. It's like ... like my life has suddenly finished."

I gulped and could not find suitable words in reply.

She turned and held out her hand "Good luck, lad. Don't let them buggers in London get you down. I know that your heart's in the right place."

She turned towards the office door. I could sense the tears in her eyes and fought to hold back my own. I was overcome with need to do something more. "Aggie – wait," I said and went over and kissed her on the cheek.

She faced me with a smile, the wistfulness gone. She touched my face. "Ee, lad, if I were thirty years younger, I'd be after you." And then she left.

* * *

A few months after her retirement, Aggie was appointed supervisor of the Retired Employees Club. She organised weekly visits for our senior people to come into the factory to meet their friends and have tea and biscuits in the canteen. She established home visits for less mobile people and ensured that club members were invited to the company's social events such as coach outings, Christmas parties and children's sports days. She organised their funerals – and, a few years later, I was privileged to organise hers. Despite the continuing pressure from the group for cost economies, the Retired Employees Club survived. Together, Aggie and I had beaten "the buggers in London!"

CHAPTER 8

THE FACTORY NURSE

The telephone on my desk rang: I could tell it was an internal call. "Robert James," I answered.

"Peggy Atwell. Can you talk?"

Peggy was one of our factory nurses. With over a thousand employees, we manned a surgery day and night to cover both shifts, and there was a SRN or SEN nurse on duty as long as there were people working in the factory. The factory doctor also attended the surgery every day to deal with minor medical problems.

I could imagine Peggy sitting at her desk, a petite brunette of thirty-five, friendly smile, clearly spoken, dressed in her dark blue uniform with the upside-down watch pinned to it and caught at the waist by the fancy nurse's belt. She was married and had two children but that did not prevent her from taking on all the employees as her other family. She took her job seriously and understood what an important role she played in keeping the factory going.

"Yes, Peggy, let's talk."

"Norman Ackroyd is down in my surgery right now, laid out on the couch. He has been having headaches for the past two months and they're getting more regular and more pronounced. There's also a swelling on his head. He won't go to his GP. I've seen something like this before and it was a brain tumour. What do you want me to do?"

"Thanks for letting me know, Peggy. Is the doctor due in shortly? If so, get him to see Norman and ask him, if necessary, to make arrangements with any specialists to confirm his diagnosis. Keep me posted; if it's serious I would like to be the person to tell his family."

Norman Ackroyd was my idea of a Yorkshireman, medium height but sturdily built, quite outspoken but likeable. He had

Tales From A Briefcase

come to the factory at sixteen, as an apprentice, and was now about thirty-four. After a four-year apprenticeship he had become a fitter in the precision assembly line producing engraving machines. About four years ago he had become a sales engineer demonstrating machines, installing them and training customers' staff. His knowledge of the machines and his pleasant personality kept the orders flowing for this important part of our business. He lived in Harrogate, and had a wife and a daughter of about eight years of age.

A little later, my secretary put her head round the door, "The doctor and the nurse are here to see you."

"Send them in, please." They entered and I waved them to chairs.

"Good morning, Doctor. Have you been offered a drink? Good. How's the health of the factory?"

"Pretty good, considering the time of year. Coughs and colds mainly. A few employees asking for flu injections. Peggy deals with most of the customers' problems."

"Peggy is vital to keeping the factory running," I said, seizing an opportunity to praise her. "What do you think about Norman Ackroyd?"

"It's a bit early to say. He should see a specialist and maybe have a scan. However, he's against any further evaluation of his problem."

"I know him and his family pretty well. I'll talk to him and persuade him to do it for his family."

Later in the day, Norman came to see me. "Hullo, Norman. I hear that our best sales engineer is feeling a bit off-colour at the moment. It was good that you went to Peggy about your problem. How do you feel now? I asked him.

"I'm OK. Just the odd headache. It won't prevent me from doing my job!"

"I know you, my friend. Nothing stands in the way of your job. However, I think you should take the doctor's advice and have a few checks. If it's a minor problem you can have a few pills and bash on. If it's more serious, the quicker it is diagnosed and treated, the better it is for you and the family. You belong to the Company's Medical Scheme and can get the best and fastest treatment at no further cost. If you need to ease up on the travelling whilst you're having treatment, we can give you an assistant and you can control him as you want. What do you say?"

"What about telling Marie?" he asked. Marie was his wife.

"We can keep this to ourselves, if you want. You can tell her after you've had the diagnosis. Meanwhile come in and see Peggy every day and get the checks done. Yes?"

"OK, Robert. If anything happens to me, I want you to take care of my family."

"Of course, old son, but it won't come to that. We're just taking precautions."

As he left, I sensed that he was not entirely happy with my proposals.

I telephoned Peggy. "I've just had a chat with Norman. He's going along with our suggestions, but reluctantly. You should see him briefly every day. Don't let him drive with a headache; send him home in my car. See that he attends specialist consultations. You don't have to carry the responsibility alone: the doctor is there to carry the final decision. You and I may have a bigger role later – with his family."

Over the next few weeks Norman saw specialists and had scans. A brain tumour was diagnosed. An operation was possible but might not prove a cure. His headaches would most likely worsen, he might become depressed and his moods would swing wildly. I was advised that I should offer him office-based work and provide transport to and from his home.

I saw him at my first opportunity.

"Norman, do you understand your medical problem? Have the doctors given you the picture?"

"Yes. They say an operation is on the cards but they can't guarantee success. They say that I shouldn't drive, that I'll become listless and moody and maybe my character will change. I find it all pretty frightening. It's like knowing that I'll lose control of myself."

"The company will look after you, whatever happens," I told him. "You've put in all those years and the company owes you. We'll see you and your family right. You can work here in the factory when you feel like it – it will be useful work. When you can't get in, Peggy will come to your home to see you daily and I will come out when I can. Marie must telephone me when she needs help. Here is my home number. Go home and tell Marie and I will visit you both this evening. OK?"

"Thanks, Robert. I appreciate your help."

After he had left, I called a meeting with Peggy and my secretary.

"Norman will have his operation next week. We three have to provide a support team for his family. The specialist feels that the tumour may have grown too big to be removed without damaging his brain. His state could swing from violent to comatose and he may have to be readmitted to hospital. We'll just have to review the position day by day."

As it turned out, the tumour could not be removed and Norman was sent home. His moods became unpredictable and he became progressively unstable. Sometimes, he descended into deep depression, swearing at those around him and even threatening violence. On a few increasingly rare occasions he became quiet and logical, and then he would plan his funeral arrangements and his family's future.

It was awful for Marie and his daughter, seeing their husband and father deteriorating from a loving, caring family man to a violent monster. Eventually drugs were employed to quieten him down and keep him in a peaceful state.

Near the end, I explained to Marie the company's pension scheme and the arrangements that Norman and the company had put in hand for the family's future. They would be able to live in their home and her daughter could continue at the same school. Their immediate family lived close by and would provide support.

We buried Norman on a sunny, cold day in Harrogate Cemetery.

And Peggy? She was distraught at losing one of her charges. But, apart from the surgery routine, in the coming months she would have to deal with a suicide in the factory, a death by heart attack and even a birth in her surgery. She would cope with them all with a quiet humane efficiency, and continue to earn the respect due to her as a committed factory nurse.

Tales From A Briefcase

CHAPTER 9

SHE NEVER CAME BACK!

Helen, my secretary, put her head round the office door and said, "John Scott wants to see you for a few minutes – urgently."

I looked up from my desk and from the financial figures I was analysing. "OK, Helen, ask him to come up now."

Like most big group employees, John Scott was a stickler for procedures and regulations. Flexibility and forgiveness appeared not to feature in his emotional spectrum. As the factory manager, I was inclined the other way. With a knock on the door, he walked into my office.

"Robert, I need to talk to you about Alf Hebden, the foreman in the Prism Department."

"Oh, yes, I remember him. Medium height and build, with glasses and sharp-features. He always struck me as being a shy person but he's a wizard at manufacturing prisms." The prisms that his department made resembled great segments of cheese. Starting from a roughly shaped piece of specially formulated glass, the operators under his control ground and polished the prisms until the angles between the surfaces were extremely precise and the surface finish could be measured in millionths of an inch. They were used in television cameras and periscopes.

"Well, you might have to think differently of him when you've heard what I have to say," John remarked. Looking into his face, his forehead wrinkled with a frown, I knew this was going to be a longer session than I thought.

"Wait a minute, John." I pressed the intercom switch. "Helen, please hold all calls and bring us some tea."

John began: "Well, Robert, it's like this. The tea-trolley lady who takes tea and buns to the Prism Department has noticed, over several weeks, that she has been short on cash after visiting the department. She advised this to us in Personnel some days ago and we've been watching since then. She leaves the trolley

Tales From A Briefcase

and takes tea and buns across to the operators' workbenches because the machines cannot be switched off for the tea break. While she's away, Alf takes buns from the trolley without paying for them."

"John, you've got to be joking! This man has been with the company for years; he wouldn't risk his job and pension for buns. I don't believe it."

"It's true, Robert. Several people from my department have witnessed it."

I sighed and asked, "What do you want to do about it?"

John replied, "Stealing is a sacking offence, Robert. I can't see how we can hush it up. He'll have to go."

"My God, John, is this is what personnel work is about – spying on senior staff for petty misdemeanours? I won't let him be sacked. Talk to him, find out if there's a personal problem."

"Very well, Robert, but I can't agree with your decision."

I looked at John Scott – a 'by-the-book' man with no time to look under the surface at the real cause of a problem, and knowing or sensing that what I was going to say would deepen the divide between us, I said, "John, I'll handle it myself."

"If that's what you wish," he said, and left the room with anger bristling out of him from everywhere.

Later, I looked at my watch and saw that it was approaching the time when the tea-lady would be making her way from the canteen on the ground floor, up by lift to the second floor, which housed the Prism Department. I pressed the intercom switch. "Helen, I'm going up to the Prism Department. You can get me on Alf Hebden's phone if you need me."

"Right, Mr James," came her reply.

The factory had been built at about the beginning of the First World War. Constructed on four floors, it had the feel of an old Yorkshire woollen mill about it. It had been modernised several times since then and was now painted in bright colours and was well-lit and well-heated. I climbed the stairs to the second floor as a token to getting fit.

Alf was in his office seated at his desk, making out some records. He looked up as I knocked and entered.

"Hullo, Mr James. What brings you up here at this time of the day?"

Tales From A Briefcase

My visits round the factory were normally signalled in advance, either formally by me or informally by my secretary.

"Oh, I was interested to know how the Hungarian order was coming along," I half-lied.

Alf said, "It's running to time, Mr James. We'll ship it next week as planned." I knew this already. He was first class at his job and would ensure that it would happen like that.

"Come and show me around, Alf," I said, looking at my watch and walking to the office door.

We circled around the department visiting each workstation, and I chatted with the operators.

"How's the new baby, Maisie?"

"She's fine, Mr James. My mother does a grand job looking after Jeannie while I'm in work," she responded.

"That's a fine arrangement for both of you."

"It certainly is. I hope Mrs James is well. How's she keeping?"

"Thanks for asking, Maisie. Just fine. Bye."

"Hullo, George, that's a large beast you have on the turntable," I remarked next.

"That it is, Mr James. It took two days' grinding and smoothing to get to this stage, but it's polishing up well; it's already down to five Newton's Rings." These rings, like miniature rainbows, showed up when the work-piece was matched to an accurate test piece, and indicated accuracy.

"Not long now, George, and the Hungarians will be looking at their colour tellies seeing pictures taken by cameras containing your handiwork."

"Ay, it makes me feel proud that we in Yorkshire can make things happen in Hungary," he said with a beaming smile.

"Japan next, George. We'll beat those buggers at their own game. Bye"

I saw the tea-lady struggling through the swing doors, the trolley laden with a big urn of tea and piled high with buns, cakes and biscuits.

"Hullo, Doris," I addressed her. "Alf and I would like two cups of your lovely, hot strong tea and two current buns. How much do I owe you?"

"Hullo, Mr James," she replied. "Up here to drink tea out of the cracked cups with the workers!" she teased. "That will be

Tales From A Briefcase

exactly one shilling and cheap at the price!"

I handed Alf a cup of tea and a bun and said, "Let's take these to your office." Once there, I closed the door and sat down. Alf remained standing.

"For God's sake, sit down, Alf – you're making me nervous," I said, seemingly joking, but inside I was nervous about raising the subject that needed to be raised.

He sat and relaxed a little, and I continued in a chatty way: "Are you going to the company dance on Saturday?"

The company dances were held in the local Mecca ballroom to accommodate the two thousand people who normally attended. These Yorkshire people loved dancing, although it usually ended in a great 'knees up'. The workers would take over, leaving managers to gather in a small corner, waiting for an appropriate time to slink away.

"No, Mr James," he said looking away.

"Why not, Alf? All your mates will be there."

He faced me and said quietly, "I haven't been out since it happened."

Ye gods, it was like pulling teeth, getting information out of this one!

"Since what happened, Alf?" I asked, trying to keep impatience out of my tone.

He turned away again, his head bowed to his chest. "She never came back," he sobbed.

I put my hand on his shoulder and said, "I'm very sorry if I'm distressing you, Alf. Only go on if you feel up to it," and I sat back in the chair and waited.

"She never came back," he repeated and went on: "It happened three years ago last summer." I waited as he sobbed some more. "There was a school outing to Scarborough, you see," he said through the sobs. "Six pupils went out in a rowing boat without their teachers knowing."

More sobbing, then: "A big wave came in unexpectedly and the boat was overturned. They were all drowned."

I looked at him, speechless.

"But the worse thing was – only five bodies were washed up. Our Millie didn't come back."

Tales From A Briefcase

I sat back in the chair, watching this poor man re-live the experience. I could never have anticipated such a terrible story.

He went on: "Since that day, my wife has lived in the house with the blinds drawn and she's never gone out." He could go no further, his distress totally overcoming him.

I looked at him, feeling great sympathy for this man and the way he came to work every day, had hidden his desperate circumstances and managed to stay sane.

He turned to look at me again, his eyes red from weeping, his voice breaking, "So, Mr James, I won't be coming to the dance on Saturday."

I sat quietly, saying nothing.

Then the purpose of my visit came back to me. Bloody buns! I thought about what I could do, should do in the circumstances.

"Alf, that's a terrible story, unbearable for you in every way. If there's anything I can do to help, let me know."

"No, Mr James, this is a situation I and my wife must live with. Nobody can help. We must live with it for the rest of our lives."

"Alf, you're a good guy, a good engineer and a good foreman. You have the respect of us all. Remember that."

"Yes, Mr James, thank you."

I stood up to leave and then turned back.

"Alf, I know you must have a lot on your mind and you might forget things. Don't forget to pay the tea-girl for your bun – otherwise she has to pay for it out of her own pocket. You wouldn't want that, would you, Alf?"

He stood up and faced off to me squarely, his eyes fixed on mine. "No Mr James, I wouldn't want that at all."

I opened the door of his office and left, totally drained by the experience.

CHAPTER 10

DIAMOND JOHN

The telephone rang; it was Ron, my engineering manager. "I think you should meet John Corder, who's here with me now. He may have the solution to our drum problem."

The drums were part of a copying machine. Originally made from aluminium rolled sheet and welded into tubes of about fifteen inches long and nine-inch diameter, they were eventually coated with selenium which was part of the copying transfer process. The problem was how to machine the dimensions of the drum very precisely and create the smoothest possible surface on the outside of the aluminium.

There was a knock on the door and Ron entered with a short well-built man with thinning hair. My eyes were immediately drawn to a facial scar which ran from his left eye down to his chin. It was difficult to drag my eyes away from it to look into his as we were introduced. I noticed the Freemason's grip as we shook hands.

"Come and sit down, Mr Corder." I indicated an easy chair among a group around a low table. I also signalled for my secretary to come in.

"Ah Helen, see if Mr Corder would like some refreshment."

I noticed that his eyes roamed over her body taking in her height, blond hair, and good legs revealed by a short skirt. Not a shy girl, Helen deeply scrutinised his face and the scar. Corder touched the scar. "Don't worry, young lady, I only look like a pirate." He smiled at her somewhat leeringly.

A little embarrassed, I said, "Mr Corder, you'll please forgive our undue interest in your scar. Maybe after we talk business, you'll tell us your story."

"Nothing much to tell, really. I was working with de Beers at the start of the war in the Far East, buying and selling diamonds

Tales From A Briefcase

around southeast Asia. The Japanese invaded and most of the expatriates were organised into a defence force which was quickly over-run by their army. We were sent to prison camps along the Burma-Siam railway to improve and extend it. You'll have seen the film 'Bridge on the River Kwai'. It was just like that.

"One day I was rather slow getting to my feet as a senior Japanese officer came up to me. An accompanying junior officer drew his sword and slashed my face. Without drugs and medication the wound became infected and took months to heal. We were eventually released by the Fourteenth Army as they headed east in 1945. I was repatriated to the UK and rejoined de Beers as a specialist in industrial diamonds. Which is why I'm sitting here now."

"Thank you for that. Ron has explained our engineering problem to you and we're keen to hear how industrial diamonds can help us solve it."

Corder explained: "As you might know, diamonds are one of the hardest substances known, and when dressed for the purpose and mounted into a tool holder, will cut metal very finely with the minimum of applied pressure. Aluminium, being very soft, will distort under pressure. I think we can do the job if we can hold the drum without movement, say with an expandable football-type holder. We'll design a double-tool holder to move along the drum surface, the first tool sizes and the second produces a two-micron finish. This is a first for us. We'll have to experiment in your engineering laboratory to get the geometry as near perfect as we can."

"What sort of budget will you need, Ron?" I asked.

"One engineer working full time with John's engineer for six weeks. We'll also need to adapt a light lathe, make the positioning device and produce about a hundred drums to experiment with. Say about twenty thousand pounds."

"Mr Corder, we'll need a price for the diamond tools. Can they be redressed after use? If we assume a quarter million drums a year, how many new and redressed tools will we need? What will our annual expenditure on diamonds be?"

"I can give you a crude estimate now and a more precise cost after we've determined the manufacturing method. As a first guess I would think between two and four pounds a drum."

Tales From A Briefcase

I weighed up the first estimate and considered the options of using other methods. There were few. To get a fine surface condition, we would have to resort to polishing techniques like we used on glass lenses; the cost would be enormous.

"Right Mr Corder, we'll give it a whirl. We'll allow six weeks to prove the method as a joint exercise and, if it works, we'll give you sole supplier status for a minimum of two years. OK?"

"OK! I'll have an engineer over from my works in Coventry next week."

"Any points, Ron?"

"I'll get an engineer on to designing the positioning device straight away. Otherwise, fine."

The experiments proved the operation to be feasible and we were soon producing precisely dimensioned, undistorted drums with highly-polished surfaces at a rate of five thousand a week, to be sent to the copier assembly factories around the world. Mr Corder responded to our orders for new and redressed diamond tools on time and with the required quality.

A few months later, when Helen came into my office to review my diary, she said, "Mr Corder was on the telephone and has invited you to a dinner in the London Hilton. You're free on the date proposed, as you're in London earlier for a meeting at group headquarters. Mr Corder is entertaining about forty clients. It'll be a black tie occasion."

I considered the invitation for a moment. Sometimes suppliers used entertaining to put the customer under an obligation or even into a blackmail situation. I would avoid this at all costs.

"Tell him I accept and will talk to him on the telephone later."

A few days later, Helen put through a call from Mr Corder. "Good morning Robert, John Corder here. I'm so pleased you can come to my dinner. There will be quite a few well known industrialists there and a few political figures with clout." Suddenly my senses went on the alert. "I'll organise accommodation. Just bring yourself and your dinner jacket," John continued.

On the prescribed day I reported to the reception desk at the Hilton. A young man soon appeared and introduced himself as my personal valet. I began to feel distinctly uncomfortable but

Tales From A Briefcase

followed him to my allocated room, which was luxurious with a large double bed and a balcony overlooking Hyde Park.

"May I open your case and hang up your clothes, sir?"

I spun round to answer him, still pondering on the luxury and its possible cost, one way or another.

"Yes, please do." I watched as he unpacked and put my clothes in a wardrobe.

"What shoes will you be wearing this evening, sir?"

"The ones I'm wearing now. Perhaps you would polish them up for me?"

"Oh no, Sir. Mr John likes his guests to be properly dressed. I will get you some patent leather dress shoes and a proper bow tie to replace your made-up one."

Later, the telephone rang. "Robert. John here. I hope that you're comfortably settled in. My guest reception is at seven o'clock in room one-zero-six. After that, we eat at eight in the Continental Restaurant on the first floor and at ten we go up to the Starlight Room at the penthouse level to see the cabaret."

"John, that sounds marvellous. I'll see you at seven."

I put the telephone back in its cradle and gave some serious thought to the position I was in. Was all this merely innocent commercial socialising between supplier and customer, or had I stumbled into something more threatening? Perhaps I had been looking for scoundrels under the bed for too long? Perhaps it was just normal hospitality?

My valet appeared with patent leather dress shoes, an unknotted bow tie and some silver cuff-links. I let him tie the bow, his face close to mine, smelling his powerful after-shave lotion. Now I was feeling really uncomfortable as his delicate hand fluttered under my chin.

"There you are, sir. Dressed to the nines, as they say. Do you need anything else, now or later?"

The question could have all sorts of hidden meanings. "No thank you. You've looked after me very well."

"Goodnight, sir. I hope that you enjoy the evening's arrangements," and he left. Again there appeared to be more behind his closing remark.

I deliberately delayed my arrival at the reception until 7.15. When I got there, the room was full of men in evening dress,

Tales From A Briefcase

mostly black but with here and there a white tuxedo. John was welcoming guests as they arrived. Standing alongside him was a middle-aged lady, expensively dressed and festooned with jewellery.

"Robert, this is Celia who is acting as my hostess for the evening. Celia, this is Robert. He is one of Britain's youngest, star industrial managers; he appears in the press and on television regularly."

I shook her gloved hand and she fluttered her eyes at me coquettishly.

"Tell me about yourself," she pressed. "You must be important if John gives you that build up. Are you married? Family?"

"Yes, I am married with a four-year-old daughter. My wife has a severe mental illness. My job takes me away from home a lot. It's difficult to be a good businessman and a good husband at the same time."

She patted my arm. "I know how it is. Be a dear and get me some more champagne." I took the glass from her hand and signalled a waiter. I noticed that Celia had returned to John and was talking to him intently, both occasionally looking in my direction. I returned to her with a full glass.

"We'll meet later but now I must go back to John to help him with receiving guests," Celia said. "Let me introduce you to some people. Lord Wokingham, this is Robert James, an industrialist. Peter Meredith, this is Robert James, an industrialist. Lord Wokingham is in the House of Lords and Peter is Conservative Member of Parliament for Hurstpierpoint."

We shook hands and immediately got into discussing the industrial scene under a Labour government: exports, union activity and exchange rates for the pound. While we talked, I racked my brain for something I'd heard about Lord Wokingham. Of course, he was friendly with the infamous Talbot twins, so the press reported. Peter Meredith had been associated with a homosexual scandal, also spread across the press. John Corder's associates were a rum lot and not the sort of people a simple industrialist like me would normally rub shoulders with.

The guests moved down to the Continental Restaurant where a long U-shaped table was set with beautiful cutlery and

Tales From A Briefcase

glassware. I noticed John was positioned at the top between Lord Wokingham and Peter Meredith. I sat at the place designated by my name card.

The dinner proceeded very much like that of a military mess night. After the main courses, Lord Wokingham rose to propose the health of the Queen with the guests standing to respond to the toast. Cigars were lit up and John stood to make a speech. After welcoming the guests and naming a selected few, he went into a discourse which had a considerable political, anti-government slant. Clearly most of his guests were Conservative supporters and it became clear that he was manoeuvring into a position.

Conversing with one of my neighbours, I was informed that John had given generously to Conservative Party funds and that a knighthood was on the cards.

"What about the Talbots?"

"They rub shoulders with the royals at horse-racing. It doesn't seem to present a problem."

I sat dumbfounded through the rest of the time in the restaurant, until there was banging of a spoon on a table and John arose to inform the party that they should move to the Starlight Room on the top floor. A small band was playing dance music as we were led to a long table with name cards placed at every other position. I took my nominated seat and waited. Celia arrived with a bevy of beautifully dressed and made-up women in a wide range of ages.

Celia approached me and I stood. "Robert. I would like you to meet Maire who will sit next to you for a time."

I turned to shake Maire's hand. She was tall, had a slight figure, brown eyes and black hair. I guessed her age at about thirty.

She sat and turned to me: "I hear that you've lived and worked in Ireland. I'm from Dublin. I also have been told that you spent time with Radio Telefis Eirrean. I know Eammon Andrews and Gay Byrne."

I listened to her voice – hardly any brogue. Protestant, I guessed, and educated at Trinity College, Dublin.

"You know a lot about me, Maire. Yes, I worked in Ireland for four years as a business consultant with Irish Sugar, and two

Tales From A Briefcase

years with RTE in the big re-organisation. Where are you from originally?"

"Ah, Robert, it's a long time ago. Achill Island, Athlone and Dublin. Trinity College and the Gate Theatre. Then I came to England to find my fortune. I'm still looking for it!"

I looked at her more closely. How did a beautiful and intelligent girl get mixed up in the hostess business? But, truthfully, I enjoyed her company. We had much to talk about. We watched the cabaret of singers, comedians and scantily dressed dancers.

"Would you like to dance, Robert?"

"Sure," and I followed her to the dance floor. The music was a romantic slow foxtrot. Her arms went around my neck and she pressed her body into mine. I looked around and saw all the other guests were similarly engaged. I guessed that Celia must have an incredible amount of intelligence on each guest; because the hostesses had been hand-picked and matched closely with their partners. We danced some more and I could feel my nether regions stirring.

Returning to the table, I could see that other guests were disappearing with their hostesses. I looked at my watch – two in the morning. I had said that I would be back in Leeds by nine. And yet... No, I knew it would be nonsensical to follow my desires.

"Maire, I think you are a beautiful girl and very desirable but..."

I fumbled for the excuse.

"But," she interrupted, "you would like to leave this right here?"

"Yes, but...."

"Don't make up excuses. I know the form. Celia pays me whatever. I've enjoyed your company. Goodnight." And she left the room.

I looked around the nearly empty room and there was John Corder still sitting at the head of the table, alone. I carried my scotch to the chair next to him and flopped into it.

"I see that your brain still controls your dickie!" he remarked.

"I suppose so. I have to be back in Leeds by nine o'clock and have to be reasonably sober to drive up the M1."

Tales From A Briefcase

"I had the feeling you wouldn't be like the rest. Are you never tempted?"

"Of course. But my family has problems and I won't risk my job for anything. I'm heading for the top. And you?"

"Yes, I have my weaknesses but I don't pursue them in public. I have too many enemies who would like to see me fall off my pedestal."

I thanked him and left. Changing into my working clothes, I called in at reception to check out but found that John had covered the arrangements. The porter brought my Jaguar to the front door and I wearily climbed in to drive the two hundred and fifty miles to Leeds.

* * *

I met John several times after that, usually in the 007 bar at the Hilton for a drink. He was normally in the company of a young and beautiful woman. He had arranged with the band that, whenever he was there, they would play "Where have all the flowers gone?" When my secretary, Helen, left to work in London, he befriended her and set her up in a flat.

* * *

I last saw John several years later, still at the 007 bar at the Hilton, looking older but this time holding hands with a young Italian boy. He had exhausted London's supply of beautiful young women and was now seeking comfort from someone of the same sex.

CHAPTER 11

THE COMMISSAR

He sat in an easy chair near a low table, drinking coffee and smoking a cigarette. Peter, my European Sales Manager, had come to my office to talk about an order he had won from the Polish state television station in Warsaw.

He was fair, with a bright open face set in an almost continual smile. I put him at about thirty-two. He was an excellent sales manager, spoke several European languages and knew the ins and outs of our products – colour television cameras. I knew little about him personally, whether he was married, had children or where he lived, though Helen had informed me that he was a ladies' man and she took pleasure at declining his invitation to a date.

"Christ, what are you smoking? Camel shit?" I asked with feigned annoyance.

He laughed. "They're eastern European, a cross between Turkish and Gauloise. Does it put you off?"

"I'll live – and forgive you because you've won the order. Give me the details."

He took another sip of his specially-made strong coffee and another puff at the foul weed. "Up to now, Polish television has been in black and white but they want to move into colour. They want to use the PAL system used in Germany and the UK, in preference to the French SECAM system. That choice eliminates half of our competition and, whereas German lenses are good, the Poles see our electronics and technical back up as superior."

Another sip and another puff. "The initial order is for six cameras to be installed into the television studios in Warsaw. If they like them, we'll get the follow up orders for the studios in

Tales From A Briefcase

Cracow, Lodz and Gdansk. In all, I would think fifty cameras over three years, half payment on delivery and half on installation, in West German deutschmarks."

"That sounds very good. What are the preliminaries?"

"We need to set up the export credits with back-to-back-cover between the Polski Bank, Deutches Bank in Frankfurt and Barclays in London. I'll organise that with our financial boys. We need also to receive an initial visit of engineers to plan the transfer of technology and fix delivery and installation dates: I've arranged this for a week during next month."

"That also sounds good. How many in the visiting party? I'll set up the accommodation and transport arrangements."

"I think there could be four engineers but I'll confirm the details and programme after this meeting. These Iron Curtain countries usually send a political commissar with visiting teams to make sure they behave, stick to the party line and return. They speak English and German, so between us we should get the message over."

Our meeting finished after discussion of a few more details. Later, dates were fixed for the visit and I started to brief my managers about the programme which, apart from instruction on camera operation, would include tours of the factory and some off-site entertainment. The Leeds City of Varieties always went down well with foreigners with limited English.

Eventually, the Polish team flew into Heathrow on their national airline and picked up an internal flight to Leeds. Peter came by my office to announce: "They're having a meal in the canteen and will be with you in about half an hour. There are four engineers and a lady political commissar. She really is a good looker. I rather fancy her!"

"You keep your hands off her. We can't afford to lose the order because you don't measure up to her amorous requirements!"

He snorted and left the office. Later, the Poles arrived and I welcomed them in German and English and announced the programme with details of administration. We had booked a guesthouse nearby, where they would take breakfast and dinner.

"Are there any questions, or comments you would like to make?" I enquired.

67

Tales From A Briefcase

The commissar intervened before any of the others could say anything. "I am Frau Natasha Weber, the leader of this team. Apart from technical discussions between the engineers, all comments and arrangements must be made by me or through me. I am totally responsible for the Polish team. You must not ask us to comment on politics, government matters or foreign policy."

I looked at Peter, who shook his head to indicate that I should leave it there.

The Poles started in on the programme and all appeared to be proceeding smoothly until Peter came to see me, red-faced and angry.

"She's slowing everything up. She won't allow us to talk to the engineers about matters other than the operation of our cameras. We need to know their studio routines and editing procedures if they are going to use our kit properly. We have to create a more relaxed environment if this visit is going to be successful."

"What do you intend to do?"

"I'll have to get under her skin somehow – get under her skin and get personal or something."

"You just watch your step. We mustn't do anything that could lose us the order."

"You'll have to trust me, Robert," he said and he left.

The relationships between the Poles and engineers became noticeably more relaxed and clearly friendships were being established. I called a mid-visit conference between Peter, the commissar and myself to evaluate progress. Peter did most of the talking with him referring to "Natasha" in glowing terms while she just sat with cow-like eyes and nodded.

The bugger, I thought, he's bedded her. She's like putty in his hands. After the conference, I had a private word with him.

"Well," he said, "something had to be done and I did it. Communications are excellent and we have no interference from the commissar."

"But at what cost, my friend? Watch for the pay-off."

He just grinned and waved me a cheery goodbye as he left the office.

Tales From A Briefcase

* * *

The time had arrived for the Poles to go home. My secretary put her head round the door of my office, "That Polish lady wants to see you. She says it's private."

"OK, put her in the diary!"

At the appointed time, there was a timid knock at the door and Natasha entered.

"Please sit down, Natasha. Before we discuss your business, I want to thank you for your assistance in making the visit such a success."

"Ah," she said, "this is what I came to see you about. I have not carried out my duties as I should have done. We have not kept our political distance. I have failed in my job. My superiors will detect this when they debrief me."

"But your team has done a good job. They learned all they needed to operate the equipment. The installation will go smoothly because of this trip. It must be recognised as a success and that is down to you."

She shook her head. "I have betrayed my party; put my personal feelings before my job. I've fallen in love with Peter. I want to stay here and live with him!" she ended tearfully.

Oh my God, I thought, the stupid bugger had taken it too far.

"Let me talk this over with Peter and we can meet tomorrow to discuss the best thing for you, the party and your team. Alright?"

I sent for Peter. "What the bloody hell have you been up to? Natasha has just left and she told me she loves you and wants to stay in England. This could blow the order. Did you say that you loved her?"

"I told her what was necessary to isolate her from the Polish engineers, to get the job done properly. I don't want to live with her. She's lousy in bed, full of inhibitions."

"Well, you've certainly stirred her up. You'd better remove yourself from the scene immediately and leave me to apply the finishing touches."

I met Natasha on the following day and explained the situation.

"Natasha, we have a more relaxed society than you do in Poland. People form more casual relationships here than you do

Tales From A Briefcase

at home. Business and pleasure is mixed but without serious commitment, without consequences. Peter admires you very much and thinks you're very attractive. He has enjoyed meeting you and enjoyed your company. But I must say this – he does not love you! I have sent him away and you will not see him again. It was wrong of him to involve you emotionally. Do you understand?"

"I don't know. I am so confused. This has not happened to me before. I still have betrayed my party and country."

"You have not damaged you party and country in any way. They will benefit from the good job your engineers have done while they were here. That's to your credit. From what I have heard none of our engineers know this story. It will not get back to Poland. My advice for the good of everyone, you, Peter, your country, my company, all of us is – go back to Poland and finish the good job you have started. If you can, remember us here as your friends. Forget betrayal. Continue to love your country. Maybe, one day, our countries will find a way of being close friends. Until then we are your supplier and you are the customer; we promise to give you the best service possible and will remember our friends from Poland."

She left, again tearfully, and with her colleagues boarded the bus to the airport. I could see her small, unhappy face through a window and noted her half-hearted wave of goodbye. She didn't look like a commissar any more. I wondered if she would survive the regime to which she was returning.

Tales From A Briefcase

CHAPTER 12

A FINE OLD ENGLISH COMPANY

Warwick

Other than a sculpted wooden eagle with outspread wings, mounted on a wooden pedestal in the reception hall, there were few clues to the origin of the company's name, Eagle Engineering. Until recently it had been a family business, started in the mid-nineteenth century as farm-cart makers and repairers of farm implements. The arrival of the internal combustion engine sixty years later made lorry making a natural diversification. The volume market brought about by standardisation of load-carrying bodies was captured by the national vehicle manufacturers, leaving the low-volume specialised markets to small body-builders, of which Eagle Engineering was one.

Although not making much of a profit for its owners, the company had established a reputation for good engineering design, outstanding after sales service, and value for money. In the workshops could be seen dustcarts and gully-cesspit emptiers, painted in the livery of many of Britain's local authorities. Just here and there was a potable water tanker for an airline, or a vehicle with a telescopic mast for relaying outside television broadcasts.

The new owners, a car sales group, had acquired the company for a rumoured knock-down price and had plans for expansion, but based on minimum further investment. They targeted the growth opportunities for specialist vehicles: aircraft servicing and baggage handling, the multi-axle load carriers for long distance motorway operations, and sky platforms for working at height.

Tales From A Briefcase

Even the design of dustcarts was changing. Waste no longer contained a preponderance of ashes swept from domestic fire grates but a high proportion of packaging and even more waste food. Trips to the tip for waste burial were to be reduced by using larger bodies with compression packing. Britain was following the USA in increasing vehicle loads from 3 tons through 5 tons to 7 tons. With trips to the tip reduced and more time spent on waste collection, the crews of the refuse vehicles needed to have on-board lavatory, washing and refreshment facilities, and crew cabs containing these facilities emerged. Whereas 'totting' had long since been a practice as perks for the dustmen, recycling put a worthwhile price on selected waste; dustcarts now carried recycling waste compartments.

The company had experienced a strong export demand from the dominions and colonies for its side-loader vehicles, where rubbish was tipped into a simple metal body covered by hinged bin-lids and exhausted by tipping via a tailgate. Water tankers for delivering fresh water to outlying African districts were constantly to be found on the order list. These could be shipped complete or in "knock-down" form for assembly by overseas factories.

The job was advertised by selection consultants as "Managing director of a small specialist body manufacturer in Warwick, with a remit to modernise manufacturing and break into new markets." I applied and, despite my previous background being in electronics and optics, I was short-listed and given a final interview. A good salary and a Jaguar were offered and I accepted the job.

On my first day, I took the train from Leeds to Warwick station where I was met by the company secretary, a kindly gentleman in his seventies. We drove through the centre of Warwick and took a downhill road running north out of the town, arriving at an old building with large plate glass windows along its front. The front door opened on to a foyer – and there stood the Eagle.

I was shown into my office, a large room without windows but with a skylight making it bright. The walls were wood-panelled and the furniture dark and old-fashioned. It looked nineteenth century and smelt liked it. I sat in an old captain's pedestal chair and wondered what I'd got myself into.

Tales From A Briefcase

"I'm Rosie Pepper, your secretary. I thought you'd like a cup of tea."

I turned and saw the owner of the voice, a short, small-built lady, greying hair tied close back to her skull and with a beaky nose emphasised by large glasses. She was an incredible contrast to the Yorkshire lassie I had left back in Leeds, who was young, tall and slim and of model proportions.

"How kind of you," I responded, noticing the absence of a wedding ring. "How would you like me to address you – Miss Pepper or Rosie?"

"Rosie is fine, but I'll call you Mr James to keep things proper. Now, you are booked into the Earl of Warwick Hotel in the main street. Here is a folder of houses on the market in Warwick and Leamington Spa. Your Jaguar is here and Jim Balding, one of our best drivers, will drive you whenever you need him."

I looked at Rosie with her bright, sharp face. A spinster, I thought, about fifty-five, born at the outbreak of the First World War, not many suitable chaps survived that show, probably an elderly mother or sister to look after.

The company was organised into four departments: Production, Engineering, Sales and Accounts. Later, on a tour of the premises, I realised that the factory consisted of long assembly sheds stretching backwards from the main office block, which was located on the main road itself. Within outbuildings surrounding the assembly sheds were a machine shop and toolroom where metal parts and components were made, sheet metal and welding shops, hydraulics and electrical shops and a paintshop. Dustcarts were made on one assembly line, tankers on a second and 'specials' on a third.

In the yard stood new chassis with cabs fitted, delivered from the manufacturers and now awaiting mounting of their bodies. Most local authority vehicles required forward control cabs with the engine mounted within the cab, which could be tipped forward to give access to the engine.

A service road led to a manned gate, through which materials arrived for manufacture and by which finished vehicles left for their ultimate destinations.

There was little evidence of modern materials handling, but craftsmanship was very obvious. Every fitter on assembly was a

Tales From A Briefcase

time-served engineer and worked from detailed drawings. 'Prufrock' of the Sunday Times, after standing in the finished vehicle yard and acknowledging the craftsmanship, wrote: "but they also do an incredibly fine job of hand painting."

On the top floor of the main office block, accessed by a rickety staircase, was the Engineering Department. Designers wrestled with the usual truck problems of axle-loading, centres of gravity, hydraulic force and body strength. Later, as we moved into new fields, they would tackle new problems of servicing the Boeing 747 jumbo jet, with its numerous toilets, high above the ground, to be emptied in minutes, baggage and cargo to be lifted to heights never before seen, and de-icing vehicles required to spray huge surfaces never before tackled. In road tankers, they would be faced with designs in glass-reinforced fibre to handle acids, and vacuum systems in which the toxic substances were never to pass through pumps.

The chief engineer was despatched to Boeing's Seattle plant to work with their servicing engineers, and came home with outline plans for a number of service vehicles. These were quickly transformed into final designs and then prototypes, so that the company could demonstrate products at the European air shows. We had beaten the competition in design time and won the early orders.

And so I slowly settled into my new job, forgetting about my past involvement with modern technologies, becoming embroiled with unions and their different requirements. The Coventry Toolroom Agreement had established that toolmakers were top of the pile and all other skills were graded into a pecking order. Skill and wages were inextricably linked, and unions and employers became engaged in long meetings for inter-job comparisons.

The nearly all-male workforce were proud of their skills and their products, despite some of the working conditions afforded by the old factory being less than satisfactory in the eyes of the Factory Inspectorate. It was clear to me that Eagle had something special to offer in world markets. It needed to employ its wide range of engineering skills on the relatively small niche specialist truck markets, sustain its reputation for fair price,

Tales From A Briefcase

quality of workmanship, and delivery on short lead times, and give top-notch after-sales service. We used every excuse to generate publicity, such as the time we sold a dozen refuse vehicles to Athens and convoyed them across Europe, with the press reporting their progress on a daily basis.

As part of our publicity campaign, our marketing consultants decided that we should try to get television exposure and that I should go on a short course to learn presenting to TV cameras. It was fascinating to see how an interviewer, co-operating closely with a cameramen, could create a wide range of audience reactions to an interviewed subject. Camera angle and close-in focusing associated with a specific difficult question could produce and emphasise body language, especially facial contortions, which a viewer could read and make a judgement on without listening to the spoken answer. The technique of participating in group discussions had to be understood; timing of saying one's piece was vital; the best slot was to be the last person asked to comment before the programme went off the air. Encouragement by the presenter to participate early was to be disregarded.

On the other hand, if introduced as a specialist or an authority on the subject under discussion, it was important to reinforce your claim to expert knowledge early but not to get rattled when challenged. I was asked to do a slot in the BBC's Money Programme on the subject of domestic waste and its clearance. It went well and I was invited back to talk about management and union problems

The positive press reporting on Eagle began to filter through to stock market analysts and the owners of the group found that the market demand for shares escalated, causing a hike in the market price. It was not long before overtures for acquisition were being made by other larger body builders and an offer which the group could not refuse was made and accepted. The acquiring organisation was not able to offer me the autonomy I had previously enjoyed and I resigned to accept a head-hunter's proposition in Poole. I had much sorrow in leaving my friends, Rosie and Jim and the guys who got their hands dirty. Together we had opened the oyster and glimpsed the pearl.

Tales From A Briefcase

The design office at Warwick was transferred to the acquirer's site in Guildford and, later, manufacturing was also moved there. A fine old English company, over a hundred years old, capable of attracting customers from around the world, was closed, its history and reputation diluted or lost in the new and emerging mission of 'growth by acquisition'. I experienced no pleasure from hearing that Eagle's acquirer was itself acquired and then progressively shut down.

CHAPTER 13

AN EAST AFRICAN ADVENTURE

Kenya

This was to be my first visit to the continent of Africa. My business was taking me to Kenya and then on to South Africa. Nairobi City Council was in the market for compression dustcarts and the commercial vehicle manufacturers at Port Elizabeth wished to purchase specialist lorry bodies.

It was not the first time that Eagle had sold products to African customers. On checking the records I could see there had been a steady flow of exports over the years, mainly for simple side-loading dustcarts and water tankers mounted on BMC and Ford chassis. The finished vehicles had been shipped to the nearest port, from where the shipper would make them ready for delivery and drive them to the customer.

Now African customers were calling for more sophisticated vehicles. Economics demanded local assembly from exported knock-down packs onto locally produced lorry chassis.

My chief engineer proposed that I take a scale model of a compression dustcart to Kenya to demonstrate the workings. The body was made in Perspex and the hydraulic rams, operating moving parts, were represented by little winding handles. Small pieces of paper loaded into its rear would be collected and rammed forward to be compressed against the strong bulkhead just behind the cab. When full, the body could be tipped up at the cab end and a ram operated in the opposite direction to sweep the rubbish out of the rear. A special carrying box was made so that it could travel without damage in a plane's cargo hold.

I had decided to start my journey from London Heathrow with East African Airways to Nairobi just after Christmas, having accepted an invitation from my Kenyan assembler to spend New Year with his family at Malindi on the coast.

Tales From A Briefcase

The evening flight took off, and dinner was almost immediately served. There were not many passengers in first class. When the meal had been cleared away, a passenger sitting immediately in front of me turned round to introduce himself.

"I'm Tom M'boya, an assistant to Jomo Kenyatta."

After years of mounting a guerrilla campaign against the British army, Kenya had been given its independence and Kenyatta had become president. There was still tribal tension between the Kikuyu and other tribes. The economy, still based on coffee and tea under British management, provided a stable level of exports. Transportation by rail and air was efficient but many country roads were still the same tracks used at the turn of the century. Nairobi had grown into a modern city housing the seat of government and commercial links with the world. Apart from white settlers, the local population of Africans and Asians were finding their escalating take-home pay allowed them to purchase adequate food, rent modern properties and acquire luxuries. In the bush, the tribal natives lived as they had always done, in mud huts, tending their flocks of cows, sheep and goats, which they moved in an annual migration pattern to find the best grazing.

"I'm pleased to meet you, Mr M'boya. I've read that you are working in economic development and Kenya's economy is beginning to lift."

"Yes, we're looking for new opportunities to employ our people and get them into useful occupations. We have a large government training programme underway for skilled workers. What are you doing in Kenya?"

"I guess, unknowingly, I'm trying to help you do your job! I'm helping to set up a factory to produce commercial vehicle bodies for assembly onto chassis already produced there – dustcarts and road tankers of all sorts. Do you think we'll be able to take tribesmen from the bush and make them welders?"

"We have to be realistic, it will take time. They won't take to the noise and smell of factory life easily, and they may find staying within factory walls for hours on end unbearable. In government we're worried that they may use drugs to make such work bearable – we call it 'being on the bang'. Then they may wander back to the bush to recover before returning for another stint."

Tales From A Briefcase

We continued our discussion for a little longer before he excused himself, giving me his card, and returned to his seat. I never saw him again and he was murdered by some dissenting tribesmen a few years later.

By dawn, the Boeing 707 was flying over the tea and coffee plantations of northern Kenya. It landed at Nairobi airport which looked newly built. Passenger stairs were rolled out to the plane and we disembarked into an already hot environment.

I collected my bag and the model and went into customs. A man in a white suit and hat atop of his incredibly black face eyed my wooden box with some excitement. He saluted and smiled, displaying a wide mouth of white teeth, "Jambo, sir. Have you anything to declare?"

"Yes, Officer, I have. In this box. It's a model truck."

His eyes gleamed as I opened the lid and lifted out the model. His hand went up to lift his cap and scratch the back of his head.

"Beautiful," he said, touching it rather lovingly. "Show me how it works."

"It's a model dustcart." I scrunched up some empty forms on his desk and loaded them into the body, winding the handles so that he could see it compressing. I then tipped the body and ejected the compressed paper all over the floor.

"Wonderful," he exclaimed, dancing about to recover the waste from the floor and repack it into the model.

After several cycles of operation, he called the other customs officers over and quite a crowd was gathered around the model. Then my customs man decided to return to the business in hand.

"How much does this model cost?"

"About three thousand pounds sterling," I replied.

His hand went to his head again, tipping his cap forward and scratching, presumably thinking about my reply.

Finally, straightening his hat, he voiced his concern: "Sah, the children will never buy it at that price!"

I burst out laughing. This was picked up by all those in the shed. "This is not for children," I spluttered, "it's for a demonstration to the Nairobi City Council. You'll see the full-size lorry on the streets soon."

"But who will wind the handles?"

"There'll be no handles. The lorry engine will have a

Tales From A Briefcase

hydraulic pump which will operate the rams. The driver has switches in the cab instead of handles. Nairobi will have the most modern dustcarts in the world, made right here."

He visibly brightened up. "Model stays in Nairobi – yes? No re-export – no? Then, no tax. Good luck for the order. My brother works in the Cleansing Department. I'll tell him this is essential for Kenya."

He shook my hand and I passed through customs feeling that telephone lines would be humming around Nairobi today.

Scott MacDonald and his partner, Mike, owned a factory in the suburbs which assembled lorries. Scott met me at the arrivals hall.

"Where the hell have you been?" he asked. "I thought customs were giving you a difficult time!"

"Not really. I had to demonstrate the model." I held up the box.

He opened the lid and whistled, "They let you through without paying tax?"

"Yes, and I've had the customs officers playing with it. The city council will have heard of this before we arrive tomorrow."

"Great! I've put you into the Norfolk Hotel, just out of town. It has a lovely setting, gardens, swimming pools and an international menu. My partner is coming over for lunch and we'll cover a few points. Siesta after lunch and then down to see the factory before dinner at my place. OK?"

"Sounds good." And business started.

They explained the plan. Tomorrow, there would be demonstrations to the senior officers of the council; the next day, demonstrations to the engineers; the day after, presentation of price and operating costs; the day after, agreement on local training programmes. They invited me to spend New Year at their beach hut at Malindi on the Indian Ocean before returning to Nairobi to develop plans to train their own staff using my own engineers.

I visited the factory later in the afternoon. In size it was very like my smallest factory just outside Farnborough. There the comparison stopped. The bright light of the Kenyan sunshine was cut off by walls and a roof making the inside relatively dark.

Tales From A Briefcase

The equatorial sun drove the internal temperature to over a hundred degrees Fahrenheit and there was no ventilation to change the air or channel away the welding gases. Tanker cylinders, laid out close together, were being rolled and welded accompanied by an ear-splitting din. The welding crews worked on the cylinders from outside and inside at the same time, with those working inside suffering the worst of the unfriendly environment.

The welders were mostly African, and were dressed in heavy leather protection gear and wearing welding masks. The quality of their work measured up quite well to that produced by my welders back in England.

Despite this, on looking closely I could see that the welders' eyes appeared dull and lifeless and their skins were sweating profusely.

"It's a hell hole," I remarked to Scott and his partner. "How do they stick it?"

"They're on the bang. It's a drug produced from a local plant from the bush. They stick it here for about three months or so with the drug buffering off the unpleasantness and then return to the bush, to their tribes, go walk about and become native again. When their money runs out, they are back to Nairobi and into the welding shed."

"What about factory inspectors and regulations on working conditions?"

"There are none. They need the money and we provide the work."

I was troubled that my company was party to these awful working conditions and went to see the commercial attaché at the British Embassy in Nairobi. He confirmed that it was a matter for the Kenyan government and that I should not get involved in local working conditions.

Dinner that evening was a pleasant enough affair with the managers of the company and their wives, on the lawn at Scott's house. Kenyan servants were very much in evidence and the food was slightly spiced but not over-hot to the taste.

At the city council presentations next day, the model proved a brilliant sales aid with everyone and discussions moved towards finalising the order for twenty-four trucks, training and spares. Time flew with meetings and arrangements, and the New Year break was soon upon us.

The beach at Malindi, three hours' drive from Nairobi, was beautiful sand for several miles, with wooden or mud houses dotted haphazardly along its length. About four families were staying at Scott's beach hut, and another eight people were accommodated at Mike's, a few yards down the beach.

It was the afternoon of New Year's Eve. After a huge curry lunch, I was laid out on a beach bed about twenty yards from the shoreline. I was too tired to read a book and just closed my eyes and listened to the Indian Ocean throwing its waves at the beach.

"All alone? Could you do with some company?"

It was Rosalind, Scott's wife, sitting on the next beach bed to mine. She was neither pretty nor graceful. She wore glasses and was on the plump side but her powerful personality shone though. There was also a hint of feline sexuality about her.

"Yes, fine. I would like to talk to you. How long have you been out here?"

"About two years."

"But Scott told me that the children were born out here. How come?"

"I'm Scott's second wife. His first wife died out here about three years ago. Scott advertised for a wife in the Daily Telegraph. I answered and came out for a trial period. I liked everything I saw, married him and stayed. Never regretted it."

"You're a brave girl and you've struck lucky."

"And you, Robert? I hear that you're quite a business tycoon. Are you married with a family?"

"Oh, dear, do I have to give you my sob story?"

"Yes, you do," she smiled. "We don't have many stories out here!"

"I married a lovely Irish girl and we have two children, nine and six. Unfortunately, she became afflicted with a hereditary mental illness which has put her through hell, including suicide attempts. Her personality has changed for the worse and she spends a lot of time in a clinic. I'm greatly supported by my parents and uncles and aunts when I'm away overseas, and I have a housekeeper-cum-nanny when I'm at home."

Tales From A Briefcase

She leant forward and stroked my face. "You poor lad, it must be difficult for you. Don't you have any girlfriends?" she asked looking into my eyes intently.

"Well, I'm not exactly celibate but I wouldn't do anything to rock the family boat."

"I'll make sure that a few of my girl friends look after you this evening. The party is in tropical fancy dress and will be held on the beach over there."

As soon as it got dark, the beach fire was lit and a half sheep was set up on a motorised spit. My fancy dress did not extend beyond my Hawaiian shirt and swimming shorts. Most of the men wore swimming trunks, straw hats and had painted their bodies. Most of the women wore bikini bottoms, and draped garlands around otherwise-naked breasts.

The children had been miraculously spirited away and high jinks had started in the large swimming pool and in the sea. I sat in a circle of people I did not know but was included in their conversation and jokes. Later, a short, pretty lady came and sat on the arm of my chair, leaning forward so that the garland fell away from her breasts.

"I'm Tricia. Ros said you were on you own, out on a short trip from England."

"Yes, that's right. And you?"

"Oh, I live out here with my husband and family."

"Does this happen very often?" I asked. It seemed as if an orgy was about to break out at any moment.

"Oh, only on high days and holidays. We enjoy ourselves and no damage is done. Would you like to swim in the sea?"

"Your husband...?" I queried.

"He's fine. One of my friends is wrapped around him. Come on," she said lightly, grabbing my hand.

We strolled down to the shoreline, past a line of date palms towards the waves.

"Oops, I mustn't get my garlands wet," she said and threw them off, exposing small taut breasts topped by pointed nipples. "Come here and give me a kiss." Her arms went round my neck and her tongue pushed into my mouth.

As I stood there, uncertain of the next move, she pulled me down into the surf and pushed her body on top of me. Her hand

Tales From A Briefcase

had snaked past the elasticised waist of my trunks and had grasped my penis.

"I just knew it was going to be large," she whispered breathlessly in my ear. "Off with these," she commanded as she removed my trunks and took off her bikini bottoms.

"We'll swim out to that small island," she said pointing out to a sand bank about fifty yards away. She swam like a dolphin escorting a boat, bending and twisting her body to image the contour of mine. Now and then she would take my penis in her hand, diverting my mind from swimming and I would sink beneath the surface.

We reached the sandbank and flopped on to it.

"Take me," she commanded with a furious urgency.

"Not so fast, we have all evening," I replied.

"No we haven't. The others will want a piece of you when you get back. I drew the short straw to be first."

"You mean I'm like a prize bull to be tried out on the herd?"

"Yes, we always try out the visitors!"

"I'm not sure I like that idea. I like to be the one who decides my partner."

"Listen, fellah, just you get on with it right now. Or we'll call it off!"

"Well, let's do just that!" I snapped back.

"You won't get a chance with the others after they hear about this," she fumed.

I headed back to the shore, found my swimming trunks, returned to the house and sat by the bar.

I could see the girls huddled together, talking avidly and glancing over at me from time to time. My boats had certainly been burnt.

A radio had been turned on. "This is the BBC World Service from London. In a minute you will hear the chimes of Big Ben bringing in the New Year."

I watched the scene as people suddenly stopped their canoodling and scurried around to rejoin their husbands and wives. It was just like a switch had been operated and the world had just returned to normal. I stood as couples poured champagne, kissed and waited for the chimes to stop – and felt very isolated and lonely.

Tales From A Briefcase

She stood before me, apparently also isolated and lonely: a woman of about thirty-five, as tall as me, with straight hair held back with a headband. She wore a shapeless dress and flat shoes. She was not beautiful and her face reflected sadness. She held out an unopened bottle of champagne. "Would you drink with me? Just drink, nothing more."

"Of course," I said and found two clean glasses and poured, handing one to her. The chimes stopped and hugs and kisses were being exchanged all round. I looked at her and she shrugged her shoulders. I raised my glass to her, "To you, to..?"

"Alison. And you?"

"Robert."

We clinked glasses.

"I suppose we could leave this right here or sit on that swing-seat by the pool and talk about ourselves for a bit. Would you like that?"

She turned her face away from me "I'm not sure. Maybe."

"No strings, Alison," I said.

"I heard that you wouldn't play with the girls."

"I'm not a prude but my life is shallow enough without indulging in meaningless party games." I told her my story: my life as a soldier, a husband and father, my struggle to finance the special treatment for my wife's depression and to keep the children at boarding school, and my wanderings around the world.

"There. That's my story. I've no idea where or how things will go. I just live it from day to day. I'm too busy to be sorry for myself but still hope that better times are around the corner, especially for my children."

Alison looked me full in the face. "Poor Robert. You must not let these superficial happenings hurt you. You need to find a spiritual dimension." She paused, then: "As for me, I'm unmarried. I came to Kenya to work in the company when I was about twenty-five and worked my way up the administration to be the manager. I'm Scottish as you can hear. I come from near Pitlochry in Perthshire, studied at Edinburgh University and decided to work overseas. Scott and Mike have been very kind to me. About six years ago I met a British Army captain in the Royal Engineers, Donald McDonald. He was building bridges

Tales From A Briefcase

all over the country. We got very close and probably would eventually have married. The Mau Mau ambushed his squad of twenty soldiers up country. Cut them to pieces with parangs. When an army patrol reached them they found a pile of heads and limbs; the wild animals had not yet got to the bodies." She shuddered and there were tears in her eyes.

"I know how it is in war and what men do to each other in those conditions," I said. "But for you, what now?"

"I suppose I'll stay here. Despite all this, I love the country and its people. I belong here. I'm not sure that I'll ever love again; even touch a man again. I don't know anybody back home or feel I've anything in common with those back in Scotland. I have my church and my painting."

We sat on the seat looking at each other, wondering what to say next. Nothing seemed appropriate. I was lost in my own thoughts, scarcely noticing that dawn was approaching.

She startled me with her question, "Have you ever seen the sun come up over the Indian Ocean and paddled down the shoreline until it is fully risen?"

"No. It sounds wonderful!"

"Come along, we'll do it. One of God's wonders."

The sun came up a blazing red, on the horizon out at sea. A pink sheen painted the sky and the rippling sea picked up its image. I looked at Alison; the rising sun had given her face a warm hue and she gave a small smile. She was as happy as she would ever be, I thought. I also felt warm inside, privileged to have witnessed the spectacle.

"Goodnight, Robert. I'll expect we'll meet in Nairobi. We may even have time to see some more wonders of the world."

I walked back to the house and my room, where I fell into a sound sleep. The next thing I knew, it was daylight and someone was pulling the curtains. It was Rosalind with a cup of tea for me. She sat on the bed in her dressing gown.

"The girls tell me that you didn't want to play last night. They were looking forward to some action with a new male. They're asking if you're a homosexual."

"I don't like to be played with as a toy. My brain controls my john and I choose with whom I take my sexual pleasures. It was all too bare-faced for me."

Tales From A Briefcase

She slid her hand under the covers. "What about me? Would you choose me?" she asked rather coyly.

"There's an unwritten rule amongst decent men – you don't seduce your host's wife in his own house. I have to do business with Scott and I would find that difficult if I had taken his wife on the side. I'm sorry; it's nothing to do with your attractiveness."

She snatched her hand from under the bed clothes. "And yet you have time for Alison, with all her hang-ups and miserable face?"

"I find her a rather special human being. Sex does not come into it. Her loneliness is rather like mine, incurable. That's all, nothing more."

So I went back to Nairobi for a few more days work before flying on. On Friday afternoon, as the work day was winding up, Alison approached me. "You fly on Sunday evening. Scott and Mike will be entertaining you this evening but they're going back to Malindi for the weekend. Would you like to see the National Wildlife Park with me on Saturday?"

She arrived at my hotel on Saturday morning in a beaten up old Honda and we rattled over the rough roads to a huge park about an hour out of Nairobi. Occasionally we would pass Kenyans running in a column, dressed in brightly coloured robes and carrying spears. "Kikuyu going to a tribal ceremony or feast somewhere," Alison informed me.

The park had no fences or obvious boundaries. Occasionally we would see park keepers in Land Rovers. Signs warned visitors to stay in their cars and not to drive near large animals like elephants or rhinoceroses.

"Have you got a camera?" asked Alison.

"Yes, I've brought along my cine camera. I've taken films all over the world to show my children. Today, I hope to get some shots of animals in the wild."

"Right. No problem. I'd better take off the windscreen wipers or the monkeys will do it for me."

We came up to a pack of monkeys sitting on the track forcing us to stop. They clambered all over the car, pulling at any projecting accessories then, realising there was nothing removable, they lost interest and moved away. There were two giraffes twining their necks together in some courtship ritual. A

Tales From A Briefcase

large herd of zebra, backside on to us, made an incredible pattern of black and white stripes until something stampeded them. We didn't see any of the big cats but had good views of a huge variety of colourful birds.

Alison caught my attention, "I've brought a picnic. Then I thought you might like to see Lake Naivasha and Mount Kenya."

Another hour's motoring brought us to an incredible panorama. In the foreground, green coffee bushes sprouted as far as the eye could see, the round black fruit, ripe and awaiting picking. In the middle distance was a huge lake where I could see hippos, water buffalo and a huge variety of birds. In the background, Mount Kenya towered to six thousand feet, its top snow-covered.

"I've brought my painting things," announced Alison. "I thought I'd paint you a water colour. Would you like that?"

I said I would and she set up an easel and started sketching-in an outline. I watched her closely. Her face appeared to shine with pleasurable expectation and I could see that she was at peace with the world.

Eventually we left to return to Nairobi. "Come back to my bungalow," she invited. "I'll cook you dinner. You can stay the night. No strings? Have a shower while I cook. Put on that light dressing gown. We'll eat on the veranda. Steaks a little pink, OK?"

I marvelled at her animation as I ate the perfectly cooked steak. "I don't have many visitors and rarely have the chance to cook for someone else," she said.

We sat on the veranda, watching the sun go down behind the mountains, the cicadas and frogs making their usual African evening chorus. She put on a record, "Do you like Mahler?"

"He's a composer I know little about, but listening to this bit I understand why you like him."

It was after midnight when she stood up. "Your bedroom is through that door. Good night." And she left.

I snuggled down into the linen sheets, struggling to fathom this lady.

It was sometime later in the night that I felt the covers pulled back and a naked body pressed to mine. Alison's hand pressed over my mouth. "Don't talk. Don't move. No sex. Just body contact." She kissed my forehead. "Go back to sleep."

I lay wakeful, and could feel that she too was still awake. We lay just like that, lost in our own feelings, sharing something special but indefinable. The blood stopped coursing through my veins and I became peaceful and went to sleep.

Sunday morning arrived in a blaze of sunshine. Breakfast on the veranda with the morning papers seemed so natural. My flight time approached. "I'll take you to the airport," she offered. I left her at the departures gate with a kiss on the cheek.

As the British Airways plane took off for South Africa I couldn't help but wonder if I had changed her views on life. I was sure that she had changed mine.

A few months later, a parcel arrived at my office – it contained a beautifully painted water-colour of a Kenyan scene, one I would remember for ever.

Tales From A Briefcase

CHAPTER 14

THE SUNSET SCAVENGERS

New York & San Francisco

I sat at my desk and thought about my impending business visit to the United States. As the managing director, I had been given the job by the owners of modernising the company, giving it new products and taking it into new markets. The trip to America was to research the garbage vehicle market and establish whether a demand could be created for our smallest vehicles for precinct work, and to assess the opportunities for supplying servicing vehicles for the jumbo jets, about to be launched into the European market. It would involve a survey of several large city cleansing departments and a trip to Boeing in Seattle. Initial appointments had been made by British market researchers, starting in New York in the week between Christmas and New Year.

With the factory order book full, I was confident that I could be absent for the three weeks that a coast-to-coast survey would take. I caught my flight at Heathrow and was soon established in a Pan American Being 707 heading for La Guardia.

My first appointment was with the Director of Cleansing for New York City, who explained how garbage was collected, loaded into barges and dumped out at sea. To reduce frequent trips to the barge docks, the American garbage vehicles were designed with high volume bodies and had high compression systems. The smallest carried 5 tons and the largest 12 tons. By comparison, English vehicles were between 3 tons and 5 tons. However, when constructing shopping precincts, the service roads had to be small and winding and their own garbage vehicles were found to be too big to manoeuvre. The British 3-tonner, with its relatively short wheel base and small turning

Tales From A Briefcase

circle was ideal. They were thus in the market for buying our vehicles. We agreed to carry out a trial and I telephoned Warwick for a vehicle to be shipped for demonstration.

My second appointment had been arranged with a person who had the nebulous qualification of 'an inside political track'. The rendezvous was to be at an Italian restaurant on the East Side, and I was to come alone. I felt distinctly uncomfortable with the whole arrangement.

A yellow cab took me to a small but pleasantly furnished bistro where I was met at the door by the proprietor, a cheery plum-shaped Italian with a long droopy moustache.

"Signor Roberto?" he enquired. I acknowledged my name and shook his hand. "I am Antonio. Frank will arrive in a minute. He likes to sit at the rear with his back to the wall," he indicated a table at the far end of the restaurant. His next question confirmed my suspicions: "Are you carrying?"

"No!" I replied, thinking back to the many gangster movies I had seen.

"Then you won't mind Alberto just checking?"

Alberto, dressed in sparkling white apron, came over and felt all over me in a very matter-of-fact way, as if this was a routine welcome for customers.

"He's clean," he reported to Antonio.

I sat at the table and waited for developments.

The bistro's street door opened, and in walked the archetypal gangster, with black suit, black shirt, white tie, fedora, and fawn overcoat draped over his shoulders. Behind him were two shifty-looking characters who I could only imagine were his body-guards. He advanced into the open arms of Antonio who let forth a stream of Italian interspersed with kisses and back slapping.

One of the bodyguards asked Alberto if I was 'clean.'

"Si, si. Very clean. Nice quiet Englishman."

This seemed to satisfy the guard, who nevertheless continued to glare at me.

Having disposed of his overcoat, hat and gloves, Frank approached me with a hand extended. "Signor Roberto. So pleased to meet you. I am Frank Trafuro."

We sat at the table while Frank ordered wine and the guards positioned themselves at commanding viewpoints.

Tales From A Briefcase

"Tell me, Roberto, what you want to do in our country?"

"Back in England, my company makes garbage vehicles: little ones which, unlike your big American ones, can go down the service roads of your shopping precincts. New York City has said they would be interested in trialling our product. I guess many of the American cities have the same problem and there could be a lot of business for us here."

"Ah yes," he said thoughtfully, "I think big business, if you are introduced properly."

"Introduced properly? What does that mean?"

He lifted his wine glass, "You say cheers? Well cheers to our co-operation!"

I lifted my glass and sipped, wondering where this was leading.

"What business are you in, Frank?"

"My work is in construction."

"How does garbage vehicles fit in with construction?"

"Ah. I see you have not been told of my other position. I am secretary to the (mumble mumble) Italian League. The garbage industry in the United States is manned and controlled by Italians. Some cities, like New York, Washington and Chicago, have city-owned cleansing departments with Italian managers, and others, such as San Francisco, are serviced by private companies owned by Italians. In America, the Italian political vote is very strong. We negotiate government appointments for Italians with our presidents. We have a loud voice. But, for you my friend, we will help you sell your garbage vehicles across America, get you the right introductions. It is for you to persuade the industry you have the best vehicle."

"Well, that's very kind of you, Frank. But I'm a businessman. I have sold these vehicles across the world: India, Greece, South Africa. In these countries, nobody has done me a favour for nothing. They all needed a reward of some sort."

"Ah, I see that you are a real businessman. We make introductions and you pay us a commission on sales. You need to do some assembly in the USA, we do it in our Italian factories for a price. We help you, you help us. That way we make the world go round, eh Roberto?"

Tales From A Briefcase

"Yes, I suppose we could come to a deal. But what if Chrysler in Detroit get the order for chassis? They may wish to buy our bodies knocked-down and do the assembly in their factories. What happens then?"

"You will then leave Chrysler to do the deal with us; you just supply them. OK?"

"Sounds OK."

"Let's eat, Roberto, and we can discuss the details of your trip."

So I left New York after the first week, with a provisional order in my pocket and a schedule to visit all the major cities coast to coast. At each, an Italian manager received me, heard my presentation and promised to follow it up.

My last stop for selling dustcarts was San Francisco. Here a private company, called the Sunset Scavengers, did house-to-house collections and delivered the waste to a railhead from where it was shipped to the Nevada desert for burial. Until recently, they had tipped waste into the Bay to land fill but now they had reached the limit of tipping. My appointment was for a Saturday morning.

I arrived at the vehicle yard where crimson-coloured dustcarts were being washed down and polished to a shiny finish. During weekdays, these gleaming monsters were to be seen all over the city, tended by smartly-dressed crews who went about their business with a special Italian cheeriness and singing operatic arias.

My appointment was with the company's president who turned out to be a twenty-eight year old. Like all the dustmen there, he was Italian and had bought shares in the company. He had worked his way up from crewman to vehicle supervisor, and then on to manager in the sales, accounting and administration departments. The company had sent him to Harvard for his Master's degree in Business Administration and made him the boss.

Frank had passed on the introductory message, as had several other city departmental managers, and it was quite easy for me to get him interested in taking our products.

"Right, Roberto, we go to meet the shareholders. Every Saturday after clean-down, we meet in the board room for lunch

Tales From A Briefcase

of sausage and bourbon. I hope you can tell jokes because the shareholders will expect it of an Englishman who is selling them his garbage vehicles!"

And for the next four hours I traded jokes with the Italians, ate foul-smelling sausage and gulped down bourbon. At the end of the session they poured me into a taxi to go back to my hotel. I woke up next morning with an enormous hangover but it was Sunday and I had a day to recover before setting off for Seattle. In my jacket I found a letter:

Dear Roberto

I hope our shareholders like your vehicles as much as they liked your jokes. Please confirm price and delivery for an initial order of six.

Vittorio
President
Sunset Scavengers
San Francisco

Tales From A Briefcase

CHAPTER 15

HOT AIR & CUTTING GRASS

Poole, Dorset

The taxi from Poole station weaved its way around the industrial estate in the harbour district and came to a stop outside a modern single-storey factory unit. I paid my fare and entered a foyer with a window looking on to an office. I pressed a call button and a young office junior came over from her desk and slid the glass pane open.

"Can I help you?" she asked brightly, her blond curls bouncing.

"Er ... I'm the new boy arriving for his first day. My name is Robert James."

The smile vanished from her face and a huge blush spread across her cheeks, her hand going to her mouth. "Not *the* Mr James, our new managing director?" she asked, in a voice loud enough for the rest of the office to hear.

At this, a middle-aged, grey-haired lady leapt up from her desk and practically ran to the reception window. "I'm Mavis Mulholland and I'm the office manager. I'm terribly sorry. The London office told us that you were coming tomorrow. We had a car arranged and a proper reception for you tomorrow." Her embarrassment was obvious as was the enjoyment of the spectacle by the rest of the office staff.

"That's alright, Mavis. No harm done. We'll leave the serious bit until tomorrow. I'll just wander off down town and check into a hotel."

"Oh, no. We have a room booked for you at the Harbour Lights. I'll phone them now to have the room ready for you today and order a taxi. Your own car doesn't arrive until tomorrow."

Tales From A Briefcase

"That will be just fine Mavis. Tell the management here that I'll be here at eight o'clock tomorrow morning."

"At eight o'clock?" she stuttered, then: "The management tend to get in later than that!"

I ignored the comment. "Yes, at eight. I'm an early riser and I like to get started early. Please warn the management."

On the following day my taxi arrived at the factory at half past seven and I found myself locked out of the office block. Walking around the factory, I found an open door into a workshop, went in, walked up to a fitter working on the assembly line and said, "Would you find a manager for me? I'm new here and would like to be shown around."

His response was immediate. "Yes certainly. Who shall I say you are?"

"Robert James. It's blowing a bloody gale out there. Is it often like this?"

"Yes, we often get sea storms and we're unprotected by a harbour wall, so it blows straight in."

"Many thanks for your help – er?" I raised an eyebrow in question.

"Oh yes, Bill Robinson. Pleased to meet you." He stuck out an oily hand and, on second thoughts withdrew it quickly.

"That's alright, Bill. Dirty hands mean you're working. I always make a point of shaking dirty hands!"

He returned with a man in his fifties, short, bald and wearing glasses. "Good morning. Are you by any chance Mr James?"

"Yes, I am. I'm pleased to see the lines up and running at this early hour. And you?"

"Mike Allsop, Production Manager. Habits of a lifetime stay with you. I get in before the bell and have a bacon butty and coffee for breakfast."

"I might join you one day in that, Mike. Please walk me around your empire."

By the time I'd finished my quick walk about the production area, a crowd of smartly-dressed men had appeared at the doors of the department and a well-spoken, well-dressed individual stepped forward with outstretched hand and a nervous smile on his face.

Tales From A Briefcase

"I'm Burt Mitchell, Sales Director and the senior executive here. We apologise. You've caught us on the hop twice! We'll make sure that it doesn't happen again."

"Apology accepted. I'm not here to catch people out but to do my own job efficiently. Programmes and timetables have their place but I prefer to work flexibly when I can. Please let's continue with the schedule you have arranged for me."

In the conference room, after introductions and coffee, I settled into listening about the company, its people, its products, its markets and manufacturing facilities. The previous managing director, who had been promoted to be a group Director, had done a good job. Everyone knew and understood their role. The plans and budgets were well defined. Without exception, each manager talked confidently about his job and his targets. I sat comfortably in my chair listening, paying close attention to the presentation which went on all day. This appeared to be the first job for some time in which the company appeared stable and not in need of surgical attention.

The company had two factory sites, the second being at Hucknall in Nottinghamshire. A subsidiary of a large and diverse engineering group with headquarters overlooking Green Park in London, it had two main divisions, heating and horticulture.

In warm air products, it offered static and mobile blower heaters. The former were for factories and the latter for space heating needs, where heat was needed to be positioned temporarily for a job such as warming marquees and drying out damp crops.

Horticultural products were grouped into domestic and commercial applications. Cylinder mowers with roller drums were offered in both markets for use on lawns and, for example, cricket pitches to produce the striped cut effect. Rotary mowers for both markets were produced in different cut widths, and either with and without collection systems for cut grass. Domestic and commercial versions of rotary cultivators were also produced, the smallest for digging over a back garden and the largest being for digging out beds in a horticultural nursery. The two-wheeled tractor was a multi-purpose machine developed for small-holders overseas. Numerous implements could be bolted onto it.

The market for domestic ride-on rotary mowers in the United Kingdom, now in its infancy, was fed by importation from American producers, later to be overtaken by British manufacturers.

Mower product demand came mostly from the northern hemisphere, where British style lawns were beginning to appear in northern and southern Europe. Heater demand was worldwide and not so heavily geared to the opposite seasons of the northern and southern hemispheres. Improvements in the business would come from broadening the selling markets, making the product look more international, and reducing costs.

On analysing factory demands, it became obvious that we were producing both winter and summer products from similar materials: sheet metal, cast iron parts, cut and bent tubing, and small wheels. We analysed the possibility of manufacturing seasonal products during out-of- season periods, switching products as necessary but using the same production equipment and the same workforce for all. With the help of stock financiers, retailer stock financing was introduced so that customer warehouses were filled at least three months before the UK's spring selling season. With stock financed and a modest price reduction introduced to encourage early stocking, most of the larger retailers followed the new buying pattern. This resulted in less switching of production, longer production runs and higher purchasing volumes, and led to economies in costs and thus more profits.

These benefits were recognised by the group directors, who started to consider centralisation of manufacture, the other great god of that era. At a headquarters meeting, closure of the Hucknall factory was debated. Of the three hundred people employed there, only a small percentage would be likely to take up the company's offer of relocation to Poole. Redundancy costs would be high because most of the workforce had been employed since the end of the war when the factory had returned to peace time products. I was given six months to complete the closure and transfer to the south. In the end only six of the

Tales From A Briefcase

workforce moved south and the group lost hundreds of years of experience. Those made redundant on what had been generous terms at the time were to suffer as the Nottingham coalfield started to close and local work became harder to find.

In Poole, a new factory unit was taken on, production flowed as planned and costs shrank. External industrial design consultants were engaged to give products a more modern look and to introduce more cost-effective materials. It was now time to broaden the markets and sell more widely overseas. Every country appeared to have its own electrical specification and our products had to be laboratory-tested locally for approval.

One day, I was sitting in my office surveying output figures with some satisfaction when Jim, the purchasing manager, knocked and came in.

"We've got two thousand Briggs & Stratton mower engines caught by an east coast dock strike in America. What shall we do?"

I thought through the problem quickly. Nobody held great stocks of engines as the manufacturer's supply had been faultless. The Italian engine was a product of noticeably lesser quality, difficult to start and prone to oiling up. Our competitors would probably find themselves in the same boat. I telephoned Pan American Cargo to get an estimate of air shipment cost; it would double the landed cost of the engines. Dare I ask the retailers for the extra cost of shipment? Should I carry some or all the extra cost? I telephoned some of my larger customers and posed the question – pay the price for on-time deliveries or miss the season? I obtained a positive reaction and flew to the United States to set up a bulk shipments deal with Pan Am. In future, all mower engines purchased by my company would be flown in; I would try to persuade all the other British equipment manufacturers to follow suit; I would try to convince Briggs and Stratton to make all their European deliveries by air.

Travelling on to the Midwest to Briggs & Stratton, I convinced them that this was the way to knock the Italians out of the UK market. They accepted the proposition and the deal came together. We became the only equipment manufacturer to deliver that season and increased our share of the market.

Tales From A Briefcase

In the three years I was in Poole, I bought a house in Parkstone, joined the Poole Sailing Club, refereed rugby matches for the Hants & Dorset Society and enjoyed the support of my wonderful team at the factory.

CHAPTER 16

"I LEFT MY HEART IN ..."

Globetrotting

The colourful, descriptive leaflet of our products lay on my desk alongside two tender documents for supply, one to Sri Lanka and one to Indonesia. If these tenders succeeded, the two orders would provide work for our hundred-strong workforce for half a year.

Amongst our products was a two-wheeled tractor designed for small farmers in developing nations. It had a number of attachments and accessories which would convert it into a rotary hoe, a plough, and a rice paddy puddler. It could drive a water-pump, a grain winnower, a coffee grinder and a seed dispenser. With a trailer it would provide the farmer with a load-carrier and personal transport for his family. The recent visit of my export manager, Peter Farley, to the ministries of agriculture in those countries had resulted in the invitation to tender for four hundred units.

I telephoned Peter to call by my office. Within ten minutes, there was a knock on my office door and he put his face around it.

"OK for a chat, now?"

"Yes, Peter, please come in."

I looked at him as he manoeuvred a chair up to my desk. He was about thirty-two, of medium height, had a bright intelligent face, thinning sandy-coloured hair, sparkly eyes and a big smile. He was a graduate, a linguist, lived locally and was married with two young children. His wife appeared to cope with his frequent absences from home: about one hundred and fifty days a year. He travelled the world and brought home the orders. I liked him immensely.

Tales From A Briefcase

"Well, Peter, you've worked the miracle again. Four hundred units would be spectacular, if we can pull it off. What are the next steps?"

"Well, first the easy bit – sign the forms. The next will be working demonstrations in the countries, as soon as we can arrange them."

"What do the demonstrations amount to?"

"Possibly at three or four locations in each country. Each in two parts: a slide presentation with economic statistics and the like, and a field demonstration, all tailored to an audience ranging from ministers down to the farmers themselves. In Sri Lanka they are proposing to increase the number of rice crops from one to two a year, and possibly even three. The government proposes to lend the small farmer the money to buy machines and purchase seed for the first year's crop. Then the farmers will pay off the loan over three years. The government will also set up repair and servicing centres and collect the rice for marketing and distribution. There are even talks of forming regional co-operatives."

"Well, that sounds impressive. Who will you take out to do the demonstrations?"

"Because the Japanese, particularly Honda, will be there with their top management, I think you need to be there too. If our chief executive is not there the buyers will think that we're not valuing the order as important, or not taking them seriously enough. I'll also take a demonstrator with me as standby, and an engineer to cover break-downs. I suggest we set this up within the next two months before the monsoon season starts."

"Fine. Let me have the programme when it's confirmed, and details of my role."

Over the next month, the plan for the demonstrations progressed and the timetable firmed up into a trip lasting three weeks. The demonstration machines were shipped out early to the two countries, and the demonstration team collected its travel visas and airline tickets: British Airways to Colombo and Garuda to Jakarta and for internal flights in Indonesia. Then, on the day before the flight to Colombo, there was a call from Peter's wife.

Tales From A Briefcase

"Mr James, I don't know how to break this to you but Peter was rushed to hospital last night with peritonitis. He's having the operation this morning."

"Well, Mrs Farley... it's Jane isn't it? Thank goodness it didn't happen when he was away. It's much better to have the problem here in England with the family nearby and where the medical staff is top quality."

"But what about the export trip?"

"Peter's done a good job planning it, and all we have to do is follow his schedule. He's done the hard part. I'll pop over to the hospital tomorrow and see how he's progressing. Is there anything we can do for you?"

"Can I drive the company car to visit him in hospital?"

"Certainly. I'll make the arrangements for you to come on to the car insurance scheme until further notice. Meanwhile you know my secretary Yvonne – keep in touch so that I know how Peter's going on while I'm away. By the way, I'm Robert. Your man is a treasure to the company. Make sure he gets well soon!"

"Thank you so much for everything, Robert. I'll keep your secretary posted."

I asked my secretary to organise a meeting with our machine demonstrator, Brian Tomlinson, and our engineer, Tom Bagley.

"Well, gentlemen, there's no time to find stand-ins. It's down to us three. I will have to be assistant demonstrator. Are the machines out there safely?"

Brian answered, "Yes, they've arrived in Colombo and Jakarta. We'll take a couple of days assembling them and testing them at the first demonstration sites. It's lucky that most of the Sri Lankans speak English!"

"Yes. I'll meet you at the airport as arranged tomorrow. Passports and visas OK?"

They both nodded and left. I started to think about my trip, nearly four weeks in all: a week in Sri Lanka, a week in Indonesia, a few days in Auckland, New Zealand, with a lawn mower manufacturer, and back to Australia for a few more days with the local heater distributor before crossing the Pacific, a social weekend in San Francisco and then home. My best friend's sister, Barbara, lived in San Francisco and had suggested I call by on my next time through. We'd become friendly on her last visit to England.

Next day, our plane landed at Colombo and we set off to our first demonstration point about fifty miles north. We were housed in an old colonial mansion now converted into a guest house, and in the early morning of the day of the demonstration we set up our slide show in the guest house and tested our machine out in the nearby paddy fields. The top officials from the Ministry of Agriculture arrived in large cars and in their white suits and panama hats; some even sported ties of English public schools. Formal introductions were made. Status and deference were evident as coffee was served.

The Minister opened with a statement about government policy and how mechanisation would dramatically improve annual crop yields. He referred to the English as "old friends" and producers of quality machines.

I responded with a reference to the special relationships which now existed between Britain and Mrs Bandaranaike's government, and praised the government's far-sightedness in respect of its plans to increase crop harvest yields. I went into the economic relationship between machine price, operating costs, yield, and income to the farmer. Most farmers had been given a small plot of land which they and their families husbanded. The rice crop, when harvested, was sold to a government agency and the government paid the farmer the pre-agreed crop price less the loan repayment. The result was that a Sri Lankan farmer with his family could live off two harvestings a year. If he was able to squeeze in a third crop or grow something else, he would be relatively well off.

The sixty people in the party moved to the paddy field where Brian and Tom were ready to demonstrate the machine in its various roles. This involved Brian taking the machine into knee-deep water, and sometimes deeper, as the twin paddy puddles spun in their reaping motion. I noticed Brian stop on a few occasions to touch his legs. After the demonstration I could see that leeches still clung to him, their bodies fat and red with his blood. The prescribed treatment was applying a glowing cigarette end to the leech which would contract and detach itself from its victim.

Tales From A Briefcase

The demonstration successfully completed, we retired to the guest house for cold beers and a meal. I could see that Brian was in some discomfort.

"Go to bed early with some scotch, old chap," I told him. "We have to leave at daybreak to get to our next site near Kandy. We'll see how you're fixed in the morning."

At six in the morning it was clear that Brian had a fever as well as very sore legs and would be in no shape to take the demonstration; I would have to take his place!

I had practiced using the machine and felt confident that I could give a reasonable demonstration. I started the TVO engine and walked the machine into the paddy. Even though my trousers were tucked into my rubber boots I could feel leeches moving about on my skin before they clamped themselves into position on my legs and nether regions.

However, the demonstration went well and was appreciated by the audience. I went to see Brian who had been seen by a doctor and was hospitalised. I left him with tickets and money to get back to England after his discharge.

After the third demonstration near the southern coast of Sri Lanka, Tom and I caught the Indonesian Airlines plane to Jakarta. Our demonstrations were to be in Palembang in Sumatra, in Bandung and Surabaya. They turned out be equally successful to those in Sri Lanka except that the leeches and mosquitoes had fiercer bites.

We heard that Brian had been released from hospital and had arrived home safely. Tom packed up our equipment, left it in storage in Jakarta and headed home. I picked up an overnight plane to Sydney.

Arriving in brilliant sunshine, I took a taxi to my hotel. On the way I talked to the cabbie, a young Australian living at Bondi. He was a university student and drove a taxi for living money. He suggested that if I wanted to have a swim at Bondi Beach, he would take the day off and come with me. So I braved the huge rollers and under-sweep at Australia's most famous beach and then laid out on the sand to watch the skimpy bikinis. We went to his digs with a take-away and there I met his flat mates, a motley mixed-race crew of students, who did not appear too interested in university attendance. The day ended

Tales From A Briefcase

with poker, numerous bottles of beer being drunk and my getting back to the hotel at midnight, having been awake for thirty six hours on the trot.

On the following day I had meetings in the downtown business quarter of Sydney and, the day after, I flew to Melbourne. As we took off from Sydney airport my neighbour in the next seat remarked, "It's raining in Melbourne today!" but when we arrived there the sun was shining. I turned round to make the obvious remark, my neighbour had already left the plane. At my appointment in the city I mentioned the comment on raining to my host. He burst out laughing, "You were talking to a Sydney man!" Apparently the weather is a subject for teasing between the residents of the two cities.

The next day I was on the plane to Auckland, and the difference between New South Wales and Auckland was very striking. The countryside had very green, rolling downs with grazing sheep, and houses largely built of wood. Apparently the New Zealanders in North Island were developing lawned gardens and wanted to create the stripe effect they'd seen in England. This had to be achieved with a cylinder mower. I was visiting their rotary mower manufacturer to sell them our designs for cylinder machines.

After a successful business meeting on the Friday in Auckland, I was off on a Pan American plane across the Pacific, an eighteen-hour flight with stops in Fiji and Hawaii. Before leaving, however, I telephoned Barbara in San Francisco to arrange to meet her. She informed me that it was Thursday there and that she was going tomorrow to Chicago and would not be able to meet me. She promised to contact her friends, who were lecturers at the University of California and lived in the Twin Peaks area of the city, and to introduce me. I decided to spend yet another 'Friday' in Honolulu and reach San Francisco on Saturday. After the long flight across the Pacific, I welcomed a lazy day on Waikiki beach drinking cold beers.

On arrival at San Francisco, I telephoned Barbara's friends, Tracy and Scott, who invited me to a party on Sunday afternoon. Dressed up in my best light-weight suit, I arrived in a hired Ford Mustang 'a la Steve McQueen' clutching a bouquet of flowers for Tracy and a box of cigars for Scott.

Tales From A Briefcase

I could hear several strains of music from within the house as I rang the doorbell. The door opened to reveal a man and woman both wearing kaftans and beads and with bandanas round their heads.

"Well hello Robert," Scott said.

"You must be Robert – you look so English," Tracy added.

Flustered, I thrust the flowers into Tracy's hands. "How quaint," she said, "How very… English!"

I handed the Cuban cigars to Scott, who looked at the box as though he hadn't seen cigars before. "Thank you. Very generous. Come right in," he welcomed with a sweep of his hand.

Inside, he continued, "We have a lot of friends in today. Black Panthers plotting their next strike against the police – don't be put off by the handguns and grenades. There's a sitar playing in another room and smoking the hookah. Meditation and pot in there – you may find the occupants difficult to converse with! There are several other rooms with 'weirdoes', and at the back there's a crowd dressed and drinking like it's an English cocktail party. Barbara's English ex-husband, Mike, is in there – have you met him?"

"No," I assured him, "I'll find my way around," and moved towards the cocktail group. I was not disappointed. The large room had picture windows opening out on to a balcony with a view over the Bay and the Golden Gate Bridge. I stood there rather dumbfounded until a male voice distracted me.

"Robert, I'm Mike, Barbara's ex."

I stuck out my hand and shook his.

"Let's get you a drink and introduce you to a few people – presumably preferably female?"

He introduced me to a pretty, tall, thin, dark-haired girl whose name was Olga. In the chat that followed I found out that she was an editor of a West Coast fashion magazine. She was born in San Francisco of White Russian immigrants and lived locally. She had met Tracy and Scott some years ago at a university function and they had been friends ever since. She introduced me to several others in the room who turned out to be journalists or professional people.

As the Sunday afternoon wore on I decided to invite Olga out for dinner. "Oh what a pity, Robert, I have another date."

Tales From A Briefcase

My disappointment must have been heavily registered on my face because she immediately added, "Just wait a minute. I'll see what I can do," and went off to telephone.

She returned a few minutes later. "Well, I have an invitation for you for dinner but it's with five girls; you'll be the only man!"

I accepted although it would lose me my only chance in San Francisco of having a romantic evening with one girl.

Olga took me to her apartment nearby, where she bathed and changed and I sat listening to jazz records. Perhaps I would be invited back later to a more intimate rendezvous?

We jumped in the Ford Mustang and I tried to emulate Steve McQueen getting the car airborne at the road junctions on the city's steeper roads; Olga was not amused.

As we pulled up at our dinner venue, Olga said, "You're going to meet Rachel, our hostess, and three other friends. We meet fairly regularly and all work in the arts. Rachel is English but has been in the States for about five years."

She pressed the bell and the door was opened by a stunning girl in her late twenties. She held out her hand, "Welcome, Robert. I hope that you don't mind being the only man at our dinner party?" Her accent was basically English but she had picked up something of that soft West Coast twang.

I shook her hand, saying, "It was most kind of you to invite me under short notice. I'll try to be an asset to the party."

She smiled at me, leaving me weak at the knees. "I'm sure we'll enjoy your company. Come and meet the others."

I turned back to grab Olga by the hand; I had been completely captivated by Rachel and had almost forgotten Olga was there.

On being introduced to the other three women, I realised that they represented a group of intelligent, cultured, beautiful ladies and that I would have to keep my wits about me to stay the course. But Rachel, ah, Rachel, she was the pick of the bunch. As she bustled about serving food I registered the close fitting emerald green dress she was wearing with its skirt tailored to just above the knee. Her long black hair had been coiffured into a relaxed, informal style away from her face to emphasise a sharp nose and firm jaw lines.

The evening went all too quickly for me, and far too soon everyone prepared to leave. Rachel stood by the hall stand

Tales From A Briefcase

waiting for her guests to collect their coats. She looked at me with a meaningful smile and tapped the telephone which had a number inscribed on the dial. I read the number, committing it to memory, and thanked her for her hospitality. Saying goodbye to the others, I left with Olga to drive her home. We parted on her doorstep with stated intentions to meet again.

I rushed to the car to write down Rachel's memorised telephone number. I would contact her in the morning for a date tomorrow, Monday, and would still be able to maintain my schedule of flying back to London on Tuesday.

It was nine in the morning and I dialled Rachel's number.

"Good morning, Rachel Thompson speaking,"

"It's Robert James from yesterday evening. You kindly entertained me with your friends."

She responded with a loud and enthusiastic, "Hello, you sound bright. Did you not stay over with Olga?"

"Er... no. I left her on her doorstep," and then chancing my arm, "I wanted to save myself for this evening. Can you make it – dinner and dancing at the Roof Restaurant at the Mark Hopkins?"

"My, my, you do know your way around the hot spots. Yes, I would love to meet up. Collect me a nine o'clock – OK?"

"Very OK and I'm looking forward to it."

"Me too," she said, and the telephone went down.

I made a few business visits but found it difficult to put that girl out of my mind. The Ford Mustang took the hills and corners of San Francisco very skittishly as I drove over to Twin Peaks. At precisely nine o'clock I rang the doorbell and Rachel opened it, dressed in another breath-taking number.

I offered the bottle which I'd held behind my back. "I thought a beautiful girl would like a glass of cold champagne before embarking on a night out."

"She would," she responded and kissed me on the lips, "You know, you're such a bull-shitting sweetie. Come in."

By then I was spinning. It couldn't get any better! We drank champagne and smooched and left for the restaurant before going out became impossible!

The restaurant took up the whole of the seventeenth floor of the Mark Hopkins Hotel. Large windows faced out over the city,

Tales From A Briefcase

its hilly contours picked out by streetlights and advertising signs. In the near distance the lights of the Golden Gate and Oakland Bridges were reflected in the waters of the Bay, and further away I could see the twinkling lights of aircraft as they took off and landed at the airport.

We talked about ourselves during a tasteful meal. Rachel came from Leicester, where most of her large family lived. Her life was centred on music; she played piano and had taken an 'A' Level in it. She responded to the call of America when she was twenty-two, spending two years with an impresario in New York before crossing to the West Coast five years ago. She was now a senior partner of a well-known impresario in San Francisco, arranging and organising classical concerts with visiting international musical groups. She knew most of the members of the small European orchestras who came to California with its responsive audiences. Her knowledge of music was extensive.

She had lived with a few men, mostly American, but none had really captured her. She was a free spirit, lost in her music and career, but admitted she had not forsaken the possibility of motherhood. She had even thought of returning to England to work with a London-based impresario.

The lights of the restaurant dimmed as the small band moved into slow mellow music for dancing close. The young Sinatra-like singer launched into "I left my heart in San Francisco," and the floor suddenly became crowded and I became aware that everyone was singing. I led Rachel to the floor where her arms crept around my neck and her body pressed against mine. I floated on sentimental music and champagne for the rest of the evening.

We drove back to her apartment, where she pulled me inside and kissed me passionately. "I'm not like Olga, you know. Fancy her letting you go! I've a late morning tomorrow; we can lie in."

I awoke to the morning sun streaming in through the window. Rachel was sleeping quietly, her body draped with a sheet, her mouth framing a slight smile. I looked at my watch. Christ. Panic. It was ten o'clock. My plane for England would be just

Tales From A Briefcase

taking off. I telephoned the airport and found that the next plane to London on which there was a spare seat was in four hours; I would have to leave immediately to collect my things from my hotel, get out to the airport, hand back the car and check in.

I looked at Rachel, who was deep in sleep, and decided to leave her sleeping, but left a note promising to phone on my arrival in England.

As my plane cruised over the mountains of Colorado, I clamped the headphones of the music system to my head. Romantic music hit me, 'I left my heart in San Francisco', 'I'm leaving on a jet plane', 'Come fly with me' – everything with a meaning for me at that moment. I really felt my heartstrings twang.

Ten hours later, I landed on a cold February morning at Heathrow, nearly four weeks to the day after I'd left for my round-the-world trip.

Rachel and I corresponded about once a month and I visited her in San Francisco a few times on my way across the Pacific. She became more fabulous with each meeting. It must have been nearly two years later that she told me she was returning to England and had got a job at the Festival Hall. She asked if I could find a flat for her in Kensington.

I did find the flat, and stayed with her during my weekly business visits to London, but I realised that the relationship had to move on into something more permanent.... or finish. We talked about this and she revealed that marriage and babies were on her agenda.

At the weekends I returned to my home in Buckinghamshire, to my children in the charge of their nanny and to my wife in the mental clinic. Sticking with my family seemed the only responsible option, shepherding my children through to university and waiting for my wife to be released from her illness or be permanently hospitalised.

I returned to London for a final rendezvous with Rachel. On the face of it, we talked my decision through calmly and without rancour. In our hearts we knew we were throwing away something which felt so right.

Tales From A Briefcase

About a year later, I and some friends were attending a youth concert at the Festival Hall. As we got up to head for the bar in the interval, I saw her. She looked as stunning as ever. Making apologies to my friends, I went over to her and spoke. She melted me with her smile. We agreed to meet for dinner so that we could catch up on each other's adventures and exchanged telephone numbers. We met in a small restaurant near King's Cross Station. She was elegantly dressed with winter fur hat, camel coat and thigh-length leather boots. She explained that she was married and was three months pregnant. Her husband had a senior position with the Hertfordshire County Council and it was obvious that she loved him and was happy with her life.

As she left, she took my hand. "I am so lucky. I go back to a happy scene, a husband who loves me, a lovely house, my music and hopefully a beautiful baby to come. You will return to your bumpy life, to business and domestic problems which will probably go on for years, and you'll be without a clear-cut future. However, we'll share memories of happy times which neither of us will ever forget, whatever our circumstances. Remember, music will help you through. Goodbye, my love."

I watched her gracefully exit through the door of the restaurant, knowing that I would indeed never, ever forget her.

CHAPTER 17

A FACTORY IN SLOUGH

The industrial estate stood west of Slough centre, on the old Great West Road. Because of that road, Slough had in its time experienced many immigrant invasions. In the thirties, Welshmen had forsaken the economic crisis of the valleys and marched up the road to London, stopping where new industrial jobs and housing were available. In the sixties and seventies, the new factories in the Thames Valley offered job seekers from Slough the opportunity to live in a green environment and in modern, newly built-houses. The vacuum which they left was filled by newly arrived Pakistanis and Indians, bringing their own customs, Asian culture and little or no English. But hard work was part of that culture and they avidly sought jobs on the industrial estate.

My acceptable past track record as a chief executive had been noted by the headhunters, and I found myself being interviewed for a job managing a large factory on the Slough Industrial Estate. The business was part of a large British industrial group with headquarters in Manchester, and most of its interests were northern based. The Slough factory produced gaskets for vehicle engines, which it sold mainly to the British motor manufacturers. In addition, the factory supplied a huge independent spare-parts industry that competed for sales with the vehicle manufacturers.

Over two thousand people were employed by the company, whose numerous brands were known better than its name. Its customers, though, were household names – Leyland, Ford. Its largest continuous production line was for the cylinder gasket for the BMC Mini. At that time, the factory had no foreign car manufacturers as customers.

Tales From A Briefcase

My job was to continue the company's domination of the UK market for gaskets, introduce more automated production and start to win foreign customers. Not recognised by my bosses was the even more pressing need to assimilate Pakistanis into our industrial community. They were quick to learn, easily trained and available to fill our vacancies, but not familiar with how our system worked. Although we didn't operate a closed shop policy, there were understandings with the seven unions that wage negotiations, consultation, disputes, dismissal and redundancies were for consultation. Our Pakistani employees were suspicious of their British union representatives and it was beginning to produce a factory-wide problem.

In addition, the Pakistanis' poor English was a core problem, underlying their criticism that, according to their culture, the factory toilets, particularly the women's, were dirty and unhygienic and the canteen food was unappealing.

One of our senior test inspectors, an older man, appeared to be their spiritual leader and I asked him to come to my office for an informal chat about the situation.

"Good morning, Mr Mukherjee. Thank you for coming to see me. Please sit down." We shook hands. He was short and slight, grey haired and had a light brown skin. "I want to learn about the Muslim community in this factory and, if possible, make their lives more comfortable. I also want our British workers to understand more about their Muslim fellow workers so that we can achieve an even better harmony. I'm asking for your advice how this might be achieved but, first, I would like to hear your own story. Would you be agreeable to help me?" I asked with caution.

"Yes, I think so. We have a small committee of elders representing the Muslims who work in this factory and we were beginning to get around to requesting a meeting with you. You have beaten us to the draw."

Mr Mukherjee paused, smiled and continued, "I was born in Karachi, went to school and university there and was about twenty-two when partition with India occurred. Some of my family had already come to Britain at the end of the war and had settled in the Slough area. They suggested I should come over

Tales From A Briefcase

and leave the economic hardship which partition was causing. After working in some local accountants offices for a short time, I worked in Mars on the production lines, rising to supervisor. I came to this factory about five years ago as a quality inspector and became a senior inspector a few years later. I was one of the first Muslims to be employed by this company.

"At that time there were only about twenty Pakistanis; most of your foreign employees at that time were West Indians. We all spoke passable English and had become a little bit anglicised. Today there are over three hundred of us, many recently arrived from Pakistani. You know the problem: the language, the different environment and the culture."

"Yes, I think I do, although I haven't got any answers. Would your committee come to talk to me informally, although we'll have to involve the unions at some stage?"

"As long as the unions are not racist and are relatively open-minded, there will be co-operation and maybe our people will see a purpose in joining a union."

"Good. Let's fix a date for that informal meeting."

When Mr Mukherjee had left the office, I thought about the discussion and concluded that we could make a start by offering English lessons out of working hours. I decided that we would pay, as overtime attendance by trainees and teachers, for Saturday morning sessions and advertised the course via Mr Mukherjee. About forty applied to attend. Teachers were drawn from both locals and Pakistanis and a syllabus produced for a ten-session course.

Our agenda for the first meeting with the committee included toilets, canteen food and union membership. Up to then, Pakistani women would not use the seated lavatory bowls, considering them to be dirty and unhygienic. They were squatting down in corners leaving little piles all over the place. As an emergency measure I had French-type squatting lavatories installed. We consulted with the committee on preferred food for Muslims and included this in our menus.

I talked to our leading union steward, and we agreed to have a meeting with external union representatives to discuss the situation. At the ensuing meeting we looked at the distribution

Tales From A Briefcase

of Pakistanis throughout the factory and discussed whether proportional representation might be achieved. A series of meetings were held in working time to put over the unions' case to those interested. A special Pakistani induction course was introduced for new recruits to the factory and an English test given to all newcomers, Pakistani or otherwise. Many Pakistanis joined the union and several eventually became shop stewards.

About a year later, the Muslim committee and the management called a press conference to report on our progress in assimilating our co-workers from overseas. Our factory became a model for the other employers in the area. In touching gesture, I was presented with a signed copy of the Koran, which still sits on my bookshelf.

* * *

Political and economic events began to impact on our industrial community: the shorter working week, power-cuts, firemen and dustmen's strikes. Sales of UK cars dropped dramatically against the background of increasing foreign imports. The company faced capacity cuts of fifty per cent involving the potential loss of over a thousand employees. It was time to consult the unions. There was an urgent need to create a small working committee who could speak for all of them.

Eventually the unions agreed that the factory convenor, a Welshman in his early thirties called Tom Williams, could work with me during the redundancy planning phase. Outside of work, he and I had a common interest – rugby, on which our mutual respect was based: he played for Marlow Rugby Club, where I often met him as I was a referee with Buckinghamshire.

It became clear that redundancies at all levels were inevitable, but we could reduce their impact by phasing in their introduction. The unions would have plenty to say on the knotty question of who should leave first. Eventually, we first released those past retirement age and offered an early retirement package to those within five years of it. For the rest who had to leave, the unions insisted on a policy of 'last in first out.' In the end we would lose nearly half of our workforce of two thousand.

The vast factory premises seemed much quieter and emptier than before. A second round of redundancies loomed on the

Tales From A Briefcase

horizon. To protect the remaining jobs, we urgently needed more sales and these could only come from abroad. The management team spent long hours analysing the sales of foreign car manufacturers and we eventually selected our future sales targets, one from France – Citroen, Germany – BMW, Italy – Fiat, and Japan – Honda. Where to start?

We chose Citroen; it was partly government owned and was probably safer from redundancies. I had also introduced a spectacular range of new cars with attractive streamlined design and an advanced suspension system. We purchased some Citroen engines and evaluated them on our test beds. The French gaskets were good but maybe we could produce better at a cheaper price. We enlisted the services of a French teacher and the management team attended language lessons until we could make a respectable presentation of our wares. Then we went to Paris to promote our British engineering skills. It took a year of meetings, tests and negotiating to land the first order and another to capture a 'second supplier' status, which gave us half the demand for the new range.

Citroen's purchasing director was called Gerard Turcat and we became good friends, initially because we were both rugby fanatics. Every year we met at Twickenham or Parc des Princes to attend the international, and after to celebrate or commiserate on our respective positions. One season when the game was played at Twickenham, the French won and Gerard and I went to my favourite West End nightclub for our evening entertainment. I arranged for the band to play the 'Marseillaise' to celebrate the French victory. All the clubbers stood and roared the anthem; Gerard, who had been smoking a cigar at the time, thinking it was extinguished put it in the breast pocket of his jacket. As the anthem progressed into a second rendering, his pocket blackened and burst into flame. The clubbers, fairly inebriated by now, decide that soda siphons were the way to deal with the emergency and it wasn't long before everyone was soaked.

Next, the company focused on Fiat. Another language course and then we were off to Turin. There was an obvious problem for us – their engine design. In Britain, the car manufacturers had favoured the small bore, long stroke, low revving engine. As

Tales From A Briefcase

cylinder head gasket manufacturers, we had met every problem of these British designs, but the Italians had short stroke, wide bore motors, known as 'square' or 'over-square', which ran very fast. The pressure and stresses in the engine block were totally different.

We bought some Fiat engines, evaluated them and designed even stronger gaskets than the Italian ones they were using. They were worried about industrial strikes in Britain closing down their supplier factories, so we agreed to establish a subsidiary plant and also to hold stocks in Italy. We set up our factory in the small mountain village of Mondovi on the Italian side of the Alpes Maritimes. The contracts worked well and it was not long before we were supplying their associated factories in Poland (Polski Fiat} and in Spain (SEAT).

Our attention turned to BMW, headquartered in Stuttgart. With the Germans, we knew that price wouldn't be the first consideration; quality would be the issue. They over-engineered their products and it was reflected in the cost; for example a Jaguar 4.2 cylinder head gasket cost under £2 and for the biggest BMW engine they paid nearly £4. We decided to go in on a 'technical ticket' to establish our technology credentials and offered special gaskets for their racing team; these turned out be superior to the German ones. Another language session and we were off to Germany to make a bid to supply their most expensive car ranges. Volume orders followed sample supplies.

We continued our attack on Europe. We were already supplying Saab and Volvo, who were orientated to British component manufacturers, and now won orders from Peugeot, Volkswagen, DAF and MAN Diesels. Within three years, our overseas order book equalled that from the United Kingdom. We started recruitment again and built up the workforce to its original size.

Our thoughts turned to Japan, whose car manufacturers had gained a substantial proportion of the UK's new car sales. A visit to Japan confirmed that no local company would supply components outside the territory. However, as they had not sold heavily into the UK's large spare parts market, they would supply us for onward distribution. The Japanese later found that,

Tales From A Briefcase

due to limited exports to Britain, they would need to establish car plants here where they had to accept a quota of components purchased locally. We appointed Japanese business partners for the spares business.

To finalise the trading agreement, our Japanese partners sent a delegation of three to Slough; I had noticed that the Japanese always travelled in flocks and no single person appeared to make a decision, which was arrived at by group consensus. The three polite elderly men, with little English and impeccably dressed, arrived after an overnight flight, jet lagged but excited. They declined our suggestion that they should rest, protested that they were not tired, but asked to be taken to a nightclub in London. They had obviously been briefed by other Japanese visitors on the naked delights of London nightlife.

We took them to the West End and a club which started early in the evening. There were topless hostesses whose sole ambition was to induce two bottles of champagne each out of the visitors. If this was encouraged by tolerating kissing and breast squeezing, so be it. We watched our guests' eyes slowly closing as fatigue overtook them. Their hands were firmly planted on breasts until heads drooped and snoring ensued. We carried them to the cars, but not before we had photographed the scene. Our Japanese spares business took off.

Not long afterwards, I was to face a disappointment. Instead of my being promoted to the group board, an outsider was appointed, a friend of the chairman. Worse, because Slough had become such an important part of the group, he was going to base himself there. It was clear from the start that he was going to shackle me to more clearly defined policies and tighter restrictions, stripping me of my erstwhile freedom to operate independently.

Ah, well. The headhunters would have been registering my progress. The tom-toms would shortly be beating.

Tales From A Briefcase

BOOK 3
AT THE CHAIRMAN'S BEHEST

CHAPTER 18

THE CHAIRMAN

"Is that Robert James?" the female on the telephone asked.

"Yes it is. What can I do for you?"

"I'm Tracy Langdon. I work for a headhunting group called International Executive Search. My chairman, James McBride, has been following your career with interest for some time and now wishes to put a proposal to you. Could you join him for lunch?"

I quickly scanned my diary and chose some possible dates. "When do you suggest?"

"How about next Tuesday at Simpsons in the Strand at 12.30?"

"Yes. I can make it."

"Good. Ask for Mr McBride at reception." The telephone clicked off and she was gone, leaving me no chance for getting more information about the meeting.

I met James McBride as planned and we were shown to a reasonably private table in the corner of the room.

"Let's order first and then we can get down to business." We both ordered rare beef and James selected an expensive claret from the wine list.

"Thanks for agreeing to this meeting," he opened. "I don't think I'll be wasting your time. Tracy probably explained that we have been tracking your career since you were with Rank Organisation in Leeds. Since then you've had a good press and our file on you has numerous press cuttings on your exploits. We judge that you may be ready for a move into the even higher echelons of larger international groups, and we've found such an opportunity which may interest you."

His presentation was interrupted by a white-hatted chef stopping his trolley alongside our table and swivelling the lid off

Tales From A Briefcase

a silver dish holding two slabs of beef, one rare and oozing blood and the other slightly pink.

"Both rare, I believe, gentlemen?" the chef asked and we nodded our assent. He then went into an intriguing display of sharpening his knives. "Thick or thin?" he asked again. We both chose thick. He carved the meat with a rind of yellow fat adhering, placed it on plates with a Yorkshire pudding, and ladled juices on top. We made our selection of roast potatoes and green vegetables. James proffered the customary tip and we were then left to our discussion.

James continued: "Well, as I was saying, our job is to find a match between recruiters and potential candidates. I've know this particular group and its chairman for some years. It's an international engineering group and is publicly quoted in the City. The chairman is Swiss; he came to Britain in the thirties with his new product, a building prop. Henri Cartier is now in his sixties and is chairman and substantial shareholder of a group comprising thirty-seven subsidiaries around the world. It has expanded both by organic growth and acquisition and has produced ever-increasing profits since its foundation.

"The City doesn't accord the group a fair price because it believes the company's destiny is in the hands of a single person. The chairman has at last bowed to City opinion and agreed to appoint an executive board from outside. What do you think about it so far?"

"Very interesting. Please go on."

"The chairman is looking for executives with experience of international operations and multi-site facilities. He has already promoted a group managing director and is now seeking two deputy group managing directors, one with a marketing bias and the other with manufacturing and engineering bias. We think you measure up to the second. The job would be to control some of the subsidiaries as chairman, take responsibility for development of the group in selected continents, and manage, worldwide, the development of manufacturing and engineering resources, including IT. Now, how do you feel about it?"

"It sound extremely challenging and I would certainly be interested in meeting Henri Cartier. But, I know from experience of working with dominant chairman that they rarely delegate.

The underling then becomes a gunslinger doing the chairman's dirty work. I want a job with a clear specification, a clear role and identifiable authority. It sounds as though the job may not offer this."

"I know what you mean. You have to remember that there is considerable pressure by the City for the group to display the team performance of an executive board if the shares are to be fairly valued. We think it is incentive enough for Cartier to demonstrate he is delegating. What do you say?"

"I'm interested. I assume the reward package is negotiable?

"Yes. The package includes a competitive international salary, generous travelling expenses, share options, senior executive car, attractive pension and healthcare cover. I have to warn you about the downside – you will be forever travelling. Apart from your executive role, the chairman will send you on errands all over the world, sometimes at a moment's notice, but he's generous to those who perform. Could your family situation cope with this?"

"Yes, they are already used to my absences from home. I have a back-up team of a housekeeper-nanny and a home handyman to deal with day-to-day problems."

"Good. Well, let's move to the next step and put you and the chairman together. I'll get his secretary to arrange the appointment with you."

A telephone call from Henri Cartier's secretary a few days later asked me to join him at a well-known West End fish restaurant.

I arrived at the planned time to find him, already seated at an isolated table, smoking a long cigar and drinking an expensive Chablis. As he stood to greet me, I could see that he was of medium height and build, had thinning hair but a well-sculptured face. His voice boomed a welcome, "Sit down, James, and have a glass of wine."

A waiter appeared at his elbow with a bottle and dispensed wine, "A nice little vintage from France. Pity we can't produce something like this in Switzerland but we produce the most important other services," and he laughed so heartily that diners stopped eating to look at the noise maker.

Tales From A Briefcase

He continued, "These bloody City people, what do they know about business life? They sit all day in their fabulous offices, buying and selling shares, telling successful people like me how to run our businesses." He looked at me for comment.

"Does this mean that the exercise of enlarging the Board is just a sop to the City," I asked intently.

He stopped puffing his cigar, knocking off the burnt end into an ashtray. "Would that worry you, James?"

What did worry me was his use of my surname in that way. It indicated that our relationship would be far from matey, would not involve teamwork, and that I would be pressurised into being a 'yes' man. He would operate at arm's length and would never let me forget that he was the boss.

"Yes, it would Mr Cartier. I am young, ambitious and already have tasted the power of being a managing director in a blue chip group. If you ask me what job I want in your group – it's yours! I'm prepared to take time to prove to you that I'm worthy of that position but I'll not be your bum-boy in the meantime. I want a defined job with prescribed responsibilities and authorities. I don't want to be your understudy. Give me a real job and I'll show you real performance."

He took some long puffs at his cigar but his face remained impassive. "Mr James, None of my managing directors would dare to talk to me like that. Why should I tolerate it from you?"

I had the answer on the tip of my tongue, "It's obvious to me that they are afraid of you and of losing their jobs; that is something I will never be. They are probably so afraid of you that they will not take normal business risks which could earn high profits, the sort of risks which you yourself took as a younger man. They are constrained by telling you only what you wish to hear. I will tell you as I see it. I'll accept your authority but I will never be afraid of you and never become a 'yes' man."

"One other thing; I'm younger than you, have more puff than you, can endure hard travel better than you and am more up-to-date in management techniques than you. Your company must present a more youthful face; you know it already; the City has told you. I can do your job."

His face now reflected anger but there was a slight hint of

Tales From A Briefcase

smile as he continued, "I see that I'll have to watch my step with you. The bloody shareholders might just listen to a rebellious youngster like you. But the company still needs me. I have what it takes to produce sales and profits; look at my record over the years."

"Nobody can take those results away from you, Mr Cartier. But can you keep it going against growing competition, for example on cranes from Japan, without people like me?"

He stood up and offered his hand, "We may meet again, Mr James."

I registered that the form of address now included title, feeling that at least we had got the measure of each other. I would accept the job if it was offered.

Tales From A Briefcase

CHAPTER 19

A SAHARAN EMERGENCY

West Africa

I looked up as my secretary, Julie, entered the office. It was Friday and, at that moment, I'd been hoping that it would be a quiet day.

"You're off to West Africa on Monday. The Ivory Coast. The chairman wants to see you this afternoon at 2.30 to brief you. You'll be away about three days so you won't have to cancel your Liverpool trip towards the end of the week. You were going to meet CFAO at their English offices on Thursday, remember?"

CFAO, Compagnie Afrique et Occidentale, was a French construction company very prominent throughout Africa. They were a big user of our equipment and, as the director of African operations, I considered them to be vital to my company's developments on that continent.

"Right, fly out Monday morning, back to Heathrow or Manchester Wednesday evening or Thursday morning, meeting CFAO Thursday afternoon and back to Heathrow to be here to report to the boss on Friday. Please investigate flights and hotels and we'll finalise my travel plan after I've seen the chairman."

I reported to the chairman. "Ah, Mr James, I want to talk to you about a quick trip to West Africa." The cigar routine followed with him using its newly lighted end as a baton, pointing out a location on the world map behind his chair. "There, Cote d'Ivoire, a French protectorate with Abidjan its capital, which is just like Paris in Africa."

It sounded romantic but, if it was going to be that interesting, he would have gone himself. He went on, "My old friend, President Houphuet Boigny has been talking to me about setting

Tales From A Briefcase

up a factory up country. They want logging tractors and vehicles to pull exotic woods out of the forests. The Americans are selling them their surplus M45 tanks, stripped of their turrets, very cheaply. I've told him that we can convert them equally cheaply to logging tractors with powerful winches if he will fund a factory, which we would run.

He puffed at his cigar. "For some time we've been thinking about a refurbishment operation in West Africa, bringing in all the broken down construction equipment lying around out there, refurbishing it, and re-selling it for about two-thirds of the new price. We could do that in the same factory and do a tax deal on re-exports."

You had to hand it to the boss; he was a clever wheeler-dealer, knew all the right people in power in these Third World nations and made money from it.

He continued, "The president's son, Pierre, is the president of the Banque de Cote d'Ivoire. He will lend us the funds and I want you to negotiate the deal with him. If he addresses you in English, reply in English; otherwise speak French. Do not refer to any personal deals and off-shore payments – leave that to me. I will see you back here on Friday after your CFAO visit. Give the president my best regards when you see him. Any questions?"

Again the 'old man' demonstrated that he had his finger on my pulse. I gave him the expected answer, "No sir," and left his office.

Back in my own office, Julie already had a skeleton travel plan ready for me. "There are no direct flights from London to the Ivory Coast. The best route is flying BA Heathrow to Brussels on Monday, pick up a connecting Sabena flight going direct to Abidjan. Tuesday for meetings. Return on Wednesday evening, Sabena to Brussels and then BA to Liverpool or Manchester. Your Monday morning flight to Brussels will be 0645"

"OK. Set that up, please. Get the ticket agent to confirm to me personally over the weekend that I can collect the tickets at Heathrow. Get the driver to pick me up on Monday at home at 0530."

I left the office early to start my weekend by spending Friday evening with the children.

Tales From A Briefcase

On Saturday the company's travel agent telephoned confirming my travel plan and that the tickets and a visa could be collected on Monday at the BA ticket desk on production of my passport. The weekend passed quickly with the children doing their favourite things, including a picnic in Burnham Beeches on Saturday and a swimming party for friends around our pool on Sunday.

Monday turned out to be a bright sunny day. I telephoned BA to ensure there were no operational delays or strikes which would make me lose my Brussels connection. I left notes for the sleep-in nanny-housekeeper. My driver arrived on time and we drove to Heathrow without mishap. I checked in and waited in the first class lounge for the flight to be called. A pretty young hostess gave a warm smile and presented me with a coffee. Well, I thought to myself, the day is starting right.

As a first class passenger on Sabena, I was shepherded to a VIP lounge in Brussels to await the flight and have some more coffee.

"Voulez-vous choisir votre chaise dans l'avion, Monsieur? Il y a seulement quatre passagers dan la première classe."

I looked up to see, standing over me, a tall, shapely air hostess dressed in a well-tailored uniform and with a pill-box hat perched above blond hair and a big smile. I could not recollect the Belgians being a beautiful race but this member of it was quite something else.

"Merci, Mam'selle. La première ou deuxième allée, devant les moteurs. C'est plus tranquille."

"D'accord, Monsieur, chaise 2A. Désirez autre chose?"

The smart answer would not have gone down well! "Non, merci. C'est tout."

The smile flashed again and I heard the swish of her stockings as she walked away.

The flight was called and four men, including me, were led on to the plane and shown to first class seats by the on-board team. Two hostesses were allocated to first class and by now had donned their aprons and were circulating with trays loaded with champagne, wine and scotch.

The captain opened the door from the cockpit and came up to me as the first passenger on his route. He was young, relatively

Tales From A Briefcase

short and thick set. His cap with gold decoration sat squarely on his head and gave him a serious look. "I am Captain Philippe de Vigier," he said, "your pilot for this trip. My co-pilot is Bernard Rickard and my engineer is Jean Leclerq. Have you flown Sabena before? Do you know the Cote d'Ivoire?"

"Yes I've flown between Britain and Belgium but not on an African flight. It's my first time to Abidjan."

"Today we fly to the coast and stay over the sea all the way down the Iberian peninsular, past Morocco and then start cutting due south over the Sahara to Cote d'Ivoire. About seven hours all told, ETA Abidjan about 1800 local time. It is an interesting trip because there is no radar positioning over the Sahara and we fly on dead reckoning and call other aircraft all the way down to get their positions. This is a Boeing 707 delivered to us in 1972 and so it's about six years old. Perhaps you would like to come up to the cockpit after we've crossed the Mediterranean? Meanwhile make yourself comfortable, enjoy your lunch and keep the hostesses busy!"

He saluted as he moved off to another passenger behind.

A short, dark-haired hostess introduced herself: "Mr James? I am Marie. Shall we talk in English? I am the cabin supervisor and Yvette is my assistant. Our job is to make your trip as comfortable as possible. We will be serving lunch shortly and maybe you would like to choose some food from this menu and select one of our fine wines?"

"Thank you Marie, the service could not be better. I'll have the asparagus starter and the chateaubriand, à point, and this claret. I don't know it but perhaps you can recommend it?"

"You should taste the wine first but I think you will like it."

After lunch, with the aircraft drifting smoothly through scattered clouds over the Bay of Biscay, I took the notes on the Ivory Coast out of my briefcase. I must have slept because I was awoken by Marie shaking my arm. "Captain de Vigier invites you to visit the cockpit. Please come this way."

I entered the cockpit to find the captain sitting in the forward left hand seat. He had removed his hat and jacket but had a headphone on his head. He turned to greet me.

"Mr James, welcome to the cockpit. This is Bernard Rickard, my co-pilot, who is at present flying the plane," he nodded to the

Tales From A Briefcase

right hand seat. "Behind Bernard sitting facing all the dials is our engineer, Jean; he keeps an eye on everything to do with the workings of the plane and Bernard and I just navigate and steer it."

I sat fascinated with the view out of the cockpit – sand as far as the eye could see. Here and there were a few white buildings and palm trees and vehicular tracks. Now and then, Philippe or Bernard talked to someone on the radio using call signs and giving figures.

Philippe explained, "Where there are airfields we check with them as we fly over and we talk to other planes on nearby routes, exchanging with them courses and heights. We make allowances for dead reckoning errors and agree aircraft separation distances. We still fly visually and keep a sharp eye on our airborne radar so our chances of mid-air collision are pretty remote."

I asked a few more questions before thanking them and returning to my seat. Then, other first class passengers also visited the cockpit.

A few hours later, when I calculated from a marked-up flight plan that we had passed Senegal and were entering Guinea airspace, I noticed the plane yawing from left to right and beginning to switchback vertically.

As a regular flier over hot arid deserts I was used to heavy thermals and planes dropping vertically but had never experienced anything quite like this. I called Marie over to ask but her arrival was interrupted by a call for her to go to the cockpit.

She looked a little worried as she re-entered the cabin. "We have a small problem. Bernard will be out to explain this to the first class passengers and the captain will make an announcement."

Bernard duly appeared and called the four of us around him. "We have a hydraulic problem," he explained. "It is affecting the flaps and rudder, making steering and level flying very difficult. We have called Brussels and been advised that we should land at the nearest emergency airfield which is Guinea Conakry. They have a Boeing engineer there and we should be able to find the cause of the problem and deal with it. We shall

Tales From A Briefcase

be making a general announcement in a minute to say that we have a minor fault and are landing to correct it. In practice gentlemen, it could be a bumpy landing as we might not be able to steer a course, or control height or reduce our landing speed. We want you to go back to the coach class so that we have as much weight at the back as possible and we'll attempt to land nose up. The hostesses will be demonstrating the emergency landing positions. Thank you."

We moved back and sat in the vacant seats. The announcements were made, including instructions to fasten seat belts. The hostesses demonstrated putting on life jackets and using pillows on laps to rest heads, and bracing against the shock of landing.

The plane's movements became more exaggerated as it lost speed and height. It hit the ground violently, bursting its tyres, and rolled to a stop just before the end of the runway. With the engines shut down, a deathly silence crept over the passengers. Even children who had been weeping and babies screaming momentarily stopped.

The hostesses rushed up and said quite calmly, "Sit still, leave your seat belts buckled. There is no fire. We have to wait for the steps."

The captain came on the loudspeaker, "We are down safely. There is no danger. We are waiting for someone to bring us a ladder or some steps. Please sit still until we have the means to empty the plane. Thank you."

Marie told the four of us from first class to go forward to our seats and we would be served coffee or tea.

"The army is here," remarked a fellow passenger casually. We all looked out of the windows as lorries and jeeps were disgorging soldiers who surrounded the plane with weapons pointing at it.

"They don't look like Africans," remarked another. "Look there a small group with a ladder including a civilian."

There was a tapping at the fuselage door opening into first class. Marie got the captain's permission to open it and in strode a very tall soldier with a red beret. The captain came from the cockpit to receive him. They saluted each other.

Tales From A Briefcase

"I am Captain Martinez of the Cuban Marines. We provide a special guard for the president. We have been asked to keep you aboard this aircraft until we have further instructions." His English was very good.

The civilian turned out be an American engineer from Boeing, based at the airfield in case of such an emergency.

Captain de Vigier spoke to the Cuban marine: "Captain Martinez. We would like to start analysing the problem and, if possible, repairing our aircraft immediately. I am sure that the president would like us to be on our way as soon as possible. We think that this will mean that we will have to go outside the plane, particularly around the wing and tail sections."

"Please go ahead Captain, but the passengers and other crew must stay aboard, for the moment. You must not however use your radio to make outside contact. Agreed?"

"Agreed."

"We wish to collect the passports of all crew and passengers as part of our immigration procedure. Please advise your crew that I will set up my base in the first class section and administer it from there."

So, we returned to the coach section of the plane where there were one hundred and seventeen passengers, mainly Belgian, including ten children and three babies. After a while, Captain de Vigier came back to speak to the four business passengers who had travelled first class.

"There are now four of us who can start searching for the problem on the plane. It will involve removing panel sections of fuselage and uncoupling air and hydraulic hose lines. There will not be time for us to deal with the passengers. There are however logistical problems, mainly of food supply and toilet emptying and cleansing. There are no service vehicles here other than fuel trucks. There are no toilet emptying and cleansing facilities, no potable water supply, no air conditioning, no mosquito control. Finally, the nights get very cold here at the edge of the Sahara – no heating.

"We have food supplies sufficient for a cold evening snack. Water will run out by the morning and the toilets will be full. My crew have volunteered to survive on a half litre of water a day.

Tales From A Briefcase

Finally, the plane's batteries will start to run down; we cannot recharge them at the moment and we must therefore conserve power."

I spoke up, "Captain, you are talking as though you expect us to be here some time!"

"It could be so. Belgium knows we're here but no one else does. In countries like this, the president and his guards control everybody and everything. He probably knows nothing about this yet and it may be some time before he gets involved. This is where you come in gentlemen. You are businessmen, used to dealing with officials at high level. I want you to persuade the Cuban Captain to take you to the President's Palace, negotiate food and drinking water and permission for the passengers to go into the trees to perform their bodily functions. It is six o'clock now and will shortly get dark. In twelve hours we could have an impossible situation on our hands. Are you willing to do this?"

We agreed without discussion.

I spoke up again, "I suggest two of us go to see the Cuban captain now. He may think it threatening if there were more of us."

It was agreed that I and a Belgian businessman, Francis Torhout, should start the representations. We went forward to the first class cabin to speak to Captain Martinez.

I spoke first. "Captain Martinez. On behalf of the passengers, we wish to make representations to the government of Guinea about the plight of the people on this aircraft. Without support, by tomorrow morning their conditions will have deteriorated to a life threatening state. As a minimum, we seek water, some food and toilet facilities. The toilets on the plane will become full before morning and will soon become a health hazard in this climate. There is no air conditioning during the day and no heating at night. We have ten children and three babies aboard and cannot provide them with the right care. We have been unable to contact Belgium to arrange another plane or relief supplies. Please will you assist us to make an appeal to someone in authority?"

He thought for a moment, drumming his fingers on a foldaway table. "You know this a communist state and that it is controlled by a president who is the ultimate authority. He lives in the palace at Conakry and has several aides who assist him in ruling the country. I could contact one of the aides who might talk to the president about your problem. To save time I suggest you two come in the jeep with me now and we'll go into Conakry and search for the right contact."

A few minutes later we were sitting in the back of a military jeep, driven by Martinez with a soldier in the other front seat. Nobody talked on the half hour journey to the palace which turned out to be the residence of an ex-French colonial governor. High walls and sturdy iron gates surrounded it. We stopped at a guard hut where Martinez appeared to be accepted, then swept up to the building's grand front entrance. There on the steps leading up to the foyer was an armed guard who saluted Martinez as he led us into the building.

"Please sit there." He pointed to some chairs in a waiting area and disappeared up further stairs.

A little later he returned and said, "One of our soldiers will now search you for weapons." The search was brief but thorough.

"Come with me, we are going to meet Colonel Obasanjo, a presidential aide."

We entered a vast office with a table and chairs placed at its far end. Four armed Cuban soldiers stood around the desk.

Martinez said, "Stand up when the colonel comes in. Just sit and wait and only speak when invited to."

An officer arrived dressed in military uniform decorated with red tabs, tassels and rows of medals. He sat down and started reading a document, then noticed that we were still standing. "Sit..."

He continued reading for a while, then sat back in his gold chair and said, "Talk!"

I stood up, knowing that it had to be short and to the point. "Your Excellency, we apologise to the president and yourself for this disturbance caused by our aeroplane emergency over the Sahara. It was critical and your airfield has been classified as available for emergency landings. The problem we, the passengers, find ourselves in is not of our own making and we cannot find a solution on our own. It appears that we have only

Tales From A Briefcase

one course of action; to place ourselves at the mercy of your president and appeal to him for assistance to survive in the short term, whilst rescue arrangements are made. We have no communication with the outside world." I searched for a simile. "We are like a tribe lost in the wilderness. We appeal on behalf of one hundred and sixteen adults of several countries, ten children and three babies. Our immediate need is food, water and toilets."

Colonel Obasanjo's response was swift enough to have been rehearsed. "Our benevolent president is mindful of your predicament. He too has suffered with his people under impossible conditions enforced by a colonial power. Other countries came to his aid," at that he waved his arms at the Cuban guards, "and now this country is settled, peace-loving and its citizens have all they need. By helping you we can demonstrate that we are a civilised nation ready to take its place in the council of nations and to discuss world affairs."

Oh my God, I thought, they are going to use us as bargaining pawns to gain political recognition.

The colonel continued: "Captain Martinez will help you with your immediate needs. My office will contact your consulate and work something out. Thank you, gentlemen." Everybody stood and he left the room with a curt nod.

Martinez was next to speak, "Come gentlemen, we will visit the quartermaster's stores to find your urgent requirements." We got back in the jeep and went to a nearby barracks. There was a small water-bowser, full of fresh water, which was hooked to the tow bar of the jeep. Another jeep with a trailer was commissioned to carry bread, tinned milk and juices, and a wide selection of fruit. "Look what I've found," Martinez said, waving at boxes of toilet rolls. "No babies' nappies, though. I'll replace the water-bowser when it is empty. Let's get back, before it gets too dark."

"What about toilets, Captain Martinez?"

"We'll let the passengers off the plane in small groups. They can visit the woods about two hundred metres away. I will delegate a party of my men to help the women and children down the ladder from the aircraft and there will a group guarding the perimeter fence to prevent anyone escaping. Please

Tales From A Briefcase

warn your people that this is a concession. They must not wander about but return to the plane so that others may have their turn. My men will shoot anyone who is not complying with these orders. We have been very patient up to now so please warn them to co-operate."

"Captain Martinez, we thank you for your efforts on our behalf. We will ensure that our charges will conform to your requirements."

We found Captain de Vigier and his crew, using torches, covered in oil from head to toe, removing panels from the aeroplane wings, tracing the path of the high-pressure oil hydraulic system controlling the wing flaps and trims. We told him of our progress and asked about his.

"No pressure in this sector. It looks like a burst hose somewhere because the pump is working OK and there is oil everywhere. You tell Marie about your success and she will tell the passengers. She'll also work out feeding and toilet schedules."

I found Marie rationing out the food and took her aside. "Marie, we should share the work load with you and give the passengers some jobs as well. You and your girls continue with the feeding of the passengers and organise toilet visits using responsible passengers. Tomorrow, we should get buckets, towels and soap so that they can at least wash. We'll try to get canvas screens and shovels and dig some field latrines nearby. Maybe we could get tents so that passengers can get some time away from the plane. Have you got disinfectant for the plane's toilets?"

"Have you done this before, Monsieur?" she enquired, then: "Yes, we have some chemicals for the toilets and we should be able to keep the smell down for a few days. After that the smell in the plane will become unbearable."

"Yes, I've done this before – when I was in the army – with refugees. Basic needs first, creature comforts second. Get everyone back in the plane by ten o'clock and settle them down for the night. You have blankets? Yes? Good."

I sought out Captain Martinez again. "You have been most kind to get us food and water for the passengers and a concession on toilet visits. I can see this lasting for a few more

Tales From A Briefcase

days yet. Could we press you to find us field washing and latrine facilities which we could set up near the plane – buckets, spades, canvas screens and soap? The passengers will feel more human and they will be easier to control if they don't have to wander so far."

"You sound like you've been a military man. Were you?"

"Yes, a regular officer. Six years, Korean War and Malayan Emergency."

"I would like to talk to you about that, perhaps tomorrow evening when the passengers are settled down for the night?"

I considered this with some trepidation. My war service was fighting communists and, as a Cuban soldier, he was a communist. "Certainly, but could we collect the other items tomorrow morning when we collect the food and water?"

"Yes, we'll drive into Conakry tomorrow at nine in the morning."

"By the way," I told him, "the passengers will be all on the plane and settled for the night by ten o'clock. The three other first class passengers are taking shifts to look after them through the night, particularly if they want to visit the toilet. The crew will want to leave the plane at daylight to resume their investigations – OK?"

"Yes, OK. What rank were you in the army?"

"Like you a captain. We captains always got the dirty work! Good night."

Tuesday

I slept in the big, wide first class seat and was awoken just after daybreak by Monsieur Torhout. "Monsieur James, Captain Martinez is back with food and water and a big truck. He says he has some news for you."

I climbed down the steps and crossed to where Captain Martinez was supervising his soldiers unloading the lorry. "I have managed to get most of what you needed. The grass starts about a hundred metres from the plane. Could you get your strongest passengers to set up the washing and toilet facilities there? Also, I have some news from the palace."

Tales From A Briefcase

"I hesitate to ask a Cuban, but would you like a mug of our coffee?"

"Thank you, I would, Captain James."

"Not a captain any more. Mr James, or if you prefer, Robert."

"Robert," he rolled my name his tongue, and held out his hand, "Fernando. We can talk as equals, maybe as friends?" he ventured, his head at a slight angle.

"Certainly, we both have a job to do; look after people and obey orders."

Marie brought us lukewarm coffee. "The plane's batteries are nearly finished. Cold meals and drinks from now on!"

"I could probably get you hot food at mid-day from our cookhouse," suggested Captain Martinez.

"That would be most helpful," I said. "You have news from the Palace?"

"Yes. They have contacted the Belgian consul and given him all the details of the problem. They now know where you are and how we are assisting you. The consul has been in touch with Sabena to see if a replacement plane can be sent. All their passenger aircraft are deployed all over the world and there will not be one free for two days. They will send a small aircraft with spare parts as soon as your plane's captain advises us of his needs."

"Well, thank you for that. We'll tell the crew and passengers."

I mustered the younger and fit men from among the passengers and explained the work to be done. Two soakaways were dug, six feet deep, one for the wash tents and the other for screened-off latrines. Logs cut from the woods served as tables for the washbasins and squatting poles on which to rest bums.

Next, I sought out Captain de Vigier. "How are you doing?"

"We have isolated the problem to a sector but not the precise component. By the end of today we should know which component has failed."

"Good news from the presidential palace. They've opened up a line of communications back to Belgium and Sabena. There are no spare passenger aircraft, but spare parts can be delivered as soon as you can define the failed pieces. Meanwhile Captain Martinez is pulling all sorts of rabbits out of the hat. We will

Tales From A Briefcase

shortly have field latrines and wash houses erected and food and water is being delivered on a regular basis. I must say that your cabin crew are bloody marvellous."

"That is all wonderful. We wish to thank the four of you for your efforts. It has enabled us to concentrate on the plane."

I took my leave and went in search of Marie. "We'll have field washing facilities and latrines before dark. They will be very primitive, quite smelly, not very private but quite usable and hygienic. Because we won't have separate male and female facilities, you will have to schedule the times. We have been able to get towels, soap, lanterns and candles. Is there anything else you need?"

"That is marvellous, Monsieur. Nothing more for the moment."

Daylight passed into darkness, and passengers and crew had cold meals. The plane's batteries started to fail and the lights would not work. Candles in saucers were handed out and lit and the inside of the cabin looked like a fairy grotto. Most people were asleep by eight o'clock.

I walked into coach class to find a seat and sleep.

Wednesday

Daybreak arrived and the passengers followed the prescribed schedules and were much happier with a firm routine to follow. Captain de Vigier came to me waving a burst length of armoured hose found in the depths of a wing section. He advised Captain Martinez who took the message to the palace.

Later we received news from the palace that no replacement aircraft could be found but a replacement for the failed part would arrive on Friday. Fernando advised me that the colonel at the palace wished to see me. We drove to Conakry, following the procedures and rigmarole of gaining entry to the palace and audience with the colonel.

I sat quietly awaiting for him to speak. "Did you get everything you want?" he asked brusquely.

"Yes, Your Excellency. Everything and more. Captain Martinez and his soldiers have given us wonderful treatment. The passengers and crew are most grateful to the president and yourself for your generous hospitality."

Tales From A Briefcase

"Good. Tell your people at home that we are not savages but responsible citizens of the world, trying to do the best for our people, wanting to extend the hand of friendship to our neighbours. You will tell them?"

"Yes, sir," I acquiesced, wondering if some sort of demand was going to follow.

"The president, generous and benevolent, has decided to help you on your journey. Tonight, he will place the presidential plane at your disposal to take you another step in your journey – to Monrovia in Liberia. It is on the main air route from America to West Africa. From there you will easily get a plane to Abidjan. We will of course advise the Belgian consul of your onward transit. Goodbye." He stood and left.

I walked from the palace to the jeep, in a daze. What was going on? Had we become an embarrassment to the president? Were there politics behind this unexpected turn of events?

Fernando hardly spoke on the journey back to the airfield. I could sense that he was angry. I called a meeting of Captain de Vigier and the crew, along with my three first class colleagues. I relayed the president's decision.

"We cannot come with you. We have to stay with the plane," said Captain de Vigier.

I replied, "You may not get out after we have gone. You and the plane could be made hostages."

"Nevertheless, we stay. You and the other passengers will be flying on an unscheduled flight in a military plane, probably antique, and have no guarantee of being put down in Monrovia. There is no guarantee that Liberia will let you in and you could become stranded. If you fly, you do so at your own risk. No insurance company in the world will cover you. You will not have tickets or local funds to buy them. As the captain responsible for the passengers' well being, I leave the decision to go or not to the passengers. We should speak to them immediately."

Captain de Vigier spoke to the passengers in the coach section using a loud hailer, explaining the pros and cons. After handling some questions, he asked for a show of hands, for and against. All the passengers without exception voted to go.

A plane painted in military colours landed on the airstrip near the Sabena aircraft. It had four propellers and the engines snorted

Tales From A Briefcase

exhaust flames about a foot long. A door at the rear of the aircraft opened and a ladder was put in place. The large coloured man who appeared at its opening called out, "I am the captain of this presidential plane. The rear cabin here is the presidential suite which you will not enter. From here forward, we have a hundred canvas seats normally allocated to the president's bodyguard; this is where most of you will sit. The rest will stand. Our flight time to Monrovia is four hours. Please ensure that you have your passports with you. We can take only your hand luggage. Please board now and be careful as you climb the steps."

I looked at Fernando who appeared distressed at the arrangements. "Are we doing the right thing?" I asked him. He shrugged his shoulders, shook my hand and walked away.

I walked over to the Sabena crew and thanked them on behalf of the passengers. "See you in Abidjan on Saturday or Sunday. Big party." This was greeted with weak, unconvincing smiles and half-hearted waves. Did they know something I didn't?

I climbed aboard the plane and took my place with others standing with my back to a bulkhead as the doors were shut. The engines roared and sputtered, emitting even longer exhaust flames. I later learned that the plane was an old Ilyushin, presented by Russia to the president. It trundled down the runway and managed to lift off at its end. The engine noise and vibration was almost unbearable and the sudden drops caused by the thermals added extra fear.

Later we could feel the plane descending, and then we landed on a long runway. It rolled to a stop some way away from lit airport buildings, now visible out of its windows. The rear door was opened and the passengers disembarked with great difficulty, down the steps to the ground. No sooner had we got off than the plane revved up and was trundling down the runway for takeoff. The passengers stood in a huddled pathetic group on the runway, being fast approached by cars and trucks with flashing blue lights.

Armed soldiers formed a circle around us. "Who's in charge?" said a voice in English. Its owner wore a large floppy hat such as those worn by police in the USA.

"I am," I replied. "We are passengers from Sabena Flight SA 46 from Brussels to Abidjan. An emergency forced us down in

Guinea Conakry where we have been on the ground three days. We have just come here on the president's plane."

"Passports and tickets," he commanded. I and my colleagues collected them. "I would like receipts for all of them, please," I requested.

"Hand them over. You are here illegally. You have no visas, no permits to enter Liberia. We have no facilities for refugees." The last word struck a note of terror for the passengers.

"Be quiet," said the policeman. "No talking. Walk to those buildings and don't try to escape."

Herded by armed men, we trailed in column to the building which was the transit lounge for short stay passengers.

There I was asked, "Are you the spokesman for the passengers?"

I looked around me and there were nods. "I suppose so."

"We have nowhere to accommodate you here. We will take you to the airport hotel which lies within the boundary fence. They will put you up until the morning when we can sort something out. That way, walk!"

The bedrooms in the hotel were almost all already occupied and many of the passenger families had to be accommodated in the poolside changing cabins and a garden chalet. The rest of us slept on the floor of a conference room.

Thursday

We all awoke early and hungry and invaded the dining room where early breakfast was being served to hotel guests. It took some time for the restaurant manager to realise we were not guests but most of our passengers got fed before the food supply had run out.

Walking around the hotel, I found an empty office with a telephone. I lifted the receiver, got a dialling tone and phoned my secretary's home number, realising it was still only 6 am in London. She answered the phone after a few rings, "Yes."

"Julie, it's Robert."

"Where the hell are you? Will you miss today's meeting with CFAO in Liverpool?"

"Have you got pencil and paper?" I explained the situation

Tales From A Briefcase

adding: "We must find out which flights call into Monrovia on their way to Abidjan or anywhere else for that matter. Try KLM and Pan American first and contact Sabena to make ticketing arrangements and visas. Assuming I can get to Abidjan by tomorrow afternoon, Friday, make business appointments for me for then and also on Saturday morning. I doubt if I will get back to Europe before Monday. You can try phoning back here on the hotel's number but someone must contact the airline desks at Monrovia airport so that we can be informed of what's been decided. Oh, yes, please inform my housekeeper-nanny and see if she needs anything. You are our only lifeline; do your best!"

"I've got all that and I'll start right away. Have fun, Robert and don't get sunburnt by the pool!"

The airport police superintendent arrived and gathered the passengers in the conference hall to announce: "We intend to hold you here until arrangements can be made to transfer you to a police compound in the city."

I popped the question, "What arrangements are you making for our onwards transit to Abidjan?"

"None," came the answer, "it is for you to make them. We'll allow you and one other into the airport ticketing hall."

"What about our passports?"

"You will get them back when you have tickets to fly out and not before. Meanwhile all the passengers stay in this room. Any food from the hotel must be purchased. There is drinking water in the washrooms."

Monsieur Torhout and I went to the ticketing hall where all the desks were closed. We found the airport manager who told us that the next east-bound plane would be Pan American Airlines which would land early Friday morning, getting into Abidjan about lunchtime. He would contact the home of the PAA representative and get him to contact Sabena about ticketing. I asked him if I could use his telephone and contacted Sabena in Brussels, explaining the need for onward ticketing and for one more night's accommodation in Monrovia. I also requested that they speak to the police chief about taking us off the refugee list and regarding us as bona fide passengers.

By the time we got back to the hotel, Sabena had talked to the hotel manager and arrangements for accommodation and feeding were being made. We returned to the conference hall where the passengers had become rather tense, and explained the position, which calmed things down.

"We'll arrange for you to use a public telephone without charge and you will be able to contact your relatives and friends and make arrangements to be met tomorrow at Abidjan airport. Check into your rooms, eat and drink what you want and take it easy by the pool. We are on our last lap. See me if you need anything; I'll probably be sleeping by the pool."

I surprised myself with my calmness. Nothing had really been finalised and we had still to retrieve our passports.

Friday

Having breakfasted, the passengers followed me to the ticketing hall. I felt like Moses leading the Israelites out of Egypt.

The Pan Am agent was at his desk. "I have instructions to allow all of you on our flight to Abidjan arriving in half an hour."

I sought out the chief of police. He was adamant: "Every passenger must have his own ticket. We release each passport when we see the ticket."

I rushed over to the airport manager, "Has Belgium got a consulate in Liberia?"

He gave me the telephone number, and I got through to some junior who played a straight bat. "I must speak to the consul himself; it is a matter of extreme urgency with political consequences for Belgium."

The consul came on the telephone and would only speak French. I handed the phone to Monsieur Torhout who explained the position and its critical timing. Meanwhile the passengers sensed a problem and began to get restless.

The PAA Boeing 707 landed and the other passengers boarded. We waited for a telephone to ring. The agent told us that he would have to release the plane in ten minutes. Then the police chief arrived with a box of passports. He appeared very angry. "You can go," was all he said and left. There was a mad scramble for the plane.

Arriving at Abidjan airport with only hand luggage, I had no change of clothes and presented myself for the high-level meetings

Tales From A Briefcase

in a crumpled lightweight suit and sweaty shirt. I made my apologies for the deferred meetings and went into my proposal for the project. It was approved by the Economic Minister for the Cote d'Ivoire.

Next, I went into central Abidjan to buy a change of clothes and then check into my hotel.

Tomorrow morning's meeting would tell us if we had the funding to do the project.

Saturday

The meeting with the president's son at the bank went smoothly and the funding was approved. I returned to the Sabena desk at the airport. Yes, there was a flight to Brussels on Sunday evening Would I like to retrieve my luggage from the baggage handling office? It had been brought in from Guinea Conakry that morning.

The cab deposited me at the hotel. It was a warm, sunny day and the residents were relaxing by the pool. I made for the lounge to get a cool drink and there was the crew of Sabena Flight 46, still in uniform, flopped into deep chairs sipping long, iced cocktails.

"Well, I'm buggered!" I exploded, "Bonjour, mes amis. Fantastique!" and we started telling our stories. On Friday a replacement for the broken armoured hose had been flown into Guinea Conakry by Sabena. They had repaired the plane, run up the engines, tested the hydraulics and refuelled. They took off early that morning and had just arrived!

They pressed me for my story. Philippe said, "We knew you were heading for trouble when you left us. Military aircraft, no visas, no onward tickets – we thought you would become stateless persons and be locked up in prison awaiting a long political process to release you. You did very well to get away."

"What are you doing this evening? When do you fly next? This calls for a party!" I said.

Philippe smiled. "We are taking you home on Sunday evening – same crew, same plane, same journey – for most of the way! We can drink tonight but right now we need some sleep. We know a superb restaurant with African food and music. You'll love it. Taxi at the hotel at eight. OK?"

So that's how I came to be playing a tom-tom with a conical straw hat on my head, singing French songs with a terrible accent not improved by drinking too much local champagne. But I really got to know the cockpit crew, Philippe, Bernard and Jean, and the cabin crew Marie, Yvette, Lysianne and Annette. I had seen them operating under an extreme emergency and admired the way they handled it as a team.

We took taxis back to the hotel and had a last drink in the lounge. One by one the crew left for bed leaving me sitting opposite Marie.

"Would you like one more drink – in more comfortable surroundings?" she asked.

"My room or yours?" I asked with feigned innocence.

"Mine," she replied and took my hand.

We arrived at her room where we sat close on a sofa drinking more champagne from her room bar.

"Are you married?" she asked.

"Yes, a wife in hospital with mental depression and two children."

"Poor Robert," she caught my hand and kissed it.

"You?"

"A lovely husband and also two children. I guess you and I are about the same age?"

I looked at her closely, probably for the first time. The other air hostesses were younger and shapelier. She was petite, had black hair and, I think, brown eyes. She looked good, dressed in a belted shirt-waister with several buttons opened down from the neck.

"Yes," I mused and popped the conversation stopper. "Are you a good Catholic?"

"I try to be. It's difficult in this job. The crew get used to the position. It's me. Sometimes I feel lonely and lost, especially if I have come through a difficult time like now. My husband could not share it with me. You could – you went through it with us."

"I know what you mean," I told her, lifting her hand and kissing it. "We could get comfortable on the bed. We will do nothing which either of us would later regret. Just being two lonely people getting comfort from each other."

"Yes, just two lonely people."

Sunday

I met the crew around the pool, but flight regulations prevented then from taking alcohol, and the need for sleep before a sleepless night took them to bed for the afternoon. Philippe came up to me and said, "If you would like, you can fly with us in the cockpit. You will find it interesting. Also join us on the crew bus. We leave the hotel at about 1800 hours."

Marie and Yvette served dinner in the first class cabin and after it I went forward to the cockpit.

Monday

The flight to Brussels was uneventful and we landed just as dawn was breaking. I said goodbye to the crew and headed for the BA flight home, a week after I'd left for Abidjan.

* * *

I wrote to the president of Sabena and praised the crew of the flight to Abidjan. A few weeks later, the London based director of Sabena visited me at my office.

"The president of Sabena has asked me to thank you for your kind letter. He has met the crew and expressed your sentiments about their devotion to duty. He wishes me to present you with the airline's VIP card which will give you special treatment any time you fly with us. Also, Sabena is a sponsor of the Miss World competition whose finals are to be held in London next month. You are invited to be our guest." And that is how I came to sit between Miss Israel and Miss Argentina, the two most beautiful of the contestants.

CHAPTER 20

I'VE NO BLOODY LEGS!

The telephone at my bedside rang. For the moment I was disorientated and then remembered that I was in a hotel in Newcastle. I wearily looked at my watch; it was nearly eight o'clock.

"James," I answered.

"It's Fiona Thompson." She was the wife of Richard, one of the youngest and brightest directors at our Sunderland plant. "The police have told me that Richard has had a bad accident in his car. He's in the King's College Hospital in Newcastle undergoing a serious operation. The staff there will not give me any information."

"Right, Fiona. I'll get over there now and telephone you when I have some news. Are you going to be at home for the rest of the morning?"

"I'm not sure if I should take Alison to school. Richard may need us."

"If you haven't told her yet, don't, not until we have some more information. If we need to, we can collect her from school later. Meanwhile stay as calm as you can. Don't drive – get a taxi. I'll phone back as soon as I can. I'm sure that they will let you see him as soon as he out of the operation."

I threw on some clothes and headed for the car park. It was a frosty morning and there was ice on the roads. I drove to the hospital's reception and explained that I was a director of a group that employed Richard; that we made it a practice of following up emergencies on behalf of families. Somehow this worked and a doctor in a white gown appeared.

"I'm afraid your man is in a bad way. He skidded on the ice going over a viaduct in Sunderland and landed on the roundabout beneath. They found him in the back seat and both his legs under the dashboard. He's having two amputations, one high on the thigh and the other just above the knee. It will be at least two more hours until they are finished and another two before his family can visit him. Will you take responsibility for keeping the family informed?"

"Certainly I will. I'll bring his wife in about four hours from now. Which ward will he be in?"

"Probably Surgical Nineteen but ask again at reception."

Thanking him for his help, I telephoned Fiona to say that I would call by to give her the information. Breaking the news to her gently as possible, I could see that she was terribly distressed and should not be left alone.

"Fiona, I'm going to get a nurse from the company to sit with you until I return to take you to the hospital at one o'clock. He's in the best medical hands possible. I'm sure that he'll survive the operation. The company will do all it can to help him and you and Alison."

I drove to the plant, a huge complex making mobile cranes and employing over three thousand. Richard, at the age of thirty-two, was the financial director. He was efficient and much respected by everyone, especially by us at group headquarters in London. His job involved financial control of five crane factories in the United Kingdom and two overseas. At that point, I had no idea whether or not he would be able to continue to hold any position in the future.

He was still sleepy from the anaesthetic when we got to the hospital. Fiona got to see him for a few minutes but was not able to speak with him.

Because I was flying nearly every day, I got a company senior social worker to visit Fiona and organised the company car and driver to take her to the hospital

Once, I visited Richard on a bad day. "Robert," he said, "I've no bloody legs! I'm useless. I'll never be able to work again. I'll never be able to have sex again. I'm inhuman. I might as well be dead."

It was some weeks before I was able to visit Richard again. He had been given the details of his amputations and the prosthetic opportunities for the future. In about a month they would fit a false leg to his longer stump and, after about six months, another one to the short stump. Meanwhile he had learnt how to lever himself out of bed and into a wheelchair.

Despite still being in shock, he was now his usual optimistic self again, keen to get back to work, and he kept pressing me for answers about that.

More weeks passed and he was discharged from hospital. I visited him at home whenever I was in Newcastle, and noticed that he slept in a single bedroom.

"How is it between Fiona and yourself?"

"She can't bear to look at my stumps, never mind touch me," he replied bitterly. "You know, I feel so bloody normal down there. I can get an erection and everything. If she could only help me!"

"I guess she's still getting over it. I'm sure time will bring her round. Now what about those artificial limbs?"

"I've got the fitting dates and the therapy schedules."

"Good. Do you feel up to a little work?"

"I'll say. What is it?"

"We need a new business plan for the Duisburg factory. You are the best guy for the job. Can you get around in a wheel chair including flying?"

"Yes, I think so."

"Well, let's have a practice. Next week you fly to London and back. Come and see some old friends at headquarters. And visit a night club?"

"Wow, that sounds great."

My secretary made the flight arrangements, including special assistance at the airports and company cars. Richard arrived at the reception of the headquarters building, beaming broadly; the inward journey had gone well. He sat in his wheelchair looking at the stairs from the ground floor to the next.

"What do you want to do Richard? Two of us can lift you in the chair."

"I've been practising on the stairs at home. I think I can manage these on my bottom, going up backwards." The small crowd who had gathered to welcome him watched with amazement as he levered himself out of the chair and placed his bottom on the lowest step, turning to face us.

With contorted face and gritted teeth, he pushed down on the next step with both arms and lifted his body upwards until it

Tales From A Briefcase

rested on the next ledge. None of us had ever before seen determination like it.

The day passed splendidly and I could see that he had not lost his spark. We had booked into the same hotel, and this time the lift eased his way. After eating at a good restaurant in W1, I asked him if he was tired.

"No, never. You promised me a trip to a nightclub!"

So we took a cab to a nightclub with hostesses and got a table on a balcony overlooking the stage and dance floor. Trixie, a well-built German girl whom I had met before, came over and sat down.

"Good evening, Robert. Brought a friend I see?"

"Yes, this is Richard. He is a very special friend and needs some very special attention. Have you a friend who would find him attractive?"

She leaned over to stroke the side of his face. "Anyone would find him attractive," she commented. "I have a Polish friend, Petruska, dark hair, petite, very simpatico – she would like to meet Richard. I'll go and find her."

Richard's face was a picture of delight. "What will I do? Will I be able to take her home?"

"Whoa, laddie. First we buy them dinner and you get to know Petruska. If you get on well and she proposes something, well just go along and do it. OK?"

The evening passed pleasantly; the food was good but the floor show of strippers was amateur and pathetic. Richard, sitting in his wheelchair, was hampered in getting close to Petruska, unlike other customers who were snuggling up to their partners.

"Petruska says she'll take me home. Will that be alright with you?"

"Yes, of course. Petruska, would you come and have a few words in private with me?"

I met her in the club's foyer. "How do you feel about Richard? Did he tell you about his accident?"

"He is a beautiful boy. Yes, I know how it is."

"And you are still prepared to go with him? He hasn't had sex since his accident. He doesn't know if he can do it but you must do your best to help him. Where do you live?"

"I live in an apartment block in Paddington. There's a lift."

"OK, here's the 'but'. Afterwards, you must get a taxi for him back to the hotel and see him into it. Deal?"

She nodded and we returned to the table. Trixie rose and said, rather understandingly, "We girls will have a little chat outside while you make arrangements with Richard."

I explained the plan to Richard and he could hardly contain his excitement. Trixie and I waved them off in a taxi and went back to the table. She linked her arm in mine, looking closely into my face, "What about you, good friend to the needy?"

"Not tonight, Trixie. But I am very grateful for your help," I said, pressing some notes into the palm of her hand and kissing her.

I met Richard at breakfast. "I did it. Got a real hard on. She was on top and......"

"For Christ's sake, its breakfast time. Spare me the details."

Later, I took him to the airport. He started to thank me but I gently stopped him.

"It's nothing. You have to fight back now. Your job's safe as financial director. Your marriage may be shaky for a while. Fiona is a lovely girl and you now know you can do the sex bit. Work at your marriage. Let me know if there's anything I can do."

* * *

I met Richard during a trip to Newcastle a year later.

"Come out to dinner with Fiona and me. I want to show you something," he said.

"Sure thing"

They took me to a nightclub, Richard without wheelchair but using two sticks. At the end of a lovely meal, Richard put aside his sticks, stood up, and asked Fiona to dance. She looked very surprised but stood up and went into his arms. Very slowly and jerkily they danced, but close together. The bugger! He must have been down in London, practicing with Petruska!

CHAPTER 21

A NIGERIAN ADVENTURE

Lagos, Nigeria

There were eight of them, standing in a close circle around us. Their smiling faces and happy jabbering did not relieve the tension created by their pointing rifles and fingers crooked around triggers.

We had just got off the Caledonian flight from London to Lagos. The heat and humidity had hit us like a brick wall as we clambered down the aircraft steps. On entering the newly-built airport building, we had to stand in line waiting to be called forward by the customs officials. I stood before a uniformed Nigerian customs officer who was intent on conveying to me his high status and the seriousness of his questioning. Did I have books, newspapers, pornographic magazines? – their importation was forbidden. How much English and Nigerian money was I carrying? The allowable amounts were strictly limited and any excess had to be handed in.

He switched the questioning to the purpose of my visit, taking down the names of people and companies I intended to visit. He fingered my passport and asked about how I had obtained my visa. By now I was beginning to believe that he would refuse me entry. I noticed he was rubbing his forefinger and thumb together and wondered if this was a sign for me to offer money – I decided against it.

"You may go!" It was a command, not a pleasant welcome for a foreign visitor to his country. I walked to the baggage hall where an equally unpleasant interview was conducted by another official, who not only went through my suitcase and briefcase but fingered my passport and gave me the same lecture about importing prohibited goods.

Tales From A Briefcase

My release was signalled with a flapping of his hand towards the door into the arrivals hall. As I stepped though I was surrounded by a throng of men and boys offering to carry my bags and get me a taxi. One went as far as to try to snatch them from my hands and quite a physical tussle ensued. I noticed a Nigerian policemen watching the incident with an amused smile on his face and his hand on the butt of his gun.

I walked to the taxi rank where there was a line of waiting cars and there I met one of my fellow travellers from the plane. "I'm going into the Eko Hotel," he told me. "Do you want to share a cab?"

After my uncomfortable arrival, it seemed a good idea to share a taxi with someone who appeared to be a seasoned visitor to Nigeria. We bundled into the cab, but the driver insisted on haggling a price for several minutes before leaving.

The airport was about twenty miles out of the city and was reached by a rough tarmac road running through wild countryside. A few miles from the airport, the group of soldiers had straddled the road and waved the cab down.

"No protests, keep calm," warned my travelling companion.

"Passengers out," shouted the corporal in charge. "Baggage out." The driver threw our bags into the road.

The corporal opened each bag and briefcase and tipped the contents on the road, all the while watching us closely for a reaction. We stood mute. He kicked through the contents and grunted, "Fine of fifty naira."

My fellow traveller handed a fifty naira note to the driver. "Pay the fine."

The soldiers drifted away into some trees, leaving us to repack our belongings and get back in the taxi. The driver started to renegotiate the fare on the basis that he had been put out.

"He's probably got the soldiers to hold us up!" said my companion.

"Is it always like this?" I asked innocently. "Constant tension and threat, and veiled bribery?"

"Yes, bribery and corruption are endemic, a way of life. There's no way that was an official fine. The soldiers were looking for beer money. Sometimes, they are drunk or drugged and a protester can get shot, later to be explained as resisting arrest. You won't be able to do business here unless you participate in what is known as 'dash' – bribery. Don't expect British law and order. By comparison, there is none, and you are on your own without its protection."

We arrived at the hotel, a modern multi-storey white building. My companion said, "I'd better help you check in. You have a reservation?"

"Yes and my company paid in advance, so there shouldn't be a problem."

"I wouldn't count on that!"

I handed the reception clerk my passport and faxes confirming my reservation.

"Sorry, sir, we do not have a reservation for you."

My companion stepped in. "I know the chief of police and if you do not allocate him a room immediately I will call him over and you can tell him why this visitor has not got a room despite following the correct booking procedure. Get me the hotel manager."

"That will not be necessary, sir. Room 407. Here is the key. The room will be ready in half an hour. That will be fifty naira for room service."

I handed him a bank note and said to my fellow traveller, "Let me buy you a cold drink at the bar."

Over a very cold beer – the glasses had been cooled in a refrigerator – he explained that the reception clerks sold reserved rooms for cash. If the booked customer strongly protested, they would eject the current room occupant into the corridor without notice and let in the reserved customer. Many businessmen, believing that they had bought a room, returned to the hotel in the evening to find all their belongings in the corridor. Their protests were met with demands for documentary proof of payment and room allocation, of which there would be none.

The room was large and basically furnished. A noisy air conditioner struggled with both high temperature and humidity and the room still had a damply musty smell about it.

On the ground floor was a large restaurant and lounge area, leading into a garden with swimming pool. The place was full of people of all races including families with children. In that respect it felt normal, cosmopolitan and unthreatening.

The following morning, I had an appointment with a government official in the centre of Lagos. A line of taxis were queuing outside the hotel. Watching the proceedings for a minute, I realised that hotel porters had to be used as part of the taxi booking procedure and, of course, required a tip for the service. During the drive into the city, a policeman, directing traffic at a crossroads, blew his whistle furiously and waved the taxi to the curb. He walked to the rear window which was open, there being no air conditioning, and saluted.

"Sir, your cab went over the central white line. It is an offence. You must pay the fine. Fifty naira."

The driver turned round in his seat," Pay the fine mister and we can go on."

I remembered the advice from my travelling companion of yesterday: no arguing, offer less but do not hand money directly to the demander. I took a twenty naira note from my wallet and threw it into the driver's lap, "You pay it, you were driving!"

There was some discussion between policemen and driver in Nigerian dialect, and the car was waved on.

I arrived on time for my appointment at ten o'clock but was still sitting in the hot and humid corridor at noon when a clerk arrived. "Senator Abalayo sends his apologies. It is now lunch time. Please return at two o'clock."

My question, "Is there any guarantee that I will be able to meet him this afternoon?" was met with a shrug of the shoulders.

It became clear to me that appointments with officials were made for a particular day – if you were lucky, for a morning or afternoon. You waited until summoned. Perhaps these practices were started in the days of the British administration and, as in India, when the locals took power they'd continued them.

I had read that three main religious tribes controlled the country: the Hausa in the north, the Yoruba in the south and the Ibo in the east. The Hausa were essentially Moslems whilst there was a smattering of Christians elsewhere. Tribal loyalties were strong and a foreign businessman had to ensure that he was represented by all three tribes to do business across the country.

Tales From A Briefcase

Furthermore, Nigerian business law required foreign companies to take on Nigerian shareholders and directors. On the following day, an appointment had been made to visit the home of a highly placed Nigerian businessman, whom my chairman wished to appoint to the board of a joint venture company, shortly to be formed. I arrived at a house surrounded by a high wall and approached through solid metal gates.

Ringing the bell brought an armed policeman to the gate. I explained the purpose of my visit only to be told that there would be no appointments today. I was later told by a commercial attaché in the British Embassy that my contact had been arrested earlier in the week, had been tried for political insurgency and was to be shot at the execution site at the tourist beach on Sunday.

Part of the purpose of my visit was to research the main construction sites throughout Nigeria, determine who were the main contractors, and establish whose equipment they were using, particularly mobile cranes, excavators and building props.

For this, I had reserved a seat on a local airline to Kaduna, an hour's flight from Lagos. I queued at the check-in desk until just before take-off time, at which point I realised, too late, that others behind me were going through the departures gate. I then realised that a purchased ticket and a confirmed seat reservation did not entitle you to a seat on the plane. Shifty-looking individuals were walking up and down the queue offering to get passengers on the plane for a fee, obviously to be shared with the check-in clerk. I gave up and returned to Lagos to the Telecom tower to book a telephone call to my chairman in England.

The call went though and I could hear the chairman's booming voice, broken English and him puffing at his cigar.

"Chairman, have you ever been to Nigeria?" I asked

"No but I have been to other countries in West Africa," came his reply.

"This is not like Cote d'Ivoire or Liberia. This country works on bribery and corruption. Making a reservation or buying a ticket does not necessarily get you anywhere. Unless I arrange private transport, there is little point in staying here. By the way, your important Nigerian contact has been arrested and is to be shot on Sunday. Shall I search for another local contact?"

Tales From A Briefcase

"Ya. Make whatever travel arrangements you need. Find me some Nigerian partners who might survive past the next election. Nigeria will become one of our best markets for equipment sales – get me market intelligence. I look forward to your recommendations. Stay as long as you like. I'll forward more money for your trip. OK?"

The telephone clicked off and I grabbed a taxi out to the airport. There I found an air taxi service and discussed my need to cover the country, over-flying the major construction sites and landing at the major cities. I was introduced to a Dutchman who was to be my pilot and shown the six-seater twin-engined Cessna which had been allocated to me.

"Do you want to sell the spare four seats?" the Dutchman asked.

I looked at him in amazement.

"See all those chaps sitting in the hut? They're waiting for spare seats. I'll draw up flight plans for the next four days and post them on the board with seat prices. You should be able to cover eighty percent of the costs."

During the next four days I flew over Nigeria, its rain forests, rivers, oil wells and cities. I visited all the main contractors of construction sites, particularly those building the new capital at Abuja. It was clear that our German and Italian competitors were firmly established in the market and we would need some attractive commercial propositions to penetrate it.

The pilot allowed me to fly the plane on the quiet legs. For light relief he would dive on fishermen in dugout canoes on the Niger, frightening them into jumping into the river. On an evening return flight to Lagos we hit an electric storm which could not be avoided. The plane dropped through several hundred feet as the thermals changed, the lightning flashed and St Elmo's fire flicked along the wings and fuselage.

Caledonian Airways had an office at the Eko Hotel and I was able to confirm my flight from Lagos to London. It had one stop, at Kano in northern Nigeria. I would again have to run the gauntlet of the customs officials. Even so, I settled into a first class seat with a large scotch served by a pretty young lady in short kilt, blouse in airline colours and tam o'shanter. I felt safe, unthreatened for the first time for days.

Tales From A Briefcase

The chief steward came on the intercom. "Ladies and gentlemen, Kano is a military airfield with military equipment positioned around it. Nigeria is very sensitive over its military sites. Please do not photograph the airport during our short stop-over." I noticed two Americans huddled close to the plane's windows, taking photographs as we landed. We flew past long lines of Russian MiG 15s and several radar sites and anti-aircraft guns. As the plane came to a standstill and the doors were opened, two Nigerians who had been sitting at the back of first class came forward to the Americans and manhandled them off the plane. I guessed that they would not be reboarding this flight.

On takeoff, the relief of the passengers became evident as the consumption of champagne increased. From this distance, England appeared such a pleasant and lawful country.

* * *

"Ya. Ya. Good," the chairman was in a generous mood as he read my report. Nigeria was going to be an up-and-coming nation as it tapped its oil reserves and its population benefited from the increased wealth. It was already encouraging partnerships with the rest of the world, east and west alike. And like many big cities in third world nations, Lagos became a honey-pot for the poor people, trying to make a living by buying and selling on the street. The last time I was there I saw a young boy with six lavatory seats on his head in the main street. God knows who his customers would be.

"Ya, we must organise to exploit this growth, have a corporate presence there, employ Nigerian staff," continued the chairman. "You will be the first director of our Nigerian company. I want us to be strongly represented at their first international trade fair in Lagos next year. They are building a new trade centre."

I didn't enlighten him with the fact that in Nigeria even foreign-managed contracts ran at least twice as long as planned and cost at least three times as much. The trade centre would never be finished in time, and many exhibits would end up in the scrubland on the site outside Lagos. The port would become

Tales From A Briefcase

blocked under the combined effects of inefficiency and bribery bids.

"My daughter, Helen, has requested to assist with the fair arrangements. Please involve her in your planning."

"You know that it's a difficult country, far from safe, and it has diseases by the legion?"

"Ya. I will tell her about security and to behave herself," he said knowingly.

I groaned inwardly. The chairman's second daughter was unhappily married to a racing car driver and spent much of her time committing adultery with all and sundry, especially daddy's staff.

It was necessary to make an interim trip to Nigeria to put some contacts in place. This time, prepared for the worst, I passed through customs without undue problem and arrived without interference at the hotel, where, surprisingly, a room awaited me.

I made the acquaintance of several well-educated Nigerians who had worked for British companies, such as Unilever. They seemed to have learnt the British way of doing things and I signed them up as consultants to help with the fair.

We upped the bribes until we were at the front of the queue at the docks and our equipment came ashore in time. Then the chairman's daughter, Marianne, flew into Lagos and demanded a meeting with me.

"Daddy wants me to take control of our operations at the fair," she announced. "I want a meeting with everyone to brief them on what I want. You should be there."

My hackles rose immediately. "Just you hold on. I am a main board director and the chairman has given me responsibility for all Nigerian operations, including the fair. Show me a written authority supporting what you have just told me."

"Daddy just told me before I left. There's no written instruction."

"Well, you just go back to the chairman and get something in writing. Until then, I'm following the chairman's written instructions and will run our activities in Nigeria as I think fit. I'll accept you as assistant fair manager, reporting directly to me and only passing orders to the staff under my direction. If you cannot accept that, I'll send you back to London on the next plane. Is that clear?"

She blushed and said, "Surely we can talk about this later under less pressurised circumstances?"

I knew precisely how she would use her femininity to get her way; I would have to play a firm and absolutely straight bat. "Our relationship is one of director and employee. I have given you my orders and you'll obey them. The chairman has said that he has told you to behave yourself and, in my book, that means no fraternising with the exhibition staff."

This hit her hard. She responded, "I've never been so insulted in all my life. I will tell daddy what you said," and flounced away.

The fair opened on time but the site was in an incomplete state. Our most popular exhibit was a water-purifying bowser; we took dirty water in, via a hose, from a hole at the site and cold, pure water came out of the back. Many visitors slaked their thirsts and it was great publicity. As a selling exercise, though, the fair was disappointing; many of the visitors came from African territories where capital was made available through aid schemes and orders would take time to be confirmed.

The Chairman's daughter stayed out of my way but did nothing to restrain herself from seducing several of our junior staff.

I reported to the chairman on my return to London and explained the low sales.

"Ya, it's all we could expect from a developing nation. But we had to be there; it will come good in the end. I see that you kept my daughter under control."

"Yes, chairman, no problem if you understand women."

He laughed and lit another cigar.

CHAPTER 22

A SWIM IN THE CARIBBEAN

Venezuela

It was a Monday morning. I had left my home in the Thames Valley prepared for a journey – to where I did not know but I would soon find out from the chairman. I sat in my car in the morning rush-hour queue on the M4 into central London, mentally checking the home situation which I was leaving behind. Mary, my middle-aged, live-in, Irish housekeeper-nanny had been briefed on the children's programme: school, outings, friend's parties, menus. She had been given cash for shopping and petrol for her little car. Later, by telephone, I would give her my contact numbers. Anyway, she had met my secretary, Julie, and would contact her if all else failed.

More than an hour later, I turned the car into the offices in Paddington and made my way to my room on the third floor executive level, where Julie was waiting for me.

"Good morning, Robert. The chairman's secretary has already been enquiring as to your whereabouts. He wants to see you at ten o'clock. It sounds like a long-haul trip somewhere. Have you got your passports and your flexible wardrobe with you?"

I carried two passports because of international political stances; you couldn't get into Nigeria with South African immigration stamps in your passport, likewise into Arabic countries with Israeli stamps.

The flexible wardrobe, carried in the boot of my car, offered me selections of clothing for whatever hot or cold climates I might find on my travels.

"Yes, thank you, Julie. All organised and ready. By the way, I want you to nip over to my home sometime and go over the worst case scenario again with Mary, my housekeeper."

Tales From A Briefcase

She nodded. She understood that there was some risk associated with my business lifestyle: delayed returns, travel accidents, kidnapping and killing, in countries far less stable than those of Europe. I could rely on Julie and Mary to keep my family and personal affairs on track as I travelled the world, and we had worked out what should be done immediately for the children, and for their mother in the Surrey mental clinic, if something should happen to me. My solicitor and the company secretary would deal with it thereafter.

The chairman was seated behind his large desk, its top clear of everything but a telephone and a single sheet of paper. "Come in, Mr James, sit down," he boomed, formal as usual, in accented, broken English. With Henri Cartier, Christian names were not used in his discussions with employees whatever their status. "I have a little job for you – in Venezuela, here."

He had swivelled his executive chair and his gargantuan cigar, after describing several circles in the air creating a spiralling smoke trail, jabbed at a large map of the world on the wall behind.

He continued, "Venezuela is a member of LAFTA, the Latin American Free Trade Association. To capture the South American market, we need to be manufacturing there. Venezuela is the most stable of the countries in that continent. Our managing director has just returned from a trip to Venezuela to acquire from a Senior Cabello, owner of a large Venezuelan enterprise, a large factory which used to make Volkswagens. The MD has returned, not only having failed to complete the deal which I had initiated but having also broken down the good relationship that I had previously built up with Señor Cabello. Your job is to go and smooth things over and conclude the deal.

"While you are there, seek out opportunities for us to sell more of our products. My secretary has got you a ticket for tonight on a Venezuela Airlines flight to Caracas and a reservation in a decent hotel. Stay there until the deal is concluded. Talk to me on the telephone if there are problems. All the details are in the file. Any questions? No? Good Luck."

I returned to my office with the file and collected a world atlas from the company library to find a few facts on Venezuela.

Tales From A Briefcase

Venezuela

Democracy with elected president

Official language – Spanish

Discovered by Columbus, 1498

Population 23.4 million

– 85% urban 65% less than 30 years of age
– birth and mortality rates equal about 25 in 1000
– 69% European, African, Indian mix, migrants from Italy, Spain, Portugal and Colombia

Natural resource – Oil, world exporter

Main cities – Caracas, Maracaibo, Valencia, Barquisimeto, Cuidad Guayana.

Enclosed newspaper cuttings indicated that relationships between Venezuela and the USA were improving and that it would not be long before United States products would be flooding into South America. The file told me that Señor Cabello was thirty-five, had attended Harvard to gain an MBA, and was owner of an extensive, family business spread throughout Venezuela, particularly strong in oil extraction and refining, and in construction of dams and power stations.

I made one last quick check with Mary before jumping into the company's chauffeur-driven car to Heathrow. With a first class ticket for the ten-hour non-stop overnight flight in a Boeing 747, I was looking forward to a sumptuous dinner with good wine, the latest released film and some sleep. My hopes were soon dashed – across the aisle from me was a young woman with two screaming young children of about two or three.

I settled in my seat, ordered a large scotch with ice, and discussed my options with the air hostess.

"She is a nanny taking Venezuelan children from their home in London to their family in Caracas. They should calm down and get sleepy after they're fed. I could put you further back in

Tales From A Briefcase

this cabin or seat you in coach class, although I doubt if you would find that more restful."

"OK, I'll accept your offer of a seat further back in first class." The flight was long, noisy and sleepless, the young children squalling all across the Atlantic and the Caribbean.

The air hostess, whose name was Juanita, came to check my comfort through the night. Her English was good.

"Is this your first time in Caracas? Do you know your way around? How long are you here for?" I gave her the name of my hotel and she gave me her telephone number, mentioning that she wasn't flying for a few days.

Landing was a relief and I settled into the back of a taxi from the airport to the city, attempting to avoid conversation with the driver who was keen to discuss the merits of Liverpool Football Club.

Checking into the hotel, I went to my room, pulled the curtains closed and got into bed. The loud voices of the gardeners and the frequent knocking of the housemaid on my door ensured that any sleep was short-lived and light. I got up and bathed before entering the dining room and gaining a window seat. Bright sunlight flooded through the windows and outside I could see large rolling lawns, immaculately manicured, and flower beds planted with exotic flowers.

After lunch I telephoned Mr Cabello's office and spoke to his secretary.

"Hola, buenos dias. Señor Cabello, por favor. Hablo muy poco Español. Do you speak English?"

"Señor Cabello no esta aqui, not here. Que hablar?"

"Robert James de la compañia Inglesa, Construction Equipment International de Londres."

"Uno momento, por favor. Habitación nombre y el numero?"

I had exhausted my Spanish, "One, zero, eight."

"Bueno. Señor Cabello telefoneara mañana. Si?"

"Si."

I spent some of the afternoon looking over maps and exploring telephone directories, but first I telephoned the commercial attaché's office at the British Embassy and made an appointment for later that day. A man of my own age with an

Tales From A Briefcase

Old Etonian tie received me. I explained the background and purpose of my trip.

"Oh, yes. I know of Señor Cabello. One of this country's movers and shakers. He's very American in his outlook. In fact I would go so far as to say he is closer to the United States than he is to the UK. I think he would prefer to dispose of his factory to an American buyer."

"Have you got our company on your files?"

He turned to his computer. "Ah yes. English, owned by Henri Cartier, Swiss. Manufacturer of construction equipment: cranes, excavators, scaffolding, pipeline valves, pressure vessels. Subsidiaries all over the world. You work for a big organisation, Mr James."

"We want to use Venezuela as our LAFTA manufacturing base. We think there may be advantages if we can establish our manufacturing facilities here, to supply South America and get preferential treatment over American sourcing. What do you think?"

"It's a good strategy. LAFTA was set up to screw the best supply conditions out of the USA, Japan and Europe. Foreign manufacturers who set up here in the LAFTA economy have, and will continue to get, preferred supplier status."

"If I wanted to assess the potential for our products in Venezuela, where would I start?"

"In the oil and construction industries, where the refineries and dams and communication links are being built. See it for yourself from the air along the frontiers with Colombia and Brazil. I'll give you lists of local companies who could become partners and customers. Come back in two days and we can talk again."

I left, thanking my lucky stars that I was British and that the UK had excellent overseas embassies to assist the British businessman.

All the next morning I waited for Señor Cabello's call, but in vain. I telephoned his secretary but got the message that he was not in. It seemed a good day for flying so I headed out to the airport. After I had explained my mission, a private charter company offered me a twin-engined Aztec with pilot. We settled

Tales From A Briefcase

on a flight plan allowing for landing at the five major cities with one-hour stops and over-flying the major construction projects. With me I had my cine and still cameras to assist me in the presentation when I got back to England. We ran into a thunderstorm in the evening on the way back to Caracas.

"Do you have many days like this? I asked the pilot, who was an American.

"The Caribbean weather can get nasty with cyclones and hurricanes in the summer and the plane can bounce around a bit. Just like that!" he remarked as we fell vertically through sixty feet.

I was silent for the rest of the trip, jaw clamped, knuckles white ... and praying.

Back at the hotel there was a single message from Juanita asking me to phone her. It was too late to make a date for that evening but I rang her anyway.

"Si."

"Hi, it's Robert James calling you back. How are you?"

"Oh I'm just fine. And you?"

"I've just flown Venezuela with a charter plane. What a beautiful country you have."

"Tell me about it when we meet. What about tomorrow? I'm off all day and the weather will be good for the beach."

"Could we meet at eleven o'clock? I have an appointment at the embassy before that."

"Sure. I'll call for you at the hotel in my car tomorrow at eleven. Adios!"

I spent the rest of the evening writing up my visit notes and having dinner. Next morning I was woken by the housemaid with my breakfast. A short taxi ride took me to the embassy where my contact had arranged a meeting that included two of his colleagues.

They presented statistics on the Venezuelan economy, details of the government contracts being placed and which companies were bidding for them, contact information with possible partners for my company, company intelligence on Señor Cabello's company, and some facts about the man himself.

Returning to the hotel on the stroke of eleven, I found Juanita just emerging from her BMW sports coupé.

Tales From A Briefcase

She came over to me. "Robert, how lovely to meet you again!" her hand brushing my cheek.

I responded by kissing both of her cheeks, trying to keep my eyes from the plunging neckline of her off-the-shoulder mini-dress.

"Would you like to come in and have a cool drink while I change and get my beach things together?" I asked.

"No, thank you. I'll wait, and you be quick. I want to make the most of every minute with you."

My God, I thought, she's coming on a bit strong for a chance acquaintance!

She drove very competently north over the mountains. Eventually, we arrived at a secluded bay with a few houses and a long curved sweep of sand being lapped by a gentle sea. Along the beach from the car park was a café where they also hired out sun-beds and sailing boats. We took a beach umbrella providing shade for two sun beds.

"I'll just put on my bikini and you put on your swimming trunks. No peeking," she ordered coyly.

I stole a look at she fumbled with a towel. She was slim with small pert breasts and her skin was a beautiful light coffee colour.

"How about a snack at the café?" I asked.

"The seafood here is wonderful and I'm starving," she replied with enthusiasm.

We had lunch and snoozed on our beach beds. At one point she crossed over to me and planted a light kiss on my lips before returning to her sun bed.

"What's that for?" I asked.

"Because I think you're a nice guy. Do you like me?"

"I think you are beautiful and sexy and I daren't tell you the thoughts going on in my mind."

"Maybe later," she said.

"Would you like to sail? I'd rather like to have a go at that catamaran over there – a Hobicat. It has a canvas platform stretched between the hulls for beautiful maidens to lie out and do nothing while we skim across the waves."

"Let's do it," she said, leaping to her feet.

The westerly wind blowing lightly across the bay took us gull winging along at about ten knots but I kept both hulls planted in

Tales From A Briefcase

the sea. We tacked back across the bay and turned on to our original course.

"These are built for speed but we need to get one hull out of the water and get our weight over the lifted hull. Are you game?"

"I've never sailed on a small boat before but I'm willing to have a go."

"Come and sit by me on this hull and push you toes under that rope."

I turned the Hobicat stern-on to the wind, let out foresail and mainsail and steered so that they filled with a snap. The hull came up and we were soon roaring along on one hull at about fifteen knots. Juanita's long black hair was streaming out in the wind and her mouth opened as she sucked in great gulps of air, unable to shout or scream. She had her arms tight around my neck, hanging on for dear life.

We reached the other side of the bay and I called out, "Watch your head on the boom," as we gibed about.

Sailing calmly on two hulls at a sedate pace we picked up a seaward tack. "You can go and lie on the canvas now and get your breath back. We'll just poodle along for a bit."

She lay out facing me, one leg stretched and one bent. I moved towards her taking the tiller extension with me and lay down facing her. The rippling of the waves against the hulls and the cool breeze provided a perfect background to a long breathless kiss as we clung to each other. She slipped off her bikini top to reveal very dark and flat-topped nipples. I lowered my head to kiss them and she moaned, pulling my head harder into her breasts.

I felt my erection stiffening and started to move my hand to her bikini bottom.

"Hey, we're still in sight of land and the people on the beach. There's nowhere to park this thing out of sight. As much as I hate having to say it, maybe we should reserve this for the hotel."

"I guess you're right. Let's make tracks!"

There was a sexual tension all the way back to the hotel. Her driving became more erratic and impatient. Forsaking an absent lift, we ran up the stairs, crashed through the door of my room and started throwing off our clothes.

"Shower," she commanded, and we pressed ourselves into the cubicle facing each other. I turned the water on and we pressed our bodies together, rivulets of cool water cascading over our skins. Open-mouthed we entwined our tongues like wrestlers trying to get the better of the other. She dropped her hand to grasp my penis, already fully erect. Turning her back to me she thrust my member into herself from behind and stated to rotate her backside, pulling my hands round to grasp her breasts. The high excitement brought us quickly to our climaxes. We dried each other off and flopped on to the bed where we slept.

I awoke with a hand moving down my body. Without any preliminaries she straddled me, thrusting my now erect phallus into her body. Her incredible movements accelerated and brought her to another climax. Flopping down beside me she pulled me on top of her and said, "OK. Your turn now!" Her hands grasped the cheeks of my bottom, pulling me deeper into her, and her legs arched over my body.

Another climax and I was ready for some dinner. Juanita left at about ten o'clock because she was on an early morning flight to Europe. I visited Venezuela several times after that trip but was unable to contact her and never saw her again. To some it might appear a promiscuous dalliance but I liked to think of it as 'passing ships'.

* * *

It was on Thursday that the telephone call came from Señor Cabello's secretary.

"Good morning, Señor James, how are you today?" Her sudden command of English rather set me back.

"I'm OK," I managed.

She confirmed briskly, "Señor Cabello invites you to meet him at the marina at the port on Sunday at mid-day. He has his yacht there and proposes to take you out for a sail. You are to bring a swimming costume and a towel. His boat is called 'Ferdinand'. Can you make it?"

Again, I was taken aback with the friendliness of the invitation and the preciseness of the instructions. "Of course, I'll be there. Thank Señor Cabello for me."

Tales From A Briefcase

With days to spare and nothing planned, I decided to fly to Cuidad Guyana and take a boat trip down the Orinoco. I would go to the coast on Sunday, of course, but what was Señor Cabello's game?

Sunday arrived and I took a taxi from the hotel to the marina, about half an hour's ride away. I asked the whereabouts of the 'Ferdinand' at the marina office and was directed along one of the wooden quays to a blue-hulled boat about fifteen metres long and with an even taller mast. A man dressed in sailor's uniform, standing by a short gangplank to the deck, saluted me and said in perfect English, "Señor Cabello is waiting for you down there in the cabin."

I stepped down into a spacious day cabin which had doors leading off it, presumably to other cabins with berths. A young, swarthy man of about thirty-five rose from a chair to greet me with outstretched hand. "Welcome aboard, Mr James, and welcome to Venezuela. Is this your first time here?"

I looked him over before answering: medium height, thick black hair, brown eyes, clean-shaven. A strong handshake and immediate eye contact confirmed his American training. No apologies were forthcoming for keeping me waiting for days, but I was not going to allow him to think that I was any old hick out of England.

"Yes, this is my first time in Venezuela. As a director of our large international group with worldwide interests, I've visited South America on several occasions before this: Chile, Argentina, Uruguay, Paraguay, Bolivia, Peru and Colombia. This week, I've been flying around your country; it is both beautiful and resourceful, Señor Cabello."

"Call me, Ferdi," he invited, a broad smile revealing immaculate dentistry, "I was named after my father Ferdinand, and hence the name of my boat."

I looked at him closely to see if his face gave away his hidden agenda, but the big smile and bright eyes masked his inner thoughts. "Vamos," he said to the sailor and the boat was let slip and pulled away from the quay under power.

"Do you have time to sail much?" I asked.

Tales From A Briefcase

"I try to get in a short sail and swim every day. Otherwise I take my family up to the islands for a week or two at a time – Barbados, Antigua, St Lucia."

The sailor set the sails and the boat leapt forward under the power of the wind, leaving the shoreline behind very rapidly.

I faced Señor Cabello across the cockpit. "I would like to get down to business. I'm returning to the UK tomorrow evening and I must have an answer for Henri Cartier by then."

He responded "I think I'll go for a swim. Are you coming?"

"I'm not a good swimmer and I'd rather talk business."

Ignoring my comments, he leapt over the side of the boat and swam with a strong crawl to keep up with the it.

He shouted over the wind, "I don't believe you can't swim. I believe you're scared – a scared, liver bellied, cock-sucking limey!"

I looked at him, rather taken aback by his change of mood, but I only shrugged my shoulders.

"A mother-fucking scared limey," he threw back at me across the waves.

I judged the distance to his back, decided I could leap on to it and sink him... and then jumped, landing on the small of his back with both of my feet. He went under whilst I floundered on the surface.

He surfaced blowing water, waved the boat away and came for me, catching me in a stranglehold and forcing my head under water until I had exhausted the air in my lungs and could struggle no longer. I lay still in the water, face down, turning my head to gasp in air.

He swam lazily towards me. "Are you alright?"

"You bastard! You set me up for this. You knew you could beat me at this game. I thought Harvard provided the world with civilised citizens but you're just a fucking killer. If we were ashore I'd bloody kill you. In the circumstances, just fuck off. I'm going to see if I can reach the shore," and I struck out in a breaststroke which kept me afloat but gave me hardly any forward motion.

He waved the yacht back. "Get into the boat. It's obvious you can't swim."

Tales From A Briefcase

"Not bloody likely," I bellowed in anger, "I'll contact the police if and when I get ashore. Attempted murder." And then, as an after-thought, "However, we could discuss conditions."

"What conditions?"

"No police and the contract signed on board the boat before we reach the shore. I have a copy in my brief case."

He nodded and the sailor brought the boat alongside and hauled me aboard. I went to my briefcase, pulled out the draft contract to acquire the factory, and found a pen.

Señor Cabello sat sullenly in the cockpit with a towel around him as I spluttered through the contract clause by clause, requiring him to say 'yes' at the more contentious points. As we arrived at the quay I thrust the contact at him. "Sign and date it. What has happened today is just between you and me. If you cross me again, I'll bloody kill you."

He returned the signed papers to me; I collected my things, got off the boat and caught a taxi to Caracas. The next day I returned to London.

* * *

"Come in," came the chairman's voice through the door. I entered to find him, as expected, seated at his desk reading documents and puffing his cigar.

I threw the contract in front of him on the desk. He picked the papers up, read them slowly, took a long draw at his cigar and looked up. "Good trip?"

"Not too bad. Nice swim in the Caribbean, though."

Tales From A Briefcase

CHAPTER 23

SHUT DOWN OUR JAPANESE OPERATION

Tokyo

My secretary was going through my appointments diary. "The chairman wishes to talk to you about the Japanese company. The meeting is fixed for three o'clock this afternoon."

"OK. I'll be there," I said.

The group had acquired a Sunderland company specialising in manufacturing stainless steel products, amongst which were pipes installed in sea tankers through which steam was pumped to heat liquid cargoes. Viscous liquids, such as molasses, were heated as the tanker approached the port to allow fast evacuation of the cargo once the port was reached and a faster turn-around in the acceptance of another cargo.

Japan was the largest producer of tankers of all sizes, including the super-tankers which were making smaller tankers uneconomical. The redundant smaller tankers were being anchored in creeks all over the world, some left to rust and sink and others to be scrapped and recycled.

Four years previously, the Sunderland company had set up a factory in southern Japan to feed the demand for stainless steel pipes, but with fewer tankers being built the orders had now dried up and the Japanese subsidiary was making heavy losses.

I knocked on the chairman's office door. A sonorous voice bid me enter. "Ah, Mr James. We must speak about Japan. You are responsible for Japan, aren't you?"

"Yes, sir, I am. In fact I am still trying to find a part of the world for which I'm *not* responsible."

"Ha, ha, very good Mr James. That's a good joke! It means that you are doing my job and I get the salary."

Tales From A Briefcase

He was indeed the major shareholder and a multi-millionaire, and I was one of three lesser mortals who did his fetching and carrying around the world. For this we were very well paid, took high personal risks, rarely saw our families and took the blame for the group's failures. The chairman took the bouquets and was rarely out of the international press.

"I've just read the report of the managing director in Japan. Super-tankers have wiped out the demand for their smaller brethren and the demand for stainless steel piping had been decimated. The factory will run out of orders within three months. Our Sunderland factory has already moved into food processing and refrigeration equipment and is not so affected, but I don't want to spend money in Japan on diversifying. I want to close the company."

I thought about the Japanese 'cradle to the grave' ethic. Britain's employers had long lost their sense of responsibility to employees and the employees had turned to their unions for protection. Loyalty in either direction had ceased to have any meaning. But Japan had a different industrial culture. Maybe we should try to work within its norms.

I suggested, "Perhaps we could get the Japanese banks to fund the diversification or sell the facility to someone else. After all, stainless steel welders and fitters are always in demand."

"Nein," he said, impatiently, reverting to his mother tongue, "Go to Japan and close it down!"

I knew better than to argue further.

"If you can sell the Japanese company, good. If not, give it to the workers. Try to avoid closure costs. Hein?"

"Yes, sir." I left knowing what was to be done.

Faxes were sent to Mr Nagumo, the managing director, to advise him of my week-long visit. The long British Airways flight across Siberia made one stop in Moscow before landing at Narita Airport just outside Tokyo. There in the arrivals hall stood Mr Nagumo bearing a card with my name it.

I signalled to him and he came over, coming to a stop a few feet away and bowing low from the waist to acknowledge my senior status. He still clung on to his Japanese customs although he had studied for his MBA at Harvard and must have become partly westernised.

I put out my hand. "Robert James, Group Deputy Managing Director. I'm pleased to meet you."

He extended his hand. "I'm very pleased to meet you. I have a difficult first name. Would you call me Mike and I'll call you Robert-san."

"I would be very pleased with that."

His face took on a serious look. "I know why you have come, Robert-san. Our English mother wishes to kill its ailing infant!"

I was taken aback by his blunt and simple understanding of my hitherto unstated mission, and didn't reply immediately, but we picked up on this conversation in the bar of my Tokyo hotel.

"It's not quite as black and white as that, Mike. We may have options."

"Robert-san, you must learn to understand the oriental mind. We think deeply about possibilities, weigh up chances, sometimes gamble but are rarely optimistic. Decisions are made after debate and consensus amongst equals. The consensus decisions are wholly supported by the group; they jointly own the selected decision; there are no dissenters. In your country you have dictator managers who decide their course of action, maybe taking into account the views of their staff - or not.

"Here, we have a code of responsibility to our staff. They give us their lives in return for us giving them a job. They are important; we care for them as part of our industrial family. We have good medical facilities, generous pensions, and retirement activities. In Britain, you have followed America in the treatment of your staff. You treat them as expendables, have no loyalty to them, and give little reward for service. You now have two sides in industry – the management and the unions, usually in conflict and rarely finding a common mission."

We talked through dinner and long into the night about the difference in our cultures. I got the feeling that Mike was determined that I understand the Japanese viewpoint before I delivered the message from Britain.

Early the next morning, after a restless night due to both jetlag and my chat with Mike, we went to Dai Ichi Bank to a meeting that Mike had pre-arranged. Four bankers were present who spoke passable English when talking to me, and Japanese amongst themselves.

Tales From A Briefcase

One of the bankers stood to make a slide presentation which he said was a summary of a business plan which would be given to me later. He went on to review the performance of our Japanese company, its strengths and opportunities. Clearly the bank had done its research in depth. He proposed a diversification programme into the food processing and refrigeration industries. Costs and timescales had been carefully assessed. Details of staff retention, marketing and promotion had been developed and even some of the bank's clients nominated as potential customers. It was a masterpiece of planning. It was as though the bank had become part of the management team. It ended with a detailed funding plan showing sources of investment from bank and government regional development funders, who had already committed to the plan. I was being brainwashed.

"Robert James-san, this afternoon, we will travel by bullet train to...... near Hiroshima. There we will meet worker representatives and present the plan in even more detail. If the workers accept the plan, we will have proposals for you to take back to your chairman in England."

I stood, bowing my head slightly. "Gentleman, I thank you for your presentation. It was first class. I have to say that I have never seen a national bank in America or Britain come to the aid of an ailing client as you have done this morning. I am most impressed. I believe that, with the proposed funding, the plan will work, jobs will be saved and the newly positioned company will prosper. However, my mission today is to convey that the British group no longer wishes to support a Japanese subsidiary. If we cannot find local support to take it on, it is to be closed. I can see that adequate local support is available. My chairman wishes me to tell you that our group will transfer our shareholding to local acquirers at no cost, providing that our costs of disposal are met by Japanese sources. What is left for me to do is to assess the costs of disposal and agree their payment by an acquirer.

"Clearly, I would like to visit the factory, meet the workers and convey to them our satisfaction at the outcome. On a personal note, I would like to thank all of you for making my

Tales From A Briefcase

task such a pleasant one and offer my best wishes for the project's success. On even more of a personal note, I would like to visit Hiroshima and Kyoto to aid my understanding of your culture before I return to England." I bowed and sat down.

Over the next three days I visited the factory and met our workers for the first and last time. I was feted and cheered and felt embarrassed by the warmth offered to me as my group's representative. I took the bullet train on to Hiroshima where I was assigned a lady guide, who spoke good English. She recounted the history of the day that the bomb dropped and the years of suffering that followed. She told me of the feelings of the survivors towards the bombing crews and the attitude of the population towards the occupying forces at the end of the war. Hate and a desire revenge, if it was ever there, had now been replaced by a quest for peace, for finding a meaning to justify the slaughter and to earning a place for Japan in the world community. Pride in their nation was returning as it conquered world markets with its quality products.

Thoughtful and humbled, I took the short journey back to Kyoto. There, I was accommodated in a guest house set in a large garden not far from the main temple area. Shortly after arriving, I was visited by a priest from the temple, dressed simply in his orange robes and plain sandals and speaking with an American accent. There was no suggestion of his wanting to convert me to Buddhism although I felt myself being progressively drawn to another world by what I had seen and learned in the last few days. We talked mostly of peoples and what made them behave as they did: amongst other things, we compared eastern and western behaviour.

I felt as though I had been spring-cleaning my soul. The priest departed without any great show of emotion and left me wondering what his motive was. I boarded the bullet train for Tokyo and marvelled at my second view of the snow-capped Mount Fuji; it was twenty years since I had last seen it, from an American cargo plane flying in from Korea.

My plane was to leave from Narita airport early on the following morning. At the airport, I was unexpectedly seen off by Mike who was elated by the decisions on the company. We

Tales From A Briefcase

shook hands and promised to meet up if we visited each other's country again; it so happened that we met several times in the following years.

Reflecting during the long flight home, I began to realise that I had just passed through an emotional or spiritual door; my view on life had changed during my trip. I could predict the chairman's satisfaction with the low-cost disposal of his Japanese problem. It was a natural reaction. As for myself, maybe I should try to lessen the gap between my business life and my own changing human standards.

CHAPTER 24

A DAY AT THE RACES

Ascot and London

"You won't forget about next Thursday – Ladies Day at Ascot. You're on parade with the chairman's old wrinklies! You'll have to sacrifice your body for the company!"

Each year, the chairman, himself now sixty-five, invited several of his girl friends to Ascot, to be entertained by the younger directors, be they married or not. Apparently the wrinklies all had flats in London and he circulated among them at frequent intervals.

I looked at Julie and groaned, "That's not bloody funny, you know!"

She giggled and went on, "There's a briefing at the chairman's office next Monday at 3 pm. Put it in your diary."

I reported for the meeting, at which Charles, the company secretary, who handled all the chairman's personal and delicate matters, gave the younger of the group's directors their instructions. My charge was to be Lady Alicia Forsythe-Smith, a widow.

Charles started the briefing. "Lady Alicia has been a close friend of the chairman, particularly since her husband died four years ago. She lives in an apartment at Hyde Park Mansions and for her age she is a very lively lady. Horse racing is her passion so she will not be hard to entertain at Ascot. A car will be sent to her home at 10.30 on Thursday the 22nd of June and bring her to Ascot at about 11.30. The driver will escort her to box A4 where you will take over. You will need to hire morning dress. OK so far?"

"Yes."

Tales From A Briefcase

"Drinks will be served in the box from 11.30 and lunch at 12.30. You will sit with her at lunch. The chairman will turn up between one and two, chat all round and make a speech. He then pushes off to the Royal Enclosure for the rest of the afternoon. Racing starts at two o'clock and finishes around 5.30. The chairman wishes to pay for Lady Alicia's betting and allow her to keep the winnings. So have a couple of hundred pounds cash on you to cover that and drinks away from the box. She'll also want to wander about, see the Queen and view the horses in the saddling enclosure; you'll just have to tag along.

"When she's ready to leave for home, drive her home in your car. If she invites you out for the evening, put on your 'best bib and tucker' and take her where she wants to go. The evening will be paid for by the chairman but you will need to clear it at the time with your credit card and claim it back later. You must avoid talking to her about the chairman's personal matters, politics and religion. She is a shareholder and you must give her the best picture possible of company matters. After Ascot Day, you must not reveal to anyone, I mean anyone, not even to the chairman himself, what went on between Lady Alicia and yourself. Is all that clear?"

"Yes, Charles – completely!"

"Understand that the chairman requires you to give Lady Alicia the best time possible. Off you go."

I returned to my office to consider the sensitivities of the assignment. I would certainly not tell my secretary about it; she was the biggest chatterbox in London.

* * *

Gold Cup Day arrived; it was warm and sunny. I sat in box A4 of the main stand nervously awaiting Lady Alicia. The door of the box was flung open and a riot of noise and colour entered, later to resolve into three aging ladies, beautifully dressed in floral flouncy outfits and large cartwheel hats.

One stepped forward. "I'm looking for Robert, who is to be my escort for the day," she announced. I put her at about sixty-five but her make-up was cleverly applied to conceal wrinkles. Blond dyed hair, expensively coiffured, topped an intelligent, rather round face wearing a broad smile. Of medium height, she was well corseted to have a waist, and a fair expanse of bosom was on view.

I advanced towards her. "Lady Alicia, it is my pleasure to be your escort," I said, holding out my hand to catch hers and kiss it like a courtier, a move that I had planned in advance.

"Oh my," she said with feigned surprise turning back to her friends, "I didn't know that British industry employed directors with manners any more, and handsome at that."

"It's my Greek ancestry," I quipped, beginning to enjoy the game.

"Oh my God, I've struck lucky this year. I'll congratulate the chairman on his choice of directors."

With that the champagne arrived and the party started. What surprised me was how well the ladies knew each other, as I gathered from their excited conversation. We sat for lunch, which waiters started to serve. Shortly afterwards, there was a huge knocking at the door of the box and Charles stepped in, resplendent in expensive-looking morning dress.

"Ladies and gentlemen," he shouted, "please be upstanding for the chairman," and in the chairman came, top hat at a jaunty angle and with an enormous grin on his face. Then, like a ringmaster at a circus, he doffed his hat with an enormous flourish and started circulating amongst the guests. The women fawned over him and there was little doubt that there was something more than casual friendship fuelling the occasion. To me it seemed all over the top, even more so when Charles stood up, banged the table and said, "Honoured guests, your chairman wishes to say a few words."

The chairman stood, and the power of his personality pervaded the room.

"Dear friends, as usual we meet on a social occasion, our most eagerly awaited event on the company's calendar. Or is that the shareholders' meeting when we announce the dividends?" Cheers from all at this point. "Thank you for coming in such splendid finery bringing with you your delightful personalities and smiling faces. The company....." At this point we had a résumé of the company's sparkling progress, spoken with passion in English tinged with his native German.

Tales From A Briefcase

At the end, after the enthusiastic applause had died down, he solemnly raised his glass and said, "Ladies and gentlemen, I give you the Queen." All in the box rose and toasted the monarch with equal solemnity. I resumed my seat, thinking that this was all a charade and did nothing for the business. It could be classified as 'chairman's amusements'.

The chairman made his apologies and left to rub shoulder's with more important or influential people in the Royal Enclosure. The box had a balcony from where we had a wonderful view of the racecourse and the finishing line.

"Lady Alicia, we need to place bets soon if we are to get on the first race," I reminded her.

"Robert, while we are on our own, just call me Alicia. I would like to go down to the bookies down there on the grass. I think I've made my selection for the first race."

She paraded up and down the bookies' stands before choosing one. "I would like to put a tenner on number six, Apple Green – to win." I handed over the tenner to the bookie who confirmed the odds at six to one.

With excitement in her voice she then suggested, "Let's go down to the saddling enclosure. The Queen has a horse running and she will be there."

There she met and talked to several acquaintances, introducing me as her escort. I felt as though they thought I had been hired from an agency and felt very uncomfortable with the idea. I was also embarrassed as she curtsied when the Queen walked past.

Alicia's horse did not win but she had two winners out of eight races that afternoon and took great delight in re-visiting the bookies to collect her winnings. In the box, the guests were either toasting their wins in champagne or drowning their sorrows in spirits. By the end of the racing, everyone was happy and slightly tipsy. The Guards band played on the bandstand at the rear of the main stand and joyful punters crowded on to the rear balconies of the boxes and sang the old songs and some from recent musicals.

"Robert, I believe you are taking me home now and out to dinner this evening." It sounded more of a command than a request.

Tales From A Briefcase

We made our goodbyes and walked to the car park. I settled her into my Jaguar and set off for Hyde Park. By the time we were on the Windsor by-pass, Alicia was fast asleep, head back and snoring. Arriving at Hyde Park Mansions, I woke her gently and we discussed the plan for the evening. Dinner at the Connaught, she thought, and on to the cabaret at the Embassy Club in Dover Street. Hell, I thought this was going to be a long session.

I changed into my dinner suit in my room at the Royal Lancaster Hotel and set of back to Hyde Park Mansions, just a short distance away. They were entered via a reception hall where a concierge checked in all visitors. He telephoned Alicia who invited me up to her apartment.

"Ah Robert, welcome to my humble abode. What would you like to drink? I am drinking bubbles."

"That will do fine for me, thank you."

"Come and sit next to me on the settee," she said, patting a place beside her. "I know nothing about you. Tell me of your adventures."

I gave her a potted version of my life including my complicated domestic circumstances.

"Does Willie treat you nicely?" she enquired.

Careful, I thought. Dangerous ground. "Willie? Oh, the chairman," pretending I didn't know his pet name. "Yes, he's a good boss, much loved by all his employees."

"Oh good. We all think he's a nice man." I conjectured on that 'we'.

"And you Alicia, do you have a happy life?" I asked.

"Oh yes! I never thought I would have a life after the death of my husband, Justin, but friends, including Willie, rallied round and I am never lonely. I don't have many young friends of your age, though. Are you about forty?" she said, rather suggestively.

"Yes I am, but I'm overseas on business for much of the year and don't have much time for socialising," I said, heading off a possible invitation.

"Oh what a pity. Then we must make the most of this evening."

The taxi dropped us at the entrance steps of the Connaught, where a uniformed doorman touched his hat and said, "Good evening, Lady Alicia. Pierre informed me that you were coming. He is awaiting you in the Restaurant Bar."

"Thank you so much. How nice to see you again, Carlos. Family well?"

"Very well, Lady Alicia, thank you. I'll take your cloaks."

We walked up a grand stairway to the next floor where we had a further sycophantic episode with Pierre, who made a big fuss showing us to Alicia's favourite table and explaining the special items on the menu. During the meal, Alicia gossiped about London social life and socialites. I was left in no doubt that she was well-connected and not short of a bob or two.

Having eaten magnificent food and drunk some memorable wines, I paid the bill and we took a cab the short distance to the Embassy Club. Doffed hats and bowing waiters ushered us to a table near the dance floor where champagne appeared as soon as we had sat down.

"Oh look, there's Richard, and Lisa, and Rod." She was waving at a famous film star, an international cabaret singer and an actor. She went on, "Richard bathes his balls in cold water just before sex; he says it sustains his erection! Lisa's a cow, pinching everybody's boy friends; you just watch out, she'll be over in a minute snooping around you. Rod is as gay as they come; he won't come over but he will soon be dancing with another fellow." She went on with her commentary until a roll of drums and flashing lights announced the start of the cabaret.

"Aren't they beautiful, Robert," she exclaimed pointing at the quartet of tall, scantily-dressed dancers who now occupied the floor.

"A bit skinny for my liking!" I commented ungraciously.

"Do you like my body then?" she asked rather earnestly.

"Oh yes," I enthused rather unconvincingly, and she settled back to watch the cabaret.

Next on was a belly dancer and snake handler, followed by a comedian, whose jokes were pathetic. The band, a small quintet, played romantic tunes to which dancers could be close and smooch.

"Shall we dance," suggested Alicia.

"Yes, let's."

She held me close, her face inches from mine, her perfume overpowering. Every now and then she would sigh and push her body even closer to mine. She was becoming aroused and I would need to be careful not to get aroused myself. However, all this time I sensed that the other dancers were comparing our ages and that I was obviously a full generation younger than Alicia.

When we had returned to our table, she looked at her watch and said, "Two o'clock, time for bed." I stood up, wondering if that too was a command.

The taxi arrived at Hyde Park Mansions, and she invited me up to her apartment.

"Be a dear and pour some champagne for us while I get into something more comfortable."

This was getting to be like a third-rate porn movie. In a minute she would appear in a black see-through negligee and the seduction would start.

It happened just like that! I was ushered through to a bedroom lit with soft pink lights and a huge bed with drapes. Holding out an empty glass for more champagne, she lay back on the bed, negligee open and with her tongue roaming over her lips. She put her arms around my neck and pulled me down to kiss me.

The next minute, she was lying full length on the bed, snoring. At first I couldn't believe it but, remembering all those glasses of bubbly she had drunk over the past fifteen hours, it made sense.

I covered Alicia up, straightened my bow tie and left the apartment, wondering what sort of a hangover she would have in the morning. With the first signs of dawn appearing over the London horizon of chimney tops, I walked back to the hotel, bathed, and changed for a very early start at the office. The thought of arriving late and facing the taunts of my secretary was just too much. At least the day of the races was over at last.

CHAPTER 25

ESCAPE FROM IRAN

Tehran and Ahwaz

"You're off on a jolly with the chairman; Iran this time; an audience with the Shah no less!" Julie announced.

"Oh, Lord. When is that going to happen?" I asked rather irritably.

"Next week. You fly out to Tehran on Monday, fly down to see the factory at Ahwaz on Tuesday, back to Tehran Wednesday, audience with the Shah on Thursday, Friday is a religious holiday, meetings with government departments on Saturday and fly home Sunday."

Bloody hell! I thought, just like the chairman to pack it in to a week, and just when I thought I would have a few weeks without dashing around the world.

"OK," I responded wearily, "tell me what I have to do."

She answered with a sigh, "You expect me to nanny you, don't you? Well here goes: your passport is valid and has a current visa for Iran; your inoculations are up to date, where you are going is not malarial so no tablets before or during your trip. Flight tickets I'll give you before you go, hotel bookings are confirmed, and I've got you a little currency so that can get around the fleshpots. It's all in this schedule," she said triumphantly, walloping the document down on to the top of my desk.

"You are just marvellous," I purred, knowing from experience that the arrangements would be perfect.

"Hmmmph," she exclaimed, turning towards the door so sharply that her skirt lifted to reveal her underclothes.

"Aha, I saw your black undies. Very sexy!" I shouted after her.

She opened the door and turned back, "You are just a bloody, sexist pig!" and she slammed the door so hard that the walls shook.

Tales From A Briefcase

I met the chairman briefly at Heathrow on the following Monday. He announced, "I'm checking-in at the first class lounge and will see you on the plane after take-off," and departed with a wave.

With my tourist class ticket – when you travelled with the chairman it was always so – I joined the queue for the Iranian Airways flight and eventually boarded the aircraft and found my allotted seat.

A usual tourist class meal was served and I settled back to listen to piped music. After a while, the curtain across the aisle between first and tourist class was swept aside and there stood the chairman, a huge cigar in his mouth and brandishing a bottle of champagne and two glasses. This was typical behaviour for him; keeping a distance from the troops for most of the time but on suitable occasions coming out with the munificent gesture.

A hostess came up and told him that cigars were banned but cigarettes were acceptable. He cheerily promised to smoke no more – but only after he had finished his fine Havana which was glowing brightly from huge puffs.

The plane landed at Teheran and we took a taxi to the Intercontinental Hotel, a modern building set in landscaped and manicured gardens with a view over the city. The chairman was greeted by the concierge and was whisked away to his suite. I waited to check in and was eventually shown to my room. Looking out of my hotel window, I could see the vast sweep of the city of mixed ancient and modern buildings, and snow-capped mountains in the far distance.

Later, the Chairman called to advise me that he had a private dinner appointment and would meet me in the foyer at seven in the morning to go to the airport handling domestic flights. Next morning, the two-hour flight to Ahwaz on the Persian Gulf passed uneventfully.

We were met at the airport by the managing director of our Iranian operation, Jim Parsons, who controlled our modern factory on the outskirts of Ahwaz city. It employed about a hundred people, nearly all Iranians, engaged in producing valves for pipelines and heavy pressure vessels for crude oil processing.

Tales From A Briefcase

Jim was originally employed as a manager in our sister Manchester factory. About three years ago, the Shah had persuaded the chairman to create a new factory in Ahwaz, near the refineries, and the Iranian government had made generous grants towards its start-up costs. I had not seen the accounts for the business but I became aware that the shareholders included not only the Iranian state but also the Shah, personally. His annual dividend was sent to a private numbered account in Switzerland.

Jim took the chairman and me around the factory, which was bright and airy despite the fume-making welding processes. There were a few British technicians who spoke a smattering of Iranian but a few of the Iranian workforce could speak English. The main difference from the English factory was that there were breaks for prayers twice a day when everything stopped and prayer mats were put down to face Mecca. Otherwise the factory appeared very efficient and the workforce quite contented.

That night we stayed at Jim's luxurious bungalow and ate splendid Iranian food cooked by his live-in chef and served by live-in servants. The following day, after a further visit to the factory, we flew back to Tehran. In the evening we had a rehearsal of our audience with the Shah, arranged for the following day. There we learned bowing, admittance to the presence and retiring protocols, and methods of addressing the Shah in the most subservient and flowery language. The audience was to be in two parts, the first with the chairman and me, which was also to be attended by several ministers, and the second being a private meeting between the Shah and the chairman.

The following day, on arrival at the palace we were ushered up to the Peacock Throne Room where the Shah was seated on his golden throne surrounded by his ministers. We were loudly announced and beckoned forward. Every ten steps we stopped and bowed low before arriving at two chairs placed before the throne on its high dais.

In perfect English, without accent, the Shah welcomed us formally and asked the chairman for a report on the operations

Tales From A Briefcase

at Ahwaz. This report contained only good news and a few requests for local assistance. The Shah then beckoned the chairman to follow him and they disappeared into a side room. Ten minutes later, they re-appeared and the chairman and I made our formal retreat, walking backwards and bowing low.

Other than saying, "We must walk in the park," the chairman at first made no comment to me. Arriving at the park we took off at a fast pace, taking paths which skirted the lake and avoided going near bushes.

"If you don't mind me asking, what's going on? Why are we playing evasion games?"

"Shut up and listen! When you speak, keep your voice low; we may be being observed by members of the Revolutionary Council."

I looked at him with amazement. The 'Old Man' had fallen off his perch at last.

He continued, "The Shah has informants planted in the Revolutionary Council which is led by the ayatollahs and supported by university students. It has, until now, not been a serious threat to the Shah and the state. However, information has now come to light that there will be an uprising in the near future when all private enterprises will be taken over and nationalized and the Shah deposed. The ayatollahs, led by Khomeini, will form a government and seek recognition from the outside world. The Shah will, at an appropriate time, make an escape with his family to America. He advises us to put arrangements in hand against that day."

"Good God! Do you think we have time to plan a withdrawal without losing our shirts?"

He went on, "I want you to fly down to Ahwaz tomorrow for a few days. Discuss a company withdrawal plan with Jim. We must try to keep the factory producing and delivering its orders for as long as possible. Also plan the exit for him, his wife and the British technicians. I have the name and telephone number of someone close to the Shah to whom we can appeal for help in an emergency. Tomorrow a package will arrive at the factory for you; it will contain open flight tickets back to London and a false passport to get you out of the country. As far as you're

Tales From A Briefcase

concerned, you can safely assume nothing will happen for two to three days and that the uprising will occur in about three weeks time. Meanwhile there will be no more official meetings with the Shah or his entourage Do you understand my instructions?"

"Yes, sir"

"I'm flying back to London this evening. Come back to England no later than Sunday evening and report to me on Monday morning with your plan."

I took the evening flight to Ahwaz. Jim met me at the airport and we played the security game: assume everywhere was bugged and no discussions in front of the factory staff or servants.

The need to keep the factory open, as a priority, conflicted with the requirements of a progressive withdrawal. The Iranian bank account would be frozen and cash transfers out would be curtailed. Company documents, especially those concerned with confidential dealing with the Shah and his government, had to be exported manually, and we listed those I should take out in a suitcase and those we would try to ship by air in the next few days.

During the following day, Saturday, we had a visit from an official of what we assumed was the Revolutionary Council. He was accompanied by a young man and a young woman wearing a black headscarf and voluminous black gown; I noted that her face was not masked as was the case with most Iranian Muslim women.

The official started asking questions about the factory and demanded details of orders and customers. We said that we were a British company with directors back in England and that we would need their permission to reveal such information. He then advised that all Iranians and registered foreign technicians should remain in Ahwaz and continue with their work. He ended with, "We note, Mr James, that you are booked on the evening flight back to London tomorrow. Be sure not to miss it!" and then the visitors left.

Jim and I discussed the position and decided that, apart from visiting the British consul in Ahwaz, there was little more we could do. The British consul was aware that something was afoot but could offer no helpful suggestions other than that Jim

Tales From A Briefcase

and the British technicians should seek refuge at the consulate if they felt threatened.

As I flew back to Tehran, I pondered on the complicated situation that was developing. Clearly, the Shah was still in control of the army and police and had his own secret service playing a background role – but for how long? The Revolutionary Council also had its agents, who were becoming better informed as each day passed and were openly signalling that an uprising was about to happen, and was already giving orders to the population. There must come a point of chaos when neither faction had commanding control. Maybe the new regime would honour the sanctity of embassies and consulates which would be able to protect and evacuate the British nationals – but only maybe.

I decided not to use the false passport and bought a first class ticket to London in my own name on a British Airways flight. I felt that I was being observed closely by customs officers – but on whose side were they? The Boeing 747 trundled down the runway and the wheels came unstuck as it became airborne. I summoned the air hostess.

"I'll now have that large whisky," and I settled back into the spacious seat to enjoy the civilised lifestyle yet again.

* * *

Jim, his wife and the technicians didn't escape. A gang of revolutionaries turned up at the factory a few days later and took control. Jim and his wife were arrested and put in prison, where they were interrogated, particularly about the Shah's interest in the operation. Luckily, Jim had not been told anything of the 'special arrangements' with the Shah and could not enlighten them. Later, at a revolutionary court, he was closely questioned on his treatment of the Iranian staff. However, several came to the court as defence witnesses. Also, he was able to produce a watch with a friendly inscription on the back, given him by the Iranian staff on his birthday. Three months later, he and his wife were released and returned to England. The technicians were offered contracts to stay on; some did and the rest were repatriated.

Tales From A Briefcase

CHAPTER 26

CONTRASTS OF INDIA

Calcutta and Bombay

The Thai Airways flight from Bangkok to Calcutta was, in first class, absolute luxury. As ever with this airline, the food and wine served was immaculate and the service faultless.

The pilot announced rain on landing; not surprising since this was the monsoon season. Customs clearance at Calcutta was officious but polite, and I was able to commission an old Austin A40 taxi to take me from the airport to my hotel in the centre of the city. The purpose of my journey to India was to visit the group's two Indian subsidiaries, one in Calcutta and the other in Bombay, now called Mumbai.

Our joint venture in Calcutta was a mobile crane manufacturer which supplied both the Indian military and commercial markets. Orders for military equipment were placed by army headquarters in Delhi, and other orders came from state procurement departments or directly from local, large construction companies.

The taxi was not air-conditioned and I opened the passenger window to create a flow of incoming air, albeit warm and humid. The driver attempted to miss the rain-filled potholes but nearing the centre of town there was little room to manoeuvre and he had to pass straight through them. Gasping for air at the open window, I managed to collect a mouthful of splash from a pothole. It was not entirely liquid; human or animal excreta were included in its contents. I spat it out and the residual taste was vile.

Driving through the city, I could see that many people were living on the streets. Some were dying there too, left on the roadside until picked up by body removers with a pushcart. The taxi pulled up to a grand entrance to a modern, multi-storey hotel. As I paid the driver, I was surrounded by street beggars. One in particular caught my eye; a teenaged girl dressed in rags, holding a crying, naked baby on her hip, it faeces running down to soil her garments. She made firm eye contact with me and held out her hand. I looked at the hotel entrance with its top-hatted Indian doorman ushering smartly dressed, well-fed Indians and foreign visitors and felt guilty. I thrust my hand into my pocket to pull out some loose change but was stopped by the doorman who shooed the girl away. "You mustn't do that, sir. You'll create a crowd and nobody will be able to go in or out of the hotel."

I checked in at reception and a young porter carried my bags to a beautifully appointed room. The big bowl of fresh fruit immediately caught my eye. I crossed to the window and right there on the street, just a few feet away, the people of India starved and died while I enjoyed the luxuries of the western world: food, hot water, a linen-covered bed and air conditioning.

My feeling of guilt deepened and I was overcome with a sense of helplessness. Was there nothing a lone westerner could do to alleviate this poverty? I had reviewed the statistics on India before I flew east:

- the population was estimated as approaching 1000 million and growing at a rate of over 20% per decade

- India represented 2.4% of the world's landmass

- India had 16% of the world's population

- 40% of the population was under 15 years of age

- 70% lived in 550,000 villages and 30% lived in 200 towns

- 83% were Hindu; there were about 120m Muslims

- the falling birth rate was 28 per 1000 and the falling death was 10 per 1000

I had also read that the Indian economy had improved by leaps and bounds. Its engineering industry was booming, it was beginning to be recognized as one of the world's major software generators, and its medical resources were gaining worldwide

Tales From A Briefcase

recognition: Indian private hospitals were treating a large number of patients from the Middle East.

Yet the conditions on the street outside my hotel window confirmed that India was still a Third World nation and would continue to be for years to come. I asked myself where was the income going? To fighting Pakistan, to squabbling over Kashmir, nuclear developments, or the ever-present disease of developing nations – corruption.

Tonight, I would attend a welcoming party given by the managing director at his house in the suburbs. The company car and driver came for me and we drove through the streets teaming with humanity, sheltering from the heavy monsoon rain and totally occupied with the job of surviving another day. We turned into a private estate, walled and gated and guarded by private security police. Huge mansions amid flowering gardens and ornamental fountains and lakes produced images of another India, the contrast with the other staggering.

I was received by the managing director and his wife, born of wealthy parents, sophisticated, educated in English public schools and behaving as one would expect from descendants of the Raj society. About fifty employees and local dignitaries had been assembled and the introductions and niceties took forever. In a large room, a hall in fact, two long tables had been laid out to carry vegetarian and non-vegetarian food. Soft drinks, mainly fresh juices, were served although here and there guests were drinking fine wines from Europe. The spiced meat dishes were especially delightful, nothing like the British version of curry which we ate at home.

Throughout the meal, I felt a deep anger and discomfort with what I was now experiencing and vowed to discuss the contrasts tomorrow with Richard, the MD. He was good-looking, immaculately dressed, beautifully spoken and would be acceptable in the best English social circles. His wife, Rona, was an ex-air hostess with Air India. She looked Anglo-Indian and was beautiful and clearly was westernized despite her sari and decorative Indian jewellery. Returning to my hotel in the chauffeur-driven car, I spent a disturbed night worrying about my involvement in India.

Tales From A Briefcase

The following morning I toured the crane factory where conditions were as good as those in the sister factory in Darlington. The workforce were dressed in smart overalls and there seemed to be a good rapport between managers and staff.

I raised the subject of contrasts with Richard.

"You know Britain pretty well and have detected that, with the introduction of the welfare state, poverty is fading and class contrasts are eroding. You will now find boys from working-class backgrounds being sent to boarding schools, their parents making enormous personal sacrifices to pay for their education. Here, in India I see a huge divide between the few 'haves' and the teaming 'have nots'. How do you reconcile this as you drive through the streets, seeing the poverty, witnessing the inhuman conditions?"

"Firstly," he responded, "I see my role, as an educated Indian, to use my skills in building factories and creating jobs. I will use my influence with state and national government to improve these conditions whenever I can. My status gives me a little power to change things locally but I cannot do anything for those poor devils living and dying on the streets of Calcutta. The food that we eat last evening, even my salary, if distributed locally would have no effect on their well-being. It's a national problem and needs to be tackled centrally.

"We need to divert our resources away from war-mongering, use foreign aid more effectively and produce more. We still are a dispersed village society and we must create factories and jobs in the villages. We must stop the migration of our population to the big towns and create houses and hospitals out in the village areas. What is obvious is that it will take years but we have started down the path."

I accepted his philosophy and took a more positive view on India's future. Taking my leave, I flew to Bombay where the airport road passes a vast shantytown of flimsy constructions of tin and cardboard and where people live on the poverty line. Arriving by taxi at the joint venture's offices, I was introduced to two elderly brothers who managed the business. The factory produced scaffolding and building props, much like its sister in Saffron Walden. Again the working conditions were good and staff relationships excellent. Until fairly recently in the construction industry, a bamboo and rope construction had been used to access the above-ground work levels. With the multi-storey structures now being built, the bamboo access structures became unstable and many workmen were killed. The demand for steel scaffolding systems had increased dramatically and the factory was working flat-out and had plans for expansion.

In Bombay, I was taken to the Taj Hotel for an evening meal and was introduced to the most beautifully spiced meal I have ever eaten. Clearly, in the United Kingdom we are rarely offered delicately spiced Indian food but eat the British army's, crude, fiery curry version.

I flew home realizing that one had to accept the contrasts of the sub-continent. Appointing joint venture partners and creating jobs was the group's practical way of contributing to improvements. I returned to India several times over the next twenty years and was gratified to witness positive changes all round, but there was still a long way to go.

CHAPTER 27

A WORLD OF PRINTING

Surrey

My business telephone at home rang. Strange, I thought, it's Saturday morning. "Robert James, good morning."

"Hello, Mr James. My name is Stuart Rigby. I'm a search consultant acting on behalf of the National Enterprise Board. We're seeking a managing director for a substantial UK group in electronics. Would you be interested in meeting so that I can give you more details?"

"Yes, I would be happy to do that."

"Could you meet in central London any time next week?"

"Yes. Thursday would be a good day for me," I answered.

"Good. Thursday at ten at our office at 15 Stratton Street, W1, first floor. I have your address and I'll send you a letter to confirm the arrangement. OK?"

"Fine. I'll see you then," I replied, amazed at how these agencies operated.

On the following Thursday, I went to the consultant's premises and was received by a glamorous receptionist and taken to a luxurious office, elegantly furnished, hung with original paintings and decorated with exotic plants.

"I'm Samantha. Would you like some tea or coffee? Mr Rigby will join you here in just a minute."

"Thank you, Samantha. Tea would be excellent."

Stuart Rigby arrived, suave, elegantly dressed and in his thirties, advancing towards me with an outstretched hand. "Thank you for coming in for a chat. Has Samantha asked if you would like some refreshment?"

"Yes, thank you." I sat in the chair that he indicated.

"You may think that this is all a bit mysterious, but confidentiality is vital to the project we are about to discuss. The

British government is involved with the project and it's therefore a bit sensitive." He named a well-known, almost household name in the printing equipment industry. "It's an old British company, in fact the only British company which is fighting for existence in the world of computerised printing equipment. It is inadequately financed to invest in research and development and to gain a technological lead over its American and German competitors. The government has decided to fund its electronic division, subject to appointment of a new management team. We are seeking a managing director to that team. Interested?"

"Yes. It sounds quite a challenge. Please go on."

"The original company has a second division in mechanical products; this will be hived off and continue to operate under existing management. The electronics company has two factories: one in Surrey and one in Scotland. It also has taken over the existing seventeen marketing and servicing companies around the world. The new managing director will report to a non-executive board led by a chairman and including representatives from the Enterprise Board, a supporting bank and academics."

"Wow, that's really a challenge. Can you give me any more details?"

The interview lasted for several more hours, with me reviewing accounts and staff curricula vitae, and asking basic questions about the business. At its conclusion, I confirmed my interest in being considered as a candidate for the position.

Over the next few weeks, I visited all the company's sites in Britain and some of its more important customers such as the Fleet Street newspapers and the university presses. I gained the impression that the company still had a high standing in the printing world, which would give support if the company modernised and produced state of the art technology.

After a final interview with the board, my appointment was confirmed and I was invited to a briefing meeting. The board felt that laser technology should be driven faster and that a research unit should be established at Cambridge. It also proposed that the company, already world famous for its fonts, should press ahead with digitisation of foreign languages such as Chinese, Japanese and Arabic to allow computerised printing techniques to be used. The board also felt that subsidiaries should be strengthened in France, Germany and Italy, and new ones created in Singapore, Hong Kong and Japan. Our interests in North and South America should be wound down. I was able to agree with all proposals and confirm my commitment to their implementation.

On my first day of engagement, I reported to the company's main offices not far from Gatwick Airport. There, I met my secretary, Brenda, a pleasant, middle aged and long-serving employee who would later dedicate her life to supporting me on my trips around the world. Following my established routine as a 'new boy', I met the new management team as a group and then individually. They were an impressive bunch, recently recruited, who I would come to admire and rely upon. Many were international marketing and sales people with a wealth of languages between them.

Particularly professional was the manager in charge of fonts and typography. The company's high reputation had kept the old company in the vanguard of the printing world, and he alone was responsible for that.

I visited the mechanical division and it was obvious that nineteenth century technology would not compete for much longer against computerised printing equipment. I was told that, in China, compositing speeds had been increased by putting the compositors on roller skates. Nevertheless, many Third World nations still could only afford the old technology and there was till a demand for mechanical typesetters, albeit declining.

Today, the first generation of laser-driven phototypesetters were installed around the world, printing books and newspapers at astounding speeds. The next generation would allow a newspaper page to be set in Fleet Street, sent digitally to Frankfurt, and incorporated in a locally produced English edition.

Our new research unit at Cambridge was established and was set to work developing the second-generation product. With China showing great interest in the technology, we appointed a

Tales From A Briefcase

Chinese professor to assist in the digitisation of the twenty five thousand symbols used in literary documents, especially poetry.

A delegation of Chinese academics and engineers was sent to visit us for a fortnight. They carried specifications for a system to be set up between Beijing and Shanghai against which we would need to quote. We had to face the problem of communication via poor quality land lines in China, but our British engineers found a solution.

We arranged leisure trips for our visitors: London museums, Oxford, and our research establishment at Cambridge. On one trip, their bus stopped at my house in Buckinghamshire for coffee. They asked how I came to be such a rich man – to live in such a splendid home. I explained that our social and economic system allowed ordinary people to educate themselves and work their way up to a point where big houses and luxurious lifestyles could be afforded. The Chinese visitors found this hard to believe after their own propaganda had put over the story that the aristocracy sent their offspring to public schools where an elite class was prepared for business management and government.

After many months of haggling over specifications and prices we received an order for the Beijing-Shanghai system. Shipment of equipment and engineers took two jumbo jets. Installation took four months, during which the system was worked up to perfection, newspapers being produced in either city with local pages added.

* * *

The laser driven typesetters, with the help of an excellent marketing and sales team, captured the markets around the world and were soon in operation in Western Europe, South Africa, Australia and Hong Kong. Eastern Europe became problematical because US manufacturers, of the computers we used in our equipment would not allow their most advanced products to go into countries under Russian influence. Here we could only offer earlier generations of product.

I held monthly board meetings in our French and German subsidiaries, in the language of their country, and regularly visited the other West European countries. I travelled around the world three to four times a year, with several ports of call and each trip lasting at least a month.

With the technology taken to its next generation, the Cambridge research unit working sweetly, world sales climbing and profits at last being generated, my work as a developer was drawing to a close. Soon I would have to deal with my family problem.

Tales From A Briefcase

CHAPTER 28

THE CANCELLED ORDER

Warsaw

I stood there totally naked, my feet close together and hands covering my genitals; they had even insisted that I take off my shoes and socks. There were two male officials in the little airport office; I couldn't tell if they were immigration officers or police.

The shorter, fatter one approached me snapping on plastic gloves. He extended the middle finger of his right hand and dipped it into a jar of white cream, at the same time as giving me a very searching look and the merest suggestion of a smile. The taller one grabbed my head and pushed it down towards my knees.

I felt the middle finger circling inside me, not a little surprised that it was causing me no pain but deeply offended that my intimate parts were being assaulted.

The finger stopped probing and I squeezed my anal muscles to eject the foreign body. I straightened up and looked around expecting further instructions. None came. I resumed my 'feet together and hiding hands' posture.

My brain went into top gear. How the hell did I get into this position?

* * *

It had started with an export newsletter pushed out by the Foreign Office. Printing equipment was being sought by the Polish National Book Printing Bureau in Cracow: in particular, type-setting equipment, the most modern available, driven by the latest American computers. Advice would be given by the Foreign Office to manufacturers regarding which computers were exportable to the Iron Curtain countries.

Tales From A Briefcase

My company had obtained the relevant export papers and sent our bid to the Export-Import Bureau in Warsaw. We were advised that Polish engineers would later visit the UK to assess the equipment and that the company would need to assist with their visas.

The visit had passed off well and, not long after, we received a communication from the Polish Embassy in London that we had been awarded an order worth over £2 million for delivery in about six months. This was a big order for us and would keep our people working through what would have been a quiet time.

As part of the order we were to train Polish engineers at our factory in Surrey and they would return to Poland with our engineers to install and commission the delivered equipment.

Six Polish engineers arrived at Heathrow via Lot airlines and were met by our managers and brought to Surrey in a small private bus. They soon settled into a small local hotel where all the meals were provided. During the week, they worked in a factory area which had been reserved for the project. At weekends, they were invited to our people's homes and for trips out to London and Brighton. They were very easy-going and seemed happy to be in England. Most spoke a smattering of English and German.

The order was manufactured on time and packed ready for shipment. It would stay with our shippers until the first of the three part-payments had been received.

We said goodbye to our Polish engineers, who had now become friends, and they were sent to Heathrow on the small bus in the company of some of our managers.

When the first stage payment had not been made at the expected time, I began to fear something had gone wrong. A letter from the Polish Embassy confirmed my concern. One of the Polish engineers, having gone into the departure lounge at Heathrow, had circled back into arrivals, reported to the immigration officers and asked for political asylum. The Polish Embassy had asked for his return but the Foreign Office had declined. I checked with the Foreign Office myself who were most reluctant to confirm the story. The letter from the Polish Embassy bluntly stated that the equipment order was cancelled.

Tales From A Briefcase

I visited the Polish Embassy in London and the commercial attaché advised me that I should go to Warsaw and discuss the cancellation with the Export-Import Agency. They offered to support my visa.

During an appointment with the Foreign Office, I told them of my decision to visit Warsaw in an attempt to re-instate the order. The advice was not to go and to be prepared to lose the order. They added that if I went, I might get caught up in a personal exchange scenario – me for the Polish engineer.

I ignored the advice, obtained a visa and flew to Warsaw. At passport control, I was singled out and led away to a small office where I was strip searched.

* * *

"Mr James, you may dress now. Is this your suitcase?"

I nodded and the case was opened and it contents emptied on to a table.

One officer searched through my personal items and found nothing of interest. The other read through my files and passed them back to me.

"You are booked into the Intourist Hotel, yes? Go there and stay there until you are called by the Export-Import Bureau. We will retain your passport. Take your suitcase. Your agent is waiting at the arrivals hall."

I walked slowly out of the office and down a corridor to join the other arrivals. Yes, there was Pieter, my company's Polish sales agent.

"Robert. What on earth is happening?"

I explained my reception by the police.

"You are a marked man. You will be under close surveillance while you are here. Do exactly as I say. Follow my instructions precisely. Don't speak to anyone. Just look straight ahead. OK?"

I nodded.

We got into his car and drove to the hotel. Pieter spoke to the receptionist. A room had been booked for me by the Bureau but for how long? One week, was the reply. I gasped. I'd expected the visit would last not longer than three days. Pieter shook his head to stop me from commenting.

Tales From A Briefcase

I was given a key for a room on the third floor. Pieter walked with me to the lift. "I expect the room will be bugged, probably for both sound and vision. Assume you are being watched all the time. Don't search for the bugs; just be as normal as you can. Meet me in the bar in half an hour."

I showered and put on a change of clothes, then went back downstairs where I found Pieter sitting on a stool at the bar, sipping a drink.

"What will you drink, Robert? I recommend only one alcoholic drink this evening. You'll need your wits about you."

I opened my mouth to protest at all these precautions and shut it when he shook his head.

"Vodka," I requested.

I was sitting at the bar, half turned towards Pieter, when I felt a shoe tapping my leg from the other side. Turning around I saw that the occupant of the next bar stool was a smartly-dressed, shapely blond in her thirties, drinking a cocktail. She had an unlit cigarette in her hand.

"Have you a light, please?" she asked in perfect English.

I felt a kick from Pieter, warning me not to get involved.

"I'm afraid I don't smoke and I haven't a light. I'm sorry," I replied shrugging my shoulders and turning back to Pieter. He got up from his stool.

"I think we should go into the restaurant to eat." I followed him and we sat at the table indicated by a waiter.

"You are definitely being set up! That was what is known as a 'honey trap'. I bet she would have inveigled you to a bedroom somewhere with two-way mirrors and a video camera. Tomorrow someone would have shown you the film and started to back you into a blackmail corner."

"Pieter, you Poles are full of imaginary spy scenes. That could have been coincidence."

"It was no more a coincidence than your shake-down at the airport. You really must take this seriously. They are trying to put you at a disadvantage; maybe over price or maybe – just maybe, technically. Your specification for Poland has Hewlett Packard second-generation computers, but elsewhere you are selling third-generation into Western Europe. Right?"

Tales From A Briefcase

"Correct. We can't get US government approval to export third generation into Iron Curtain countries."

"So, maybe they are trying to renegotiate the price or upgrade the specification as an off-set against the asylum for their engineer and anything else that they can pin on you. It sounds more a commercial ruse than a political one but they will dress it up as political because it is more frightening for you personally. Can you see that you must not put a foot wrong nor give in to threats?"

"Yes, I see that. But they have my passport. I don't appear to have much room in which to manoeuvre."

"I'll telephone the Bureau in the morning and see if we can get the interview chain started. Be in your bedroom at 10 am and I will phone you there. I'm off now. Straight to your room. OK?"

I nodded my agreement and walked to the lift. Standing there, I first became conscious of her perfume.

"Was your dinner bearable? We still have food rationing, you know. No meat on Fridays. But we are a proud nation and have retained our cultural links. Do you know any of our composers or musicians?" She had hit on my musical interest in one. Maybe Pieter was right. Maybe they had a file on me.

I turned to her, "Please forgive me if I appear rude not chatting with you but I have some work to do in my room. Good night." I entered the lift.

In my room I thought about the contact. Was she just 'on the game' or was there a more sinister motive in her friendliness? I bet myself there would be a telephone call later. The telephone rang.

"James speaking."

"Robert. It's Isabella. We met downstairs. I would like to talk with you. Could we meet in your room?" She not only knew my Christian name but my room number.

My eyes swept around the room, over mirrors and wall fittings. Could they see me now?

"I'm very sorry. I'm tired from travelling and am now going to bed. Good night!"

The telephone rang several more times before I disconnected it, and the door was knocked on several times during the night. I ignored the intrusions and eventually got to sleep.

Tales From A Briefcase

I reconnected the telephone in the morning. Pieter called as promised, and told me: "Get some breakfast in the dining room and I'll be round to pick you up at eleven. Meet you in the foyer."

He arrived in the foyer as planned and hurried me off to his parked car.

"Anything happen after I'd left last night?"

"The girl met me at the lift and I brushed her off, as I did the following telephone call when she suggested we talk. I ignored all the door knockings."

"Good! You have a meeting with a Mr Kalasinski at the Export-Import Bureau at 11.30. He is very junior but I'm sure that he is in on the game. The questions will be simple and rather non-committal. Tomorrow, Wednesday, you will probably meet his boss and the questions will be more elaborate. On Thursday, it will be the departmental head, who has clear-cut objectives to extract the last bits of information out of you. On Friday you will meet the director of the Bureau. He will pretend not to speak English and will speak through an interpreter, at first, anyway. He will attempt to close a deal with you suggesting that your passport and ticket home depend on a satisfactory outcome."

"Wow. What a circus! The way I feel now, I would promise anything just to get home."

"You can't play that game. They will get you in a position where you'll have to deliver. You will not be safe until you're back in England!"

Mr Kalasinski spoke good English and wished me to recount details of the security arrangements for the visiting Polish engineers. I had to remember if there were opportunities for them to be on their own in public places where private contacts could have been made or have access to public telephones where private communications could have taken place. He asked me about the arrangements for delivering them back to Heathrow and the possibility of getting back to arrivals from departures. His questions indicated that he was not a clerk but an intelligence officer seeking information.

After two hours he requested that I meet his chief on the following day at the same time. This man's questions were similar but more in depth. He asked me about the absconder and

Tales From A Briefcase

had I noticed any changes in his attitude as the course progressed? I had not. His break away came as a complete surprise. At the end of our meeting, he too suggested that I meet the departmental head on the following day.

On Thursday, I was introduced to the head man involved in importation of technical equipment. He was totally familiar with the equipment ordered, and started to question me on the specification of third-generation computers used in our latest typesetters. I could see that he had our West German brochure and would have already drawn the comparisons between the generations. I answered his technical questions but decided against commenting on the British and US governments' policies of not letting their latest technology go eastwards for use in weapons design and targeting.

On Friday my appointment with the director was at nine. I checked out of the hotel in a rather vain hope that I would be on the evening plane back to London via Stockholm. I reported to reception at the Export-Import Bureau and was asked to wait.

A short dark-haired lady in her forties approached me and said in perfect English, "Good morning, Mr James. I am the translator, Frau Ried. Director Paulus is expecting you. Please follow me."

Nice bum, I thought, as I followed her wiggling up several flights of stairs and along lengthy corridors. She stopped at a large wooden door bearing an important-looking nameplate and knocked.

"Herein!" came a loud and deep voice from within. I registered the German.

The room was huge, both wide and long and the ceiling high and ornate. A roll of red carpet had been laid from the door to a large desk positioned at the other end of the room. I started down the carpet, feigning interest in the portraits of, I supposed, previous directors and trying to avoid eye contact with the large man with bushy eyebrows seated at the desk and now observing my progress down the carpet.

I stopped immediately in front of the desk and nodded my head in an acknowledgement, "Herr Direktor,"

"Wilkommen, Herr James. Nehmen sie platz, bitte," his hand sweeping to the single upright chair opposite. He signalled to the translator to take a chair alongside his, then broke into Polish with the translator nodding at frequent intervals. When he finished, she started to talk.

"The Herr Direktor apologises that his English is not good enough for these proceedings and, although he knows you speak German, for political reasons the interview must be conducted in English. Do you understand?"

"Yes. Please thank the Herr Direktor for his consideration."

The meeting started very affably with the director asking very similar questions to those from the previous days, the questions and answers being fed through the interpreter. Later, I detected a slight incline of his head at which the interpreter left the room.

When she had gone, he leaned forward with his elbows on the desk and said in perfect English, "Well, Herr James, let's get down to business and forget about cat and mouse games." He tapped a file about an inch thick sitting on his desk.

"You have made many visits to our Eastern Bloc in the past ten years. Russia, Hungary, Czechoslovakia and several times to Poland. In fact you have proved to be a good friend to Poland. Your work on our Massey Ferguson factory a few years ago was exemplary and today it is a showpiece of East-West co-operation."

He opened the file at the beginning. "Ah, I see that you have a wife and two children and live in the Thames Valley. Unfortunately your wife is mentally ill and you cannot afford to be away for too long." He looked up, his bushy eyebrows signalling an unasked question.

I decided not to respond but let him continue. "I see that you were in the Regular Army. Service in Korea and Malaya. Fighting communists with whom today you seek to do business?"

Oh, Christ, I thought. This is where it all hangs out – SAS; signal codes, special operations with embassies. They'll pin me like a butterfly to a display board. They know everything! Mouth tight shut, no facial movements, just stare.

"But we need not rake up old scores, eh Mr James? We are about business today, between our two great nations, friends in trade. Why did you let our man escape?"

The question was direct and forceful and needed a response.

Tales From A Briefcase

"Herr Direktor, you will already know that I respect your country and its politics, that I love your people and their great culture. It would serve no great purpose to me personally, my company or my country to allow your engineer to abscond from a programme on which so much depended, not the least being work for my people in the factory. You cannot believe that there could have been any advantage accruing to anybody. I am surprised that you suggest it!"

"Once we become involved in politics we can be led into believing anything."

"I have to say that I am a businessman, I have no interest in politics. You might say that I am driven by capitalism, the great god of profit but political games are definitely not my scene. We supply the finest printing equipment in the world. It will generate books to educate future generations of Poles and thus contribute to the future well-being of your country. We want this to happen and have no political ambitions to block Poland's progress. As an educated and worldly-wise man you must already know this. The world is getting smaller. Today, we need to help each other in basic matters, tomorrow it will be in matters of environmental preservation and politics will even less of an issue."

"You may be right. But enough of these semantics. I want you to deliver third generation computers. The West Germans get them, why can't we?"

"We buy the computers from America and install them in our systems. We have to honour the purchase conditions about onward distribution. My company would be finished if the Yanks found out that we were involved in shipments to the Eastern Bloc. However, I am prepared to ask for a special concession but that's all. I doubt if it will be granted."

"OK – you do your best. Now a fine for the trouble you have caused for not looking after our engineer. It will be 15% discount off your price. No argument. The order will not be re-instated unless you can confirm this by fax this afternoon."

I did some quick sums in my head – a price reduction of £300,000. It was not negotiable – a take it or leave it situation. If I left it I might not get my passport back or even get back to

England. I wrote the fax to be forwarded back from England and drafted the order confirmation that I needed from the director to secure the transaction.

"We can take a little schnapps on a satisfactory deal, Herr James. It was good to do business with you. There, we are not such bad people after all!" He opened a drawer in his desk and took out my passport and airline ticket. "There, you can get back to look after your family – they need you."

"Thank you, Herr Direktor. How much information do you have on me?"

"I know that your mother was a Greek Cypriot, that she married your father in Jerusalem in 1927, and a lot more besides. I would use this intelligence if we ever had to be on opposite sides of the table again. I hope that will not be necessary!"

"I am sure it won't. The table is getting narrower and one day it will become round!"

We shook hands and I left.

I drove with Pieter to the airport. "It was a set up, you know, Pieter. He got half of what he wanted. But I get to go home!"

CHAPTER 29

CITY OF STEEL

Sheffield

It was a long drive up the A1 motorway, arriving in South Yorkshire as it got dark and snow was falling hard. I turned off the motorway at the Tynsley viaduct to pass by the headquarters of the steel group which I would be joining tomorrow. My heart sank as I saw the buildings for the first time – dark, dirty, grim and in need of repair, just as I had remembered Sheffield from long ago.

I made my way to the Hallam Towers Hotel, which was modern, well run, and situated in a nice residential section of the city. Any damage caused by the day was repaired by a hot bath, a fine meal and a large bedtime scotch.

Arriving at the group's headquarters at the appointed time the following morning, I was met by a secretary and taken up to John Hepplethwaite's office, tucked away high in the building and reached by narrow stairwells that were brown-painted, scratched and scuffed.

John's office was modest, with utility furniture giving further credence to the opinion that the steel industry was tottering and short of cash for re-investment.

"Welcome to Sheffield," John boomed. "Sit yourself down," he pointed to what had been a rather splendid leather chair but which was now worn and losing its stuffing.

I had met him once before at the recruitment's consultant's office in the West End of London. I was struck that, despite being a large man with a loud voice, John came over as gentle, kindly man, not one's idea of a steel baron. He was managing director of a large steel empire spread across Yorkshire and into

Lancashire. Although he ran it day-to-day, he reported to a family board of directors who carried a famous steel name.

"Did you have a good trip up and was the hotel comfortable?"

"Yes, thank you. A little snow on the way up from London but the hotel is very hospitable."

"I want to take you off-site to brief you where we can't be overheard. It's important that you know the score from the very beginning." He pressed a button on his desk and his secretary entered. She was of medium height, busty, had blond curly hair and an open happy face. "This is Joyce, my personal assistant; she knows most of what I'm going to tell you. Joyce we are just off to Baslow. You have reserved a table for lunch?"

"Yes, John, for one o'clock. Will you be back?"

"Probably about four. Have the kettle on."

Her returned smile had a warmth which went deeper than a boss and PA relationship, and the easy use of Christian names confirmed that the relationship was personal and established.

We drove past the rock outcrop at Hathersage and on into Derbyshire, pulling up at one of the attractive inns that are very prevalent in the Peak District. We were shown to a small but comfortable sitting room where coffee and biscuits on a tray awaited us.

"Well," John began, "this must appear very mysterious but you need to hear the history before we can start any constructive discussion." He went on to recount that the group was started by the family in the centre of Sheffield in the mid-nineteenth century. There were three brothers, sons of a Methodist clergyman, who took over a dilapidated steel mill and forge and, by sheer hard work, got it working efficiently. All three had died by the turn of the century but two of their sons went into management and drove the company forward for another fifty years. During two world wars the company had expanded, acquiring several small enterprises on the way and diversifying into armaments and munitions.

The group had remained independent during the nationalisation of the steel industry after the war, concentrating on the low volume, specialist sector which was of little interest to the government-owned resources.

Tales From A Briefcase

Apart from a steel mill in Manchester and a forge in Sheffield itself, all its subsidiaries were engaged in relatively low volume production. In domestic tools, little manufacturing units spread around Sheffield produced hammers, saws, pliers, screwdrivers and gardening hand tools. Another factory produced knives for the paper and leather industries and provided a knife-sharpening service. Just off the Tynsley viaduct was a factory producing railway crossings and points; these needed high carbon steels to reduce wear. Next door was a small unit producing cutting tools from sintered powder-mixes of carbon and titanium and other hardwearing metals for use in lathes, rotary mills and planers. In Halifax was a stainless steel factory producing parts for the food and atomic energy industries.

The group's chairman was the great, great grandson of the original family founders. He belied the generation tale and was a respected steel businessman, sitting on committees representing the industry. He left the detailed running of the group to John and concentrated on the national and local politics surrounding the steel industry at that time.

The steel industry in and around Sheffield was manned by a heavily unionised workforce, controlled tightly by a regional secretary who was reputed to be a communist. Apart from generally poor working conditions, there were frequent strikes over pay and working hours, a dispute in one factory spreading to another or at least gaining sympathetic brotherly support.

It was rumoured that the chairman supported a group of steel mill owners in "putting a contract" out on a union troublemaker who was losing them thousands of working hours, in which the alternative to death was a bribe to leave the country!

John produced the financial figures for the companies in the group. Several were loss-making, some for years. Overall, the group was making a small but declining profit, but no spare cash for investment in modern manufacturing techniques or repairing old buildings. Predators in the shape of other independent steel groups, some foreign, were making approaches for acquisition at a knock down price or hovering for the collapse.

The chairman and his family wanted to see the group survive and eventually flourish, initially by the introduction of new

Tales From A Briefcase

management. I had been selected as the first of a new management team recruited to regenerate the business. The options to sell off the business as a whole or in bits had not been entirely rejected. The immediate job was now to produce a survival plan, cost it and take it to funders. The stock market was handling a minority representing public shares, but the group's directors had supported acceptable dividend pay-outs and the industry analysts were too busy elsewhere to give it a thumbs down.

"Well, there it is, Robert, warts and all. We have to decide whether we can pull the chestnuts out of the fire or manage the group's demise. The family are totally loyal to the management and will not take any action unless it is discussed with us. For me, I've been in steel all my life; I know nothing else. I'm approaching retirement age and am out of new ideas; in fact I'm bloody tired of fighting rearguard actions. You are young and energetic, come from a wide industrial background and have already experienced the horrors of rationalisation elsewhere. You have no preconceived ideas of a solution; you will think it through and plan the action accordingly. Are you game?"

"Yes I am, John. Thanks for being so blunt. How long have we got to produce a plan?"

"About six months. Then we'll run out of cash and find it difficult to secure financial backers. Let's have some lunch and we can continue talking. They'll serve it in here. Is soup and roast lamb OK?"

Over lunch, we decide that I should spend one or two days at each site and the site directors should produce their business plans at headquarters at the end of my month-long tour. My visiting schedule was agreed and was to be given to Joyce to set up.

We discussed the formats of the business plans, which were to be short-term rather than long. There would be no new investment and improvements had to come entirely from application of management skill. We discussed the personalities within management, highlighting weaker and stronger people. Where a site was almost in business free-fall, we would remove the ailing manager and select a brighter spark for promotion.

Tales From A Briefcase

Our own management style would be informative, positive, and delegative. The gauntlet would be thrown down and the ambitious would pick it up.

We drove back in silence until John dropped me at the hotel. "Your car will be here tomorrow. I'll send my driver for you at eight o'clock. You know, I've enjoyed today. It's been the first time for many years that hope has appeared on the horizon. I feel I'm no longer alone and that we have a chance of succeeding. Thank you for that."

"I like your style, John. It suits me. It gives me the best possible environment in which to succeed. There's no easy way forward; the road ahead will be hard and we may not win through. The timing is tough. As a southerner, I've worked in Yorkshire before and was impressed by the doggedness and endurance of you lot up here; it's a big factor towards winning."

We shook hands and I felt that a special bond had been forged between us.

For six months we strived to improve the group's performance. It did improve but not enough: we ran out of time. The bidding company's offer needed an immediate response if our shareholders were not to lose out heavily. We recommended that they accept the offer.

I packed my bags once more and drove south.

CHAPTER 30

A LANCASHIRE INTERLUDE

Blackburn

His name was Sam. He was rather short and his round face was topped with a mop of white hair. I guessed, as we sat in the coffee shop of one of my favourite London hotel meeting places and I listened to him talking enthusiastically about his business, that he was in his late forties or early fifties.

"Northern Lancashire is the place to be," he told me. "Plenty of space for new factories, good hard-working staff, lovely countryside up in the dales, the seaside just nearby and the Lake District just up the road."

He was proud of his Lancashire birthright and spoke with an emphasized Blackburn/Accrington accent in a soft voice, which had charm for me as a southerner.

"I don't know the area really," I responded, "but I can see that, once you clear the Manchester conurbation coming northwards, the countryside is markedly more beautiful. I've worked in Wigan and found the people delightfully warm and friendly."

Quickly leaping to the defensive, he said "Well, you'll find us from Blackburn even more so."

"Tell me about your business."

"Most of it is located in Blackburn and Darwen, in the area where I was raised. There are, in fact, four businesses: building, building products, residential and nursing homes, mainly those I have built, and screen-printing and embroidery, all based in my new Blackburn factory, which I also built. I run them as four separate companies and borrow money for them from four separate banks."

His pride in his 'local boy makes good' success shone through, but he was generous enough to give credit to his staff.

Tales From A Briefcase

"On my building team, I have a good architect and a first class building foreman. In my nursing and residential homes I have excellent site managers. I have Jeannie who manages the screen-printing and embroidery business; we buy in T-shirts and pullovers and apply logos. The embroidery is computer-controlled and we get a lot of corporate business, such as bus companies. The engineering company manufactures and installs raised access flooring. Most modern office blocks now have raised flooring under which power, telephone and computer cables feed. We have a semi-automated production line producing floor units and a team of installers operating across the country."

I thought I had detected a special affection for Jeannie!

"What about financial control?"

"I have a very good chartered account financial director, Simon, who operates across the group and is supported by a qualified company secretary, Gordon."

"What do you need money for?" I asked.

"It's mainly for the building work, to fund the land purchase and building development. Once the properties are built we can repay loans from mortgages, which themselves are repaid from own company's operating income or from proceeds of sale. I think I need about two million pounds."

"As it's such a diverse business, we may have problems in giving security. The lenders will want to secure the loans by taking charges on the group's property assets. Are the accounts for the separate companies up to date?"

"I think so. I'll ask Simon." Warning bells were ringing in my head – a businessman who did not know the state of his accounts!

"Are you the outright owner of all the businesses?"

"My wife is a minority shareholder but otherwise yes."

I considered the project and its risks, decided to chance it. "I'll be happy to assist you to get funding, and I'll make a start in ten days. In the first instance, I'll come up for a week and put up at a local hotel. My deal is three per cent of the funds raised and all travel and hotel expenses covered. I'll put the terms in a contract. OK?"

We shook hands on it and parted.

Tales From A Briefcase

Some days later I made the long drive via the M1 and M6 to Preston, where I took the road into central Blackburn. The offices and factory were newly built and were of a good standard. The first meeting I attended was with Simon, the accountant, and Gordon, the company secretary.

We started by reviewing the accounts for the four companies. I had an instant dislike for Simon, with his loud voice and bumptious attitude' quite unlike any other accountant I had met before. My feelings were accentuated when I smelt drink on his breath; not beer from a lunchtime drink but spirits. I watched him more closely. His body movements were unusually quick and his hands trembled. Was he an alcoholic, I asked myself?

Gordon, a Scotsman, was a dark-haired, stout man with glasses who also appeared nervous, but he was milder in his manner and more sincere.

"Can you explain to me why you account the four companies independently and do not consolidate them into group accounts annually? Accountancy rules on conglomerates with common directors and inter-company trading require consolidated reports. How do you get round them?"

There was much foot-shuffling under the table and eye contact between the men sitting opposite me. "With much difficulty," Simon eventually said smugly, with a smile.

"I see from the accounts there is considerable inter-company trading between the building company and the care homes activities, double profits are being taken and there are no off-sets between balance sheets. The balance sheets therefore overstate the value of the group. Does the auditor not comment on this?"

"We have four different auditors and they do not co-operate," admitted Gordon.

I reacted, "Well, gentlemen, tricky accounting games. We might just modestly fund the building company as a stand-alone business using local high street banks, but you should be aware that for two million pounds we may be talking to a merchant banker who will do his due diligence in depth."

Sam came into the conversation, "Have we done anything illegal, Simon?"

Tales From A Briefcase

Jovially, Simon responded, "No! I wouldn't let you take the risk, Sam. We've done some creative accounting and most of us wide-awake accountants are doing this all the time."

Sam looked at me for confirmation. I was not an accountant but felt uncomfortable; I shrugged my shoulders. I took the accounts back to the hotel and analysed the figures. Taken as a group, the reported profits and assets were overstated. In fact, the group was loss-making.

The next day, I toured the factory and was impressed with the management team and all I saw. Jeannie was a rather plain, talkative, peroxide blonde with a strong personality. It was plain that she had Sam twisted around her little finger and that the relationship extended beyond business. Well, what Sam did in his spare time was his business and none of mine.

I prepared the funding proposal and submitted it to various funding organizations in Manchester. Surprisingly an offer of funds came very quickly and the money was soon available. Sam suggested that my assignment should continue and that I should be involved in improving the profitability of the least profitable businesses. I rented a house in Longridge, a pretty little town not far from Clitheroe.

Sam and Jeannie would often be absent together for afternoons, and it was clear, not only to me but to all the staff, that they were sharing some leisure time somewhere. Jeannie had an assistant manager, Brenda, a tall thin, pleasant divorcee and it was suggested that I make up a foursome for dinner. On one occasion, dinner was at Brenda's house while her children stayed with friends for the night. Sam's intention was abundantly clear – I should partner Brenda in one of the two bedrooms. After Jeannie and Sam had gone upstairs, Brenda and I agreed that we would not comply with Sam's suggestion.

The bank money arrived and the next phase of building work started. Meanwhile, Sam met a Canadian who wanted to sell him a boatyard and I was dispatched to Toronto to buy it with money borrowed from a local bank.

The boatyard was set on the southern shore of Lake Huron. It built and repaired boats, and lifted them out of the water and stored them over the long Canadian winters. The skilled workforce was very dedicated to the business, and the order book, some for government work, was impressive. The accounts were up-to-date and showing a profit; I considered the asking price very reasonable.

The bank manager I visited was, like me, a veteran of Korea and we got on famously. There would be no problem borrowing the purchase price while still retaining the overdraft. I returned to Blackburn triumphant.

Then things began to go wrong. Severe winter conditions hit the north, preventing building work and shortening the lives of many residents and patients in the care homes. Orders for floors and embroidery fell away and the group started to run out of cash. Simon took to his bed and then checked into a rehabilitation centre for alcoholics. Gordon was unable to take Simon's load, cracked under the strain and committed suicide. Sam decided that Canada offered him more opportunities and went off with Jeannie to live there, leaving his wife and two children in Blackburn.

Although not a director of any of the companies, I felt obliged to manage the mess and protect my professional reputation. I called in insolvency advisers. Seeing the complex group position, they advised notifying the five banks involved, which I did. All put in receivers at the same time, who fought over the ownership of the assets; many times I found myself arbitrating disputes between receivers.

It was another three months before I loaded all my worldly possessions into the car and headed south. Fortunately, or so it appeared at the time, an old client wanted me to sort out a financial problem in his company and lent me a house in Crawley. He, too, had run out of cash and would soon after run away to South Africa, leaving the VAT office and Inland Revenue to fight over the company's assets.

Tales From A Briefcase

CHAPTER 31

UP A WELSH VALLEY

Hirwaun, South Wales

I sat in my office, revelling in its opulence: the smart furniture, my desk and adjoining conference table, the comfortable seats set around a low coffee table, the live vegetation and the well-chosen framed prints. In the next office my secretary and her assistant provided my communications to the outside world and refreshments for me and my visitors. Outside in a prime position in the car park, sat my Jaguar being tenderly polished by my suited driver with peaked hat. It told my visitors that I had arrived, although I knew that such material benefits did not come cheaply. Perched at the top of the pile, whilst the authority was immense, with it went responsibility, the need to achieve targets, and a great deal of personal sacrifice.

From here I could hear the hum of machinery emanating from the company's three factory units in which over three thousand employees now applied their skills in making television sets and music centres. The estate sat on the Heads Of The Valley Road, west of Merthyr Tydfil.

But, to go back, I had been appointed chief executive of this joint venture company just a few weeks ago, following interviews by the chairman of the British owners in London and the vice-president of the Japanese owners in Tokyo.

On my joining day I met the man from whom I was taking over. "I'm sorry that I've got no time for you at the moment," he said. "The unions are going on strike for more money and it looks as though it's going to be a long drawn out affair."

Stepping quickly in, I said, "Hey, hang on a minute. You are about to leave the site. The negotiations you undertake will have

Tales From A Briefcase

repercussions between management and the employees long into the future, which will span my term as chief executive. I should sit in on the negotiations and even be leading them."

He looked at me hard. "Are you serious? Don't you think that I should clear up this issue and hand the company to you on a clean plate?"

"No I don't. I feel very strongly that I should take this on as my first job here. I will immediately talk to the chairman on the telephone and tell him that I propose to take over the company from you this afternoon, including the union problem."

I sat in an empty office waiting for the chairman's call, wondering if this is what our Japanese colleagues would call hari-kari. The phone rang and I picked up the instrument. "It's Robert James, Chairman, speaking from Hirwaun. The unions are threatening to walk out if their claim for more money is not settled this afternoon. I cannot accept that we negotiate under this threat, and I wish to take over the company now and handle the negotiations from now on. You will know from my c.v. that I've been involved in successfully settling several multi-union actions and I am confident that I can do it again here in Hirwaun."

He asked incredulously, "You're asking me to confirm you as chief executive right now and you handle the problem from here on?"

"Yes, Chairman. You selected me for the job because you thought I would be competent – that applies in two months time or today. I want it to be today."

"I hope that you know what you're doing, laddie. This could cause a long shut down."

"What I want is your backing to my telling them that if they walk today, the gates will clang behind them. I have a plan which will pay them more money but they'll have to earn it. I know that you have many acquaintances down here who will soon be on the telephone to you, asking if I have the authority to close the company. I want you to confirm that I have."

I heard his sharp intake of breath and the tapping of his pencil on his desktop. "Right, you've got it but I'll have your scalp if it doesn't come off." The telephone was slammed down from his end.

Tales From A Briefcase

I went to the outgoing director's office. "The chairman has agreed to my proposals. I take over as from now. You can telephone him to get this from the horse's mouth. I want an all-union meeting called in the works canteen in one hour. Until then, you should brief me on the background to the problem."

"Should I attend your meeting with the unions?"

"No, thank you. This is my show. If I mess it up, it's down to me and not you."

I found out that there were fifteen unions, supposedly co-ordinated by a factory convenor. In practice they each pushed their cases separately, and rarely agreed with one another. They wanted an annual pay hike in double figures, a rate which was two or three times the national average. I thought out my arguments and went down to the canteen where there were about fifty men and women. I stood at the front and waited until the chattering had stopped.

"My name is Robert James; I am the new managing director, as from ..." I looked at my wristwatch to emphasise the point, "twenty minutes ago, confirmed by the chairman."

I stared at them as this sank in.

"Is our old managing director involved in the negotiations this afternoon?" someone asked.

"No, he's leaving right now. There will be no negotiations today. I'm told that you'll walk if you cannot get the result you want. Then hear this. If you walk this afternoon, the gates of this company will clang behind you and will remain shut and employment will be terminated. Many thousands of families will be without a bread earner as a result of your action.

"You can avoid this. You will need to indicate that you are prepared to negotiate without putting management under duress. Do you hear me? I will take no questions now. I need your answer to this question one hour from now – are you prepared to come back to the negotiating table without preconditions? I think you should consult your regional convenors before then. I am prepared to consider more money for more work. In one hour then."

I left a hushed canteen, wondering if the factory convenor could pull them together to at least avoid the walk out.

Tales From A Briefcase

About forty-five minutes later my secretary came into my office to report that George Williams, the factory convenor, wanted to see me. I stood up as he entered and indicated a seat. I carried a chair to his side of the desk and sat in it, facing him.

"Well Mr Williams, I'd have given anything to have avoided that confrontation in the canteen and that you and I had met under different circumstances. We are not really on opposite sides of the table with conflicting viewpoints, you know. Your members can have more money under certain conditions but not while they are making threats. What have your members decided?"

"As you might have imagined, a few of the seniors, who knew Sir Arnold when he worked in this factory, have phoned him about your threat and he said you have his backing. As a result the hotheads have climbed down and we're working normally. Where do we go from here?"

"Starting tomorrow, a small management team will listen to representatives of each union to get the beefs on the table. I would like you to be present at each of the individual union meetings. Where the beefs are common across the unions, I will call a meeting with you and your representatives to list them and agree action points. I will also table a plan for performance bonuses. You know that our Japanese masters have furnished figures to show that our productivity is one third less than is achieved in Japan. We're going to have to promise them something. Can you live with that as long as we agree a short timetable for action?"

"Yes. I'll convey this back to the boys and girls. One question – is it true that you're a rugby referee and have transferred your membership from London to South Wales?"

"Yes, it's true, but that should have no bearing on the matters in hand. I foresee some difficult matches up the valleys when they know an Englishman is refereeing the game!"

He smiled and stuck out his hand, "Good luck, Mr James."

I returned to the managing director's office where my predecessor was packing up ready to leave for London.

"The chairman has a job for me back at headquarters. He thinks your immediate take-over is the right way. Good luck, old man!"

Tales From A Briefcase

I shook his hand, "Just stay for one meeting – with the management team. I'll summon it straightaway."

It was a bit shotgun, all this coming and going in a single day. The management team paid its compliments to the outgoing director; they also accepted the logic of a fast changeover, but I felt them eyeing me up cautiously.

Meeting over, I summoned my driver to take me to the country club which was to be my temporary home until the lease on an apartment at Porthcawl on the coast could be arranged. We went up a long drive, over rolling countryside with grazing sheep, and arrived at the main building, a large mansion from the turn of the century. Extensions had been added over the years but the graciousness of the buildings and view across the countryside had not been disturbed.

A male voice from the reception desk interrupted my thoughts, "Mr James, is it?"

"Yes, I suppose I'll be here for a few weeks."

"We have regular visitors from your factory and we've reserved a nice suite for your stay," he said in his lilting Welsh voice. "By the way, I'm Fred. I'm the owner and live here with my family. Dinner is served between seven and nine and here is the menu for this evening. On some evenings we have entertainment for single gentlemen." This last was accompanied by an obvious wink.

At dinner, the chops of Welsh lamb were perfect and superbly accompanied the Welsh bitter and the following large scotch. In the morning a huge cooked breakfast awaited me and my driver arrived spot on time.

Days ran into one another as we worked through numerous union meetings, proposing and negotiating the new wage structure. The representatives were very reasonable and certainly not as aggressive as I expected. It was clear that they carried their responsibility to the local community seriously. I met many of the external union secretaries at branch and national level and we soon found agreement on reducing the negotiating committees down from fifteen to three. One national general secretary made proposals for a single in-factory representational team. This was accepted by all and became the

Tales From A Briefcase

blueprint for later arrangements in multi-skilled factories throughout the UK.

Fred at the country club was concerned by my non-participation in the evening entertainment. "Blue movies on Thursday at eight o'clock!" he suggested.

"No thanks Fred. It wouldn't do for me to be sitting next to one of my salesmen shouting along with a blue movie."

"Next week we have a 'grab a granny' night. I'll arrange something, discreetly, with a very sympathetic matron from the old people's home. She drinks scotch just like you! I'll get her to come at nine o'clock."

"Fred you're very persistent. I'll try to be here."

On the following Thursday, I went down to the lounge where two ladies sat, obviously waiting to meet me. When they stood to shake hands I could see that one was about forty, tall, bosomy with dark hair and was called Megan. The other was slightly younger, short and quite plump and was named Lillian. They both talked with a valleys lilt.

Dancing to records played by a DJ had started and several couples were getting quite friendly already. Megan, Lillian and I decided that we were not dancers but talkers and drinkers. During the evening they explained that they ran a nursing home, Megan being the matron and Lillian being her assistant matron. Megan later revealed she liked gambling at the casino in Cardiff. Awash with scotch, the girls left in a taxi and I retired to my room with Megan's telephone number.

Megan and I had several dates in the following weeks, during which I moved into a flat at Porthcawl. It was owned by a charming old couple, Norman and Dorothy, from Lancashire, who had moved to Wales on retirement to pursue their common hobby, golf. They adopted me as a long-lost son and took great interest in my girl-friends. Megan got invited for tea with them, and they extracted all there was to be known about her background – or so they thought.

On one very stormy night with the rain bucketing down and high winds felling trees across roads Megan suggested that I should stay the night in her bungalow.

"I have two bedrooms; one is mine and the other for guests.

Tales From A Briefcase

You have a choice – mine or the guest room. Make up your mind while I wash in the bathroom."

I selected her room at the end of the corridor, entered, threw back the covers on a large double bed and stood there with my mouth open – black satin sheets. By God, I thought, this was going to be an exceptional night!

Throwing off my clothes, I slipped between the satin sheets, their silkiness already starting to give me an erection. With the bedroom light off and the sheet tucked under my chin, I waited for Megan to appear.

"Who's a naughty boy then?"

The voice came from a figure back lit by the corridor light, dressed in black leather. Long black leather thigh boots were surmounted by a tunic adorned with silver chains and a swastika armband; on her head was a peaked cap with a skull and crossbones badge. The leather whip thwacked between the leather-covered palm of her hand and the thigh of her boot.

Answer me," she commanded. "Who's a naughty boy?"

By now I was getting quite frightened by the apparition and the whip's deafening cracks. "I've done nothing wrong," I squealed.

"Have you not been punished before?" she asked calmly.

"No and I don't fancy it now."

"Let me show you my little gadget," she said, pulling open the doors of a deep cupboard and trundling out something akin to a vaulting horse with a cruciform attachment "Jump up and put you chest to the wooden cross. I'll lash your back for being un-cooperative."

"Not bloody likely. I'm not into this punishment game," I said pulling the sheets tighter under my chin.

"You disappoint me. You have a broad back and chest, just the job for punishment and, afterwards, I can tie you to the bed and make love to you."

"Not bloody likely," I yelled back at her, as I leapt from the bed, snatching at my clothes. I was completely dressed by the time I flung open her front door and was heading for my car.

When I next saw Fred, he couldn't stop laughing. With tears flowing down his face and much coughing and spluttering he explained, "Megan and Lillian are the biggest lesbians in the area. They and all their nurses are at it. The leather and the whips are just an aside: I wish I could have been a fly on the wall."

"You, bugger! You set me up. The least you can do is not spread this around."

For the rest of my time in the Valleys I lived in fear of the story getting out.

* * *

As in most big companies, budgeting time came around once a year. In this case, the budget was prepared by Welsh and Japanese staff and submitted to directors in England and Tokyo.

Having submitted the budget in advance, I appeared in Sir David's office to review it with him. As usual, he demanded improvements and changes, leaving the carefully considered management figures mauled, with sales moved upward, costs downward, and profit upward.

"Stop bloody arguing with me, James. You're always arguing. You will do what I want!"

I always left feeling that the exercise was a complete waste of time. Now I had to face the Japanese with their big meetings and consensus decisions. Arriving by air after an overnight flight over the pole, I was met at the airport by a manager whose job in Japan was equivalent to the one I held in Britain. He took me to the company guest house just outside Tokyo and we arranged to meet for lunch. The setting was a dining room with flowers and low tables at which I squatted.

"Robert-san," he started in good English, "we must be friends and have a good understanding between us. You call me Mitsu."

I noted the instant familiarity, unusual in Japanese early relationships.

"Certainly, Mitsu. Have you read my business plan? We should discuss it."

"Yes, yes. I have read it but we should drink together before we discuss more serious matters. You are a whisky drinker aren't you?"

"Yes," I replied, wondering how he acquired this information and how the whisky would give a better understanding of my budget.

"We have a very good Japanese whisky – Suntory, OK?"

Tales From A Briefcase

I had heard of the brand especially distilled for the Japanese lower body weight and metabolism. In theory I should be able to drink him under the table.

"OK," I responded.

The meal of several courses was served with extreme politeness and deference by kimono-garbed waitresses. I noticed that Mitsu talked down to them almost to the point of rudeness. By the time we started on the budget we each had downed about four glasses of Suntory and Mitsu had become belligerent. After a few more glasses he started to weave about on his crossed legs and to mumble a mixture of English and Japanese words. I could see it was leading to a drinking competition. Glasses were refilled the instant they became empty.

"Kempai!" Mitsu's glass was emptied in one gulp, and I felt obliged to respond in kind. As I watched, I saw his eyes closing and he toppled forward on to the table. The waitresses sent for two manservants who quietly carried him away to his bed, hardly having discussed my budget.

The next morning I met Mitsu, who clearly felt that he had lost face during the evening. "I have been pleased to write a complimentary report on your budget to my superior whom you will meet this evening."

Oh my God, I thought, not another drinking competition! A smart chauffeur-driven Lexus met me at the guest house and took me to a Japanese restaurant set in rather splendid gardens with waterfalls and cherry trees in blossom. My host was older than Mitsu and more formal. He had read the business plan and had some comments on the budget which we got around to discussing before the Suntory was produced. Several Suntorys later, he slowly sank beneath the table murmuring, "I have approved your report."

My report was reviewed during the following two days, in normal working hours, by managers from two more senior levels, and received approval.

On my last day I was received by a vice-president of the Japanese partners. Formalities were swept aside. He had been at Cambridge University before the war and had become friends with an English undergraduate who later had become a Lord and

Tales From A Briefcase

was a director of our British group. After the war they had met again and discussed the possibility of totally merging the Japanese group with a British group with a view to creating a dominant international group in electrical products. Sir Arnold had reviewed the proposal but suggested that a limited joint venture should proceed before a full integration, and the joint venture in South Wales was created using an existing factory of the English partner.

I learned that, prior to this, Sir David had nearly scuppered the project at the eleventh hour. After months of planning and legal negotiations, a delegation from Japan had arrived in London to sign the agreement. On the eve of the signing, Sir David had called the British board together and told them he could not proceed with the agreement. When pressed for a reason, he replied, "You can't trust those Japanese buggers, they bombed Pearl Harbour, didn't they?"

The British board was obviously horrified at Sir David's inadequate excuse and prevailed on him to sign the agreement. After several cancelled meetings, Sir David was persuaded to meet the Japanese delegation, who, by now, had waited over two days for a meeting. He turned on the charm and beamed at the Japanese, saying complimentary things about their nation and group, and signed the agreement with a flourish.

The factory in Wales produced TV sets and music centres badged with their respective group's emblems but with common internal electronics designed with superior Japanese technology. The Japanese had the last laugh because the designs incorporated components which could only be purchased from the Japanese group. The agreement assumed almost equal supply of products to both. However, by now the Japanese promotional campaign in Europe had convinced the viewing public that their products were superior, and they penetrated the English group's share of the market to such an extent that the English-badged sales all but disappeared. Inevitably the factory's output became biased towards the Japanese.

"Robert-san," ended the Japanese vice-president, "The Japanese directors are delighted with your management of the Welsh company. You have given us budgeted output, sales and

Tales From A Briefcase

profits. We, your Japanese colleagues, accept your budget and share the ownership of it with you. We notice that you request one million pounds investment in new automated production lines and subject to our UK partner's approval, we are happy to approve this investment. Good luck for your return journey."

* * *

The chairman had obviously heard from the Japanese vice-president on the outcome of my budget meetings in Tokyo. I had a very irate letter from him saying that I had no right to negotiate a capital expenditure deal for new equipment, and reminding me that my duties lay firstly with the English group. This was basically untrue because my contract of employment was with the joint venture company. But my relationship with Sir David had clearly deteriorated and he was obviously going to take the Japanese to task over a variety of issues. I could guess that the chairman might wish to withdraw from domestic products and, for other reasons, might wish to break up the joint venture.

It was some months later that I was summoned to meet the chairman at the London headquarters and was shown into his office with the minimum of ceremony. He was sitting behind his large desk wearing a striped blue and white shirt, red tie and red braces. He looked at me over the top of his half-lens spectacles.

"Tell me, Mr James, what percentage of the output of your factory goes to the Japanese?"

We both knew what he was getting at and where it would lead. "About 72%, Chairman."

"And Mr James, what is your total annual sales rate and profit?"

"Seventy-five million and twenty million respectively."

"And, Mr James under the joint venture agreement, the Japanese get a half share of the pre-tax net profits?"

"Yes, Chairman"

"What is your total component spend to achieve seventy five million pounds a year?

"About twenty-five million pounds."

"And how much of this is bought from the Japanese?"

"Twelve million."

Tales From A Briefcase

"Aha," he exclaimed, his eyes gleaming above his spectacles, his hooked nose pointing at me accusingly, "it's hardly a joint venture in the application. They knock us out of the market and take a second profit on components."

"We have to remember, Chairman, that the agreement gives the English group a fifteen per cent differential, the Japanese having to price their products higher."

"James, you are just a bloody Jap lover. You've supplied more sets to them than they deserve. You encouraged them to wreck my European sales and destroyed my television market." At this juncture he stood up and pointed at me. "You're bloody well fired. Get out!"

I drove back to the Welsh valleys, said goodbye to my staff and went on to Porthcawl to pack up my belongings in the flat. I resolved that if I did not get my agreed year's severance pay, I would fight the case on grounds of unfair dismissal. I couldn't afford to lose; I had a depressive wife in an expensive clinic, a daughter at university and a son at boarding school. In the end, my barrister won my case on the steps of the court.

Decision time had arrived. Would I go on being the lackey to chairmen of large groups, bow to their enormous egos, hop on planes at a moment's notice and circle the world, sacrifice my personal life and contract out caring for my children? Or should I regain control of my life and my destiny, become a father again and find a different purpose in life? It would be the latter. I would start my own business consultancy in the south west, where the values of living had not yet been totally eroded.

Tales From A Briefcase

BOOK 4

TALES FROM CONSULTANCY

I found consultancy a very different sort of activity to managing a business. I now gave advice, and hopefully got paid fees for it; it was the client's choice whether to accept or reject my proposals. What gave the job interest was the wide spectrum of assignments, their widely spread locations and the interesting entrepreneurs who ran these small client companies. Some of the projects were highly enterprising and unusual, to say nothing of entertaining!

Tales From A Briefcase

CHAPTER 32

BULL'S SPERM AND HARBOURMASTERS

FUNDING FOR BULL'S SPERM

"Do you see this?" the bull owner handed me a short length of plastic tube like a straw, "It's called a 'straw' in the trade, mostly because it looks like one. Can you see the liquid in it? Well, that's bull's sperm. We sell that for about £100."

The liquid was almost colourless. I was told that the sperm was mixed with a glucose product to keep it in a fluid form and the straw was stored in a refrigerator. When a cow needed to be impregnated, a vet or the farmer broke the tip off the straw and deposited the contents into the cow's rear end. With luck she would become pregnant and eventually produce an offspring or several. The sperm came from a bull registered on a database containing his hereditary line and data on the milking performance of his female progeny. The price of the sperm was fixed on his daughters' milking performance.

The best sperm banks for Holstein cows are to be found in the USA, where a computer-aided selection can be made. A refrigerated embryo of likely bovine parents can be flown in by air and selected cows are impregnated. From the resulting births in the UK, a male is selected and put into the test programme. His female progeny is monitored for milking performance over several cycles of lactation to prove the quality of the UK bull.

But to get to that point, five years of trials had to pass before the bull had proven himself as a potential father. A bull with proven quality sperm would, after the testing period had elapsed, have a capital value of millions of pounds. The bull would produce millions of straws of sperm each year. Annually, these would be worth millions of pounds of sales and profits.

Tales From A Briefcase

"I want to set up an investment club to buy bulls' sperm, breed prize bulls and make profits on the sale of sperm. The problem is that it takes five years to prove that we have a champion on our hands and before we start earning good money. If we get the selection wrong or have bad luck, we end up with an animal that won't yield a return. Our investors know the score, accept the odds and are prepared to gamble. I want you to write the investment prospectus. I think you should come up to the insemination farm in Worcestershire and see the process."

At the farm, I met the owner of the bull who started to explain the process of collecting the animal's sperm.

"The bull is so heavy that a cow or heifer would collapse under his weight. We use a young bull to take the strain. The donor bull is made enthusiastic by walking him around on bark chippings which stimulate him sensually, and when he is sufficiently horny we take him over to the young bull."

He pointed to a small man about the size of a jockey standing nearby. "Do you see that man there, wearing a riding helmet and carrying that conical receptacle? He dashes under the donor bull and collects the semen."

Two men led 'Malvern Lad', a bull that weighed about two tons, into the barn and started to walk him around on the bark chippings. The bull started to snort and stamp his feet and I could see his excitement reflected in the growing size of his penis. Once thoroughly aroused, Malvern Lad was led over to the small bull where he leapt on its back and his desire changed to fury, with great snorts and stampings. The little man in the helmet ducked under the bull's belly, avoiding the mass of swinging animal legs, and caught the semen as it was ejaculated into the conical stainless steel collector. After the climax, the man and collector ducked back from under the animals and Malvern Lad stood quietly to be led away to recuperate until the next session.

The prospectus that I wrote for the business gave potential investors the chances and probabilities of success and the planned return on investment. The business plan involved breeding one potential champion a year, and there was a 25% chance of an outstanding bull.

Tales From A Briefcase

I didn't follow up the project, but hopefully the investors were eventually satisfied with their investments and the progeny of the selected bulls produced remarkable milking results.

A SCOTTISH PORT OPERATION

"I'd like you to come to Perth for about six months, help me install the new computer and software and get our accounts straight. Maybe you'd look into the operations and see where you think we might improve."

I looked at the person offering me this opportunity. Craig Finlayson was a hefty Aberdonian, his accent difficult to understand, but the handsome fees I would negotiate would help me overcome that. He ran his own port operating company from the quayside at Perth and lived in the centre of town. Making money and golf were his two passions.

I booked myself into a local hotel and started the consultancy assignment. Craig gave me the run down on the local personalities, and as I later found out, they were all wild, sometimes outrageous and on occasions outright barmy, but more often than not drunk, as the following story illustrates.

The port could accommodate up to three or maybe four coasters. On one particular sunny autumn day, with low tide on the River Tay and no ships in port, I went up to the local pub, the 'Inn At The Port', for a lunchtime sandwich and a beer.

The harbourmaster, Hamish McDougal, sat on the terrace of the pub, surveying his kingdom. From there you could see the River Tay, as it rounded the last corner between Dundee and Perth and flowed under the road bridge, the last bit of navigable river before the port. Hamish was proud of his port; each year it handled over a quarter of a million tons of goods, in and out: cement from Gdansk, wood from Latvia, tractor parts from France and Holland, rape seed and whisky out to Holland and Germany, and electronic components bound for all over Europe.

Aye, the Port of Perth played its part in the local economy and Hamish undertook the responsibility of his position very seriously. Woe betide any coaster captain or pilot who fell foul of his wishes. Now he finished his fourth pint of beer and called for the landlord to bring his bottle of whisky, the Famous Grouse. Its label carried descending biro marks to signify the level when he last supped from it. Quite a few more drams left, he thought, and poured three fingers into a glass. He had just got the glass of whisky to his lips when a voice called out from the pub's door. It was Donald Kirkpatrick, the manager of the port's warehousing operation.

"I see I'm just in time to share the dregs of that fine whisky with ye."

Hamish scowled, "You buy your own bloody whisky. This is medicinal. I'm just building up my spirits to receive that bloody German captain from Frederikshavn. He's bringing in a load of cement on his ship... God, what's it called?"

"Seehund. It means seal. It hasn't seen a coat of paint in the last decade and is so dented and battered it's amazing it floats. He's carrying 200 tons in bags and I'm unloading and storing it. Captain Schmidt will be picking up the Dundee pilot and, as usual, they'll be swapping whisky and schnapps all the way down the Firth of Tay." Donald tossed down a big slug of Grouse from his own bottle which had suddenly appeared.

They both sat morosely contemplating the Seehund's arrival but still enjoyed the whisky's burn down their gullets and the warming sun on their near-bald heads.

"Drowning our fears for the impending onslaught, are we?"

It was Rory McMichael, the manager of the transport company that handled the goods inland. He had organised beer with whisky-chasers as he sat on a terrace bench. "Bet you a fiver that they're pissed when they arrive. Bet you another that they can't moor the ship first attempt."

"Good odds," observed Hamish.

"Take ye on," shouted Donald.

They relapsed into silence, lost in their thoughts and trying to anticipate the havoc Seehund's arrival would cause.

"Captain McDougal. Ye're wanted on the phone. It's your assistant."

Hamish was very proud of his honorary title 'Captain' and made his way into the pub at a decorous pace befitting a superior about to communicate with his inferior.

Tales From A Briefcase

He returned to the terrace. "The silly bugger has dug himself into the river bank on the ebb tide and can't pull off. He'll have to wait for the next flood tide this evening and arrive as it gets dark. With that and the fact he'll have drunk a lot more between now and then, we'll be in for some fun and games during docking. Thank God there are no other boats in port!"

The three drinkers decided not to return to their offices but sat on the pub's terrace until the sun went down. They drank quietly but continuously until the coaster's arrival was heralded by long blasts on its siren and frantic sweeps of searchlights mounted on its bridge.

Hamish returned to his small shack on the quayside, from where he collected a hand-held loudhailer. His friends from the pub joined him and he gave them a running commentary on the progress of the coaster, now with only three hundred yards to the dock.

"Just look at that silly sod! His line is all wrong. He's sailing into the shallows near the riverbank." And then into the megaphone, "Hello, Seehund. Did ye nay pick up the pilot at Dundee?"

A megaphone blared back to him from the ship's bridge, "It's me, you silly bugger, Jimmy MacFadden. You've no put the harbour lights on and we can't see a bloody thing."

"Serves you bloody right for sticking her in the mud and missing the tide! Fine pilot ye've turned out to be!"

Captain Schmidt had a bridge loudhailer and joined in the exchanges, but in German. Needless to say the three participants had had their fill of spirits. The ship reached the right-angled bend, the wheel was spun and it hit the bank. The engines were put into reverse and eventually she pulled off.

Hamish was not to be restrained from a volley of abuse down the megaphone. "Ye silly bastards. If you do that in the dock, the quays will cave in and block the port. I'll come aboard and steer the bloody thing!"

The pilot could take no more abuse of his authority and bellowed back on his megaphone, "Ye'll do no such thing, Hamish McDougal. Ye haven't a licence to drive this boat. I'll have ye put away for breaking the law, ye auld weasel!"

Tales From A Briefcase

Captain Schmidt, megaphone in hand, also joined in: "You bloody Englanders. Immer trunken!"

The ship's engines were revved full ahead and it hit the quay first with the bow and then with the stern. Then, with engines running 'full astern' it hit the south quay removing large chunks of concrete before juddering to a halt, its bow resting against the north jetty. By now Hamish McDougal was dancing liked a whirling dervish, his face a full-blooded red. Those on board and the on-shore spectators were folded up with laughter, once they knew that the coaster had not been holed. A tug from Dundee was summoned and arrived with the next tide to position the little ship snugly against the undamaged quay and moor it securely.

While his cargo was being unloaded, over the next few days, the German captain and the pilot retired to a period of serious drinking at the pub. Not to be denied his daily refreshment, on the first day Hamish McDougal entered the pub with a great banging of the door, ordered his drink at the bar and sat at a table away from the others. Fortified with a shot of whisky, he then marched over to the table where the German captain and the pilot were sitting, removed a document from his coat pocket and slapped it down on the table in front of them.

"To show there's no hard feelings, there ye are. A summons for both of ye to appear in court tomorrow to pay for the damage to the quay, the cost of the tug and compensation for lost business by your blocking the port."

With my assignment completed and the new computer and accounting system successfully installed, I headed back home to the south. Nobody would believe my story about the port and how it handled a quarter of million tons of goods each year.

CHAPTER 33

THE BIKERS CAFÉ IN BRIGHTON

We sat in the Grand Hotel at Brighton, sipping tea from beautiful chinaware and surrounded by grey-headed, fur-dressed ladies for whom this was a regular pastime if not a daily occurrence.

"You're telling me that you want to set up a bikers' pub café on the sea front at Brighton and you can make it an economic success?"

The two men sitting opposite me both nodded. One was of medium height and had a cheerful engaging face; he was a writer, musician, video producer and had a general interest in things maritime. The other was tall, thin and wore glasses, acted, played guitar and was typical of many of the floating, single, middle-aged population which you can find in Brighton.

"You want me to get you funding for the project which involves renting the large Victorian premises at the end of Madeira Drive?"

They both nodded again.

"Do you know anything about running pubs? Do you ride motorbikes? Do you know anything about biking culture and what bikers spend their money on?"

This time they shook their heads. The tall thin one, Danny, said, "We do know that Brighton is not only full of bikers but they come down from all around London and they have money to spend."

"You tell me the premises are owned by the council. Are you sure they wish to lease them? Have you talked to the council's decision makers?"

They shuffled in their chairs and the shorter of them, Nick, explained, "I've a friend who works for the Entertainment

Department. He said we would be welcomed with open arms if we could offer a project bringing leisure business to Brighton."

I thought for a few minutes and then said, "Well, gentlemen, I can see that you have a dream and enthusiasm for it. But you have no experience, have done no market research and haven't formally approached the council for the premises. And you've given no thought to funding the project. What can I do for you?"

"You've come recommended as a planning and funding consultant. We would like to engage you to develop the plan and handle the negotiations with the council and with a brewery that could become involved."

"How do I get paid for my input?"

"We'll give you a commission for raising the funding. If you throw in your management experience we'll give you some shares in the company."

"What company?" I queried.

Danny responded, "The company you are going to form for us!"

"I see. You'll bring nothing but enthusiasm to the party and I provide the management experience, raise the funds and negotiate the deals, taking the risk that if it doesn't come off, I won't get paid. No down-side for you but plenty for me."

"We'll give you a third of the shares," offered Nick trying to be encouraging.

"A third of nothing is nothing. The company has no value until it has traded. Anyway, we'll have to take on a pub or catering professional to manage the day-today running of the site and he'll want a cut. It will have to be a four-way split," I warned.

"OK," agreed Nick, "a four-way split it will be."

I poured myself another cup of tea and sat back in the armchair, weighing them up. They had arrived at middle age with no track record of business success and with little accumulated wealth. Their present skills were not relevant to the project now being discussed. They would, however, require important roles in the business and there would be conflict between them and the professionals to be introduced. A strong chairman or chief executive would be needed to pilot the project through the early stages of planning and trading.

"I'll tell you my conditions from coming in. One – I am appointed chairman and chief executive and you will obey my operational commands. Two – you will be shareholders but there will be no benefits and power for you in the earlier years. Three – you will also be directors and will abide by the board's majority decisions; as chairman I will have the casting vote in the event of a hung vote. Four – you will have employment contracts with modest salaries and expenses and can be voted off the board for misbehaviour. Five – you will required to input twenty hours a week and attend board and operational meetings. Six – as directors of a company seeking bank funding, you will be required to submit your curricula vitae and be credit investigated; if anything unsavoury is found, you might not be able to be a director.

I will also want a funding contract as well as an employment contract; my fees for funding will be 10 per cent of funds raised and my expenses will include a rented flat in Brighton.

Those are my terms and they are not negotiable. Take it or leave it. I'll go for a walk on the front for a quarter of an hour and you can give me your decision when I return."

Rather smugly, I left the hotel and crossed the busy coastal road to the seafront parade; I had certainly stated conditions which made my involvement worthwhile. I would get little management help from them and the choice of the catering professional would be a key feature to the success of the business.

On my return I found them with a raft of questions needing answering, an acceptance of my conditions and a suggestion for a catering specialist. Kevin Thompson, they told me, was a café manager in Brighton but had been a publican for several years. He was looking for an improved position. We agreed to interview him.

We agreed that I would write the business plan for the bank and brewery funding, that we would have an early meeting with representatives of the local council, and would inspect their dilapidated building. We met the chairman of the Seafront Development Committee and the entertainments officer, and presented our short written proposal. They confirmed that the council were looking for a tenant for the building in question. There would be a stipulation in the lease that the tenant would have to administer the public toilets and operate the lift all the year round. They agreed to advise the council of our interest at the next meeting, and suggested that we submit a comprehensive proposal at the meeting following.

Standing on the promenade at the end of Madeira Drive, the brick building with Victorian wrought ironwork stretched for a hundred and fifty feet. It had a large terrace at roof level connecting to an elevated pathway and a green domed tower loomed further upward carrying a lift from the promenade level to the main road above.

There were two entrances, one at the western end of the building and one located about two thirds along, leading to the lift and public lavatories. The basement was large and fairly dry. Whereas the structure was in reasonable condition, most of the large Victorian style windows were holed or cracked; the toilets were in need of modernisation and the whole needed decorating. The wrought ironwork was much rusted in places. The place would need rewiring, re-plumbing and new ventilation geared to its prospective use. My guess was an investment of £200,000 to recondition and another £100,000 to fit it for use as a café and bar.

I started to develop a crude funding plan. As we would only be licensing the use of the building from the council, nearly all the cost of reconditioning the building would be lost to the company. The only deal that made sense was to get the council to carry the refurbishment costs and recover them from rent over a longish lease. If we could negotiate an annual rental of £64,000 and a ten-year lease, our financial plan might start to look economic.

I felt that the beer consumption might be sufficient to attract a ten-year brewery loan of £100,000 to cover fitting out, and I started to approach the major chains to discuss possibilities. I decided I would approach banks for a further £100,000 to cover working capital, including promotional costs which would be substantial. With £400,000 as our funding target I started to work on our proposal for the council.

Tales From A Briefcase

There were numerous meetings with the council at various levels and with different committees. There was one official who suggested a personal consideration for support; the board was divided on this and I used my chairman's casting vote to decline to participate in this activity. The final approval eventually came through.

We decided that the building should be divided into three ground floor operating areas, bar with stage, kitchen and café, and the public amenities. The basement would contain beer and food cellars.

It was high time we appointed our catering person. We summoned Kevin Thompson to attend an interview at the Grand Hotel. He came over as an affable chap, knowledgeable about the catering industry, and gave the impression that he would manage the operation efficiently. His experience of running pubs and restaurants turned out to be ideal for our purpose, but as an added bonus he was known to the licensing justices and the local police, a fact which we felt would ease our passage to obtaining drinking and entertainment licences. We engaged him on a contract involving a shareholding, a nominal salary and a cut of the takings.

The business plan written, we were able to find a bank and an equipment leasing company to provide adequate funds and the future of the project rested entirely on the council's agreement to a lease. We did a financial deal with a national brewery company and established contracts with food suppliers.

Whereas the bar and café would provide income from the general passing public and local bikers, Danny and Nick felt that important income contributions would come from special bikers' events attracting visitors to Brighton from far and wide, and from entertainment events using the stage in the bar. They set about promoting these as the contractors moved in to refurbish the premises. After four long months and an overspend on the budget, the contractors moved out and we had a press launch and an opening night.

Our problems with Danny started early on. He was being pursued by the tabloid press because he was the father of an up and coming page three starlet and actress; there had a been a messy divorce from her mother, and he had been a less than attentive father in her young teens. The press had cottoned on to the fact that he was a director of our company and we were plagued for stories.

Danny also had numerous contacts with bands and groups in the London area and signed them up for concerts in Brighton on enormous fees leaving little profit for the business. The time had come to remind him of his directorial responsibilities, particularly as he had taken to drinking at the bar and not paying for his drinks. He began not to turn up for meetings and disappeared from Brighton for long periods of time. At one board meeting I proposed that he should be sacked as a director but was outvoted by my colleagues. He was eventually excluded from all the important decision-making and refused to sign director's guarantees required of all directors in funding matters. He wrote to the bank explaining his lack of cohesion with the rest of the management team and the bank consequently became sensitive to the lack of unity at board level.

Meanwhile, Nick had been working steadily at a marketing plan involving special events. He arranged a London to Brighton mass bikers' rally in aid of the Variety Club of Great Britain. It was planned for 5,000 bikers to pay an entrance fee to start at Hyde Park in London and ride at controlled intervals to the front at Brighton. We had planned the event in detail, involving the police at both ends and the army to help with the organisation. Observers were positioned along the route, which was helpfully signposted by the AA. At the Brighton end, we had arranged marshals to handle parking arrangements.

Communications were established along the route by means of mobile telephones.

At nine o'clock on the day, we received our first call from London, "Hello Brighton Base, London Despatch Centre here. We have just despatched the first thousand. I think we have more than five thousand wanting to join the run."

At ten o'clock another call, "Hello Brighton Base, London Despatch here. We're bit under pressure. We now have despatched five thousand and there's a huge crowd of bikers queuing up all around Hyde Park, waiting to join the run. Maybe

Tales From A Briefcase

there's another five thousand! They've all paid their five pounds entrance fee."

We hurriedly revised our parking plans on Madeira Drive. At eleven o'clock, London telephoned again. "We've sent off another five thousand and there's still more to come!"

The telephoned reports started to come in from observers and police on the route: the first arrivals would be with us in just a few minutes. By one o'clock nearly twenty thousand bikers had arrived in Brighton and were parking up Madeira Drive to the Black Rock Car park, which soon became full-up. Bikers then started to fill the public car parks and side streets in central Brighton.

The bar and cafe did a roaring trade from those who actually could get in, and the other visitors swamped the kiosks all the way down the beach road. In Madeira Drive, lorry trailers carrying bands played every conceivable type of music and kiddies' amusements did a roaring trade. During the afternoon, relief supplies of beer and food were ferried into the place via the lift.

After a rainy start, blue skies appeared in time for the Red Arrows to do a spectacular low flying display over the sea. The party went on into the evening and visitors with tents pitched on the racecourse continued it until dawn.

The event raised sufficient funds to purchase four buses for the Variety Club and make a contribution to the costs of refurbishing a children's home.

There were many such events planned by Nick. Another memorable occasion was the Save the Children event in November. BBC Television hooked the Bikers' Café into the national network and a live broadcast was transmitted from Brighton. Again thousands of pounds were raised for the charity. Later, several country music radio broadcasts were made from the premises. The Bikers Café had really been put on the map and bikers came from all over the world, from America as part of bikers' European tours, and for weekend rides out from Holland and Germany via the Channel ferries.

Sales continued to rise, mainly from bikers' activities, but disquieting problems emerged and political rumblings had

Tales From A Briefcase

started. The public lavatories on the site had become the haunt for drug trading and taking. We co-operated with the police in supervising them more closely. One morning a cleaner found a dead body. And the Brighton tearaways began to use Madeira Drive as a course for car racing and skid turns; CCTV was installed but it continued until there was a serious crash and deaths.

Danny had taken legal advice on his employment contract and a summons was lodged against the company for wrongful dismissal. Maliciously, he had also involved the local press on this and the other problems, not the least being the local citizens concerned about disturbance caused by the low-flying Red Arrows to the herring gulls during their breeding period.

Whilst all this had very little impact on the company's sales, the brewery curtailed their loan and stopped its supply of beer: their loan contract prevented us taking beer from other breweries. The suspended brewery loan in turn stopped the development of the property. The bank, losing confidence in the directors, called in the overdraft. The council then became concerned over the adverse press publicity and they halted property development and started to review the property contract on the grounds of breaches of undertaking. It was not a coincidence that a major pub chain made an approach to acquire the lease of our building from the council whilst we were still tenants.

This chain of events took place over three months culminating with the start of the summer sales season. The receivers appointed by the bank operated the facility through the high income summer season to their considerable financial advantage.

I departed Brighton without personal financial damage but with my reputation severely dented, resolving to remain a consultant and not participate again in managing a client's businesses.

Tales From A Briefcase

CHAPTER 34

HATS, WRAPPING AND VENDING MACHINES

NORTHUMBERLAND: HATS IN THE BELFRY

"I'm under terrible pressure from the bank. Originally they promised an extension to the company's loan but they have retracted that. My UK customers, like Selfridges, Debenhams and John Lewis, are taking longer to pay but my business is still growing. I need you to prepare a new business plan and find me some more funds."

Sitting across the table from me was a thin, dark-haired man with brown eyes and a very angular nose. From his curriculum vitae I gathered that he was a graduate in business management, had spent time in marketing for a number of clothing manufacturers and had bought the fashion accessory company about four years ago. A factory employing about two hundred people was based in a Northumberland village just north of Newcastle.

Seasonal orders for fashion accessories were taken from the major high street stores. The products were knitwear, such as gloves, scarves and knitted hats, or were cut and sewn from cloth and made into clothing items. The stores favoured the small company as a supplier because it delivered on time and had a sustained good quality. Clearly the company's good reputation would permit it to feed other accessories down the same channels.

Clive Redford was well dressed, articulate and had an attractive speaking voice. However, he was not flashy, drove a modest car, had a modest house, and with his wife was often the first in and last out of the factory every day. His ideas for expansion were sound and logical. I should be able to produce a convincing business plan which would get debt funding from banks and equity funding from the venture capitalists.

Clive's expansion plan involved investing in faster and more modern production equipment, introducing more accessories such as leather gloves and sunglasses, and exporting to America. The equipment in the factory had been bought a decade ago, needed considerable operator attendance and was wearing out. By contrast, the new knitting machines on offer were semi- or fully automatic and produced four times faster than the old ones. The cost over four years would be half a million pounds.

The Co-op, which had its own factories, was selling them off. Clive had his eye on a leather glove factory in Wigan which might be acquired at a very economic price. Also, a hat retail group in America, 'Hats in the Belfry', had been offered for sale and might be used as a market entry.

Using invoice discounting as a means of funding debtors, and leaving aside the cost of new equipment, the company needed another quarter of a million pounds for working capital, such as the cash needed to fund the supply and stocking of raw materials through to the point of sale to the stores.

Within a month, we had our plan, based on many assumptions, ready for presentation to funders. There were many estimates that had to be proved, particularly the cost of the glove company and the American retail chain.

With Clive busy just running the business, I was given the task of negotiating these acquisitions. The glove factory in Wigan was a light, airy building in a good state of repair. Most of its operatives were women, the male employees being toolmakers and maintenance engineers. There was little complicated machinery, which mainly consisted of presses for material cutting and industrial sewing machines. The products varied from multicoloured leather fashion gloves to heavy gauntlets for riot police. The deal was to acquire the business 'lock stock and barrel' taking over the customer orders, management and staff for a negotiated price.

I flew to the USA to visit the owners of 'Hats in the Belfry' at Annapolis. They had a chain of seven retail stores from

Tales From A Briefcase

Florida to Boston and San Francisco and two in New York City, one in the old quays area now turned into a shopping mall. They retailed every kind of hat imaginable, from high fashion to comical. It was clear that the English company's hat range would fit nicely and that other accessories could be added to the offer. During my stay I was invited to a passing out parade at the Naval Academy. The owners and I arrived at a mutually agreed price for the business and I headed back to Northumberland.

In my absence, Clive had been presenting our business plan to venture capital funders and had generated interest in inward investment. With our acquisitions defined, our factory extension planned and investment in new equipment specified, we were in good shape to close deals with potential investors. Two City investment companies made offers for a minority share interest and it was time to select our future investment partner.

The deal went through successfully after a six-month funding exercise, the money became available, the acquisitions were made and the expansion began. Clive offered me a senior job, but Northumberland was a bit too far from my family focus in the south.

NORWICH AND WRAPPING MAGAZINES

My bank manager had promised to introduce me to some companies who might become clients. His name was Brian and we had developed a social relationship involving visits to each other's houses and our children playing together.

"I have one client in particular whom I'd like you to meet," Brian told me. "He's a likeable fellow but his level of debt has become uncomfortably high: we shouldn't have let him go that far. The company administration and main factory is in Norwich. They're in wrapping of magazines – you know, your Sunday newspaper supplements come wrapped in clear plastic and many monthly institute journals are wrapped with a printed label inserted, sometimes with an advertising insertion included. He has automatic machines which do the whole job at forty thousand copies an hour.

"The success of the business is geared to machine loading and he's such a smooth talker he seems to keep the orders flowing and the machines loaded. However, he's a bit of a playboy and one helluva boozer; champagne's his tipple. Are you interested in taking him on?"

"Sure. I'll have a go at him." I responded. "What are you trying to achieve?"

"Losing a difficult client! He has a six hundred thousand pound overdraft with us. We'd like somebody else to take on the risk and get the bank repaid. It's getting too risky for us."

"Are we thinking of replacing the bank loan with equity funding? I hear Norwich Union has gone into venture capital. They may give preference to a local investee."

"Yes, that sounds interesting. The bank would be following a conventional funding route and come out of it smelling of roses. I'll ask him to give you a call."

It was a few days later when I had a mid-morning call from the bank's client. "Hello," a cheery voice blasted down the telephone, "I'm Clive Woodward, owner of the magazine mailing company in Norwich. Brian at my bank in Paddington has suggested we should meet up for a chat. Can you meet me at the International Press Club in the City at two o'clock tomorrow afternoon?"

"Yes."

"Good. Ask at reception; they'll know where I am." He sounded very confident and not like a man with his bank manager trying to call in a loan.

I called at the Press Club on the following afternoon and was shown to a large round table in a lounge where four men were sitting. One stood up and proffered his hand, "Robert James, I presume."

Shaking his hand, I said "Correctly presumed," and waited for an introduction to the others, surveying the tabletop covered with empty champagne bottles.

"Gentlemen, this a Robert James, my bank manager's spy. He's here to see that I don't run off with the bank's money and to ensure I live a less riotous life."

The table erupted with laughter and comments like, 'that'll be the day', and 'let's have another bottle of champagne'.

Clive took up the mood, "Yeah, let's have another bottle." He nodded at me, "You'll have a glass and then you're corrupted."

Tales From A Briefcase

So for the next hour the jollities continued, until Clive's guests thought they should return to their editorial desks for an hour, before retiring to the pub.

"Well," he said, fixing me with a rather glassy-eyed stare, "what are you going to do about it?"

"Well, I'm certainly not a spy. My job is to help you find some investors who will put sufficient money in the business to repay the bank and leave you some spare for expansion. Despite your...," I waved my hand over the table top, "heavy expenses, you have a good business, plenty of orders and modern equipment. We should be able to find someone who'll put three quarters of a million pounds into it for a minority stake or, for a larger sum, buy it outright."

"Sounds good. When do you start?"

"I live in Bristol. I'll motor over next Monday morning. But, before that, we'll have to agree terms – fees, accommodation and travel costs."

He looked aghast, "You mean I have to pay you for doing the bank's job?"

"The bank won't pay me, for sure. Here are my proposals which you should talk over with the bank manager; he'll increase your overdraft to cover my costs but I won't start without my contract being signed."

Later in the week I received a signed copy of my contract from Clive and made my preparations to drive across England to Norwich.

The company office was tucked away in a backstreet and the factory was on an industrial estate near the airport. Each of the four automated lines ran nearly the length of the factory and had loading stations along its length. The literature to be wrapped was continuously fed into a loader near the start of the line, which was also fed by a large roll of plastic with a second roll standing by to be laced in at an appropriate time. Auto-inserters were positioned along the line to interleave advertising flyers within the literature. About halfway down the line, a computer printed out addresses and inserted a label into the package which moved into the final process of heat sealing and trimming. With an average run being processed at forty thousand pieces an hour, few went longer than three hours.

The production manager was key to the operation, ensuring supplies and operators were available when needed, and Clive had selected well. Sometimes a nightshift was organised to meet tough deadlines or overcome backlog problems caused by machinery breakdown. All in all, the factory worked like clockwork.

Apart from a sales manager, who handled the repeat business, Clive himself established the new customers and accounts. He would disappear for days at a time, normally to London, ostensibly on business but I felt sure that boozing with his cronies in the Press Club and dalliance with a few girl-friends featured strongly in his timetable.

We produced the business plan and financial proposals for the venture capital funders and made our representations. Three funders became interested and an investor in Norwich was first to make an acceptable offer – eight hundred thousand pounds for thirty per cent of the equity. We accepted the offer and the bank was repaid.

Clive decided to celebrate the funding with a month long holiday in Malaga. He returned with the news that he had bought a luxury motor-cruiser for one hundred and fifty thousand pounds. At this point, I decided to move on before he had spent what was left of the funding and ran into debt again.

WIGAN AND VENDING MACHINES

I was surprised to receive a telephone call from the Norwich funder inviting me to a meeting which could lead to more consultancy business. They had invested in a vending machine manufacturer in Wigan along with the local development agency. The vending machine company, located in a local factory estate, had just finished the development of a range of vending consoles, had starting taking orders and employed about twenty people. My job was to review the company's progress, assess the management and rewrite the business plan.

Turning off the M6 motorway just north of Manchester, I headed for Wigan and the offices of the development agency. Their supervising manager, Jim Harborn, was a big, burly man

Tales From A Briefcase

with a beard and glasses. He was softly spoken but had a direct, open approach.

I opened with, "I guess you've received information from the Norwich investor about my assignment?"

"Yes. There was a review meeting on the performance of the company recently, during which we agreed that an outside professional evaluation was needed. Both investors were dissatisfied with the company's performance and we think it may be down to the inadequacy of the managing director."

Jim went on to explain the reasons for the concern. "The MD was a bright young scientist at the local technical college and had worked on the development of a computerised vending machine. It had everything – sophisticated change-giving mechanisms, stock recording, a modem so that a remote operator could read a vending stock and count the change in the mechanism, a local printer to read out transactional details by product and a fault detector. But when it came to marketing and production he didn't have much of a clue. We've had to give support from the local college."

"It sounds as though, technically, he's produced a winner. What's the problem?"

"The market is not the sweet and snack producers, but the vending machine operators who acquire sites at motorway and railway stations. They rarely have funds, and have to borrow the money to pay for the machines and get a credit rating for supply of vendibles. The company's customers are economically unstable and unreliable. Also, the machines have to be technically acceptable to, for example, the chocolate manufacturers – Mars and Rowntrees. Rowntrees have just specified cold storage compartments, increasing the complexity of the product, extending the maintenance requirements, and putting up the price. All of this should have been researched before investment, but wasn't."

"Yes, I can understand the problem. It needs fairly formal market research and that will cost. The problems of production can be easily settled by recruiting the right people. I'll get down to the factory, make an initial assessment of the position, and determine options and costs for moving forward. We should meet in about a week to review my report, which will be pre-circulated to investors."

The factory was modern, covered an area of about four thousand square feet and was almost empty because not many orders existed. I asked for the managing director by name, Doctor Ronald Simmons, and was shown to his office. There I met a tall, thin, dark-haired man with glasses who was about thirty years old; he looked like a professor!

During our first discussion, I found out that, after gaining his first degree, he had stayed on at university for a master's degree in computerised control of machines and then went into lecturing. Later he had obtained a grant to explore the vending machine technology and produced an acceptable prototype. The development corporation had funded the project into manufacturing and involved the Norwich funder as a venture capital investor.

Ronald had no clear idea of marketing and manufacturing, and even lecturers from the local technical college were advising him from textbooks. That evening I checked into a local pub with rooms. Substantial and wholesome evening meals were on the menu and I retired early to bed with a scotch.

Visiting the factory early on the following morning, I found the staff cheerful and helpful and those in technology knowledgeable and competent, but it was clear that there was not an experienced businessperson in sight. My report was finished and circulated three days later. It proposed recruitment of a management team, plus market research and re-engineering of the vending machines. I estimated the cost at a quarter of a million pounds to add to the half million already invested and used.

The review meeting was arranged in a Birmingham hotel and there were two representatives from each investor. My comments and proposals were quickly accepted without reservation until we reached the suggestion for further investment. The development corporation was adamant that they had no further funds to invest and the Norwich company would not put in any further funds unless a third investor was found.

Tales From A Briefcase

Eventually, a third venture capital company willing to invest £250,000 was found and a deals were struck between the three investors. The condition from all was that a new management team was to be recruited. I was given the job of caretaking the company until I had found the new team and settled them in.

Tales From A Briefcase

CHAPTER 35

FREE NEWSPAPERS AND CONCRETE PLANS

HAMPSHIRE AND FREEBIE NEWSPAPERS

Hartley Wintney is a small village on the A30 in Hampshire, south of Reading and north of Farnham. It was an ideal location from which to compose and distribute a free newspaper into the towns and villages of North Hampshire. I was approached by the owner-editor, Raymond Varney, to help him with his cash flow problem.

It was to be my first funding assignment in newspapers, and for me there was much to learn about this industry: news-gathering and reporting, editing, composing, printing and door-to-door delivery. Raymond was part-time editor and had a small, permanent team housed in offices located amongst a row of small shops on the High Street. The business ran on tight deadlines: delivery to the general public by Thursday afternoon, print-run Wednesday night, typesetting Tuesday, all copy, photographs and advertisements ready by Tuesday morning.

The paper was delivered without charge and was entirely funded by advertising fees from different types and sizes of advertisements. Motorcar sales and the large DIY stores provided a regular flow of income, and garden centres and toy shops generated welcome seasonal revenue. Otherwise, there was a steady demand for 'classifieds': things for sale, things wanted, births, marriages and deaths, which were booked by post, telephone and e-mail.

The business was very sensitive to cash flow; whereas most of the small advertisers paid up-front, the larger retailers took one month and sometimes two to pay. In the small end of the

Tales From A Briefcase

newspaper industry, services were provided on a payment up-front basis and any delay in payment by the larger advertising customers immediately produced a crisis, normally on a Tuesday just prior to typesetting and printing.

Raymond and his wife, Fiona ran a successful; bookshop and art gallery, also located in the High Street. She vented her feelings to me on a fairly regular basis.

"I don't know why he wants to be involved in the newspaper. It's more trouble than it's worth. It's always running short of cash and I doubt if it makes a profit anyway. He takes a rather glamorous view of the position of owner-editor yet the business is not worth a bean. We do well on the books and gallery and I need Raymond to help me there."

Raymond and I set about discussing a plan to put the business on a sounder footing. "It's about raising cash from one of two sources," I told him, "private investors or the bank. The business is unlikely ever to pay an investor an acceptable return so we are seeking individuals who feel there is glamour or personal fulfilment in being associated with a local newspaper. Have you any friends who may be interested?"

"No I don't think so but I'll ask around. I've tried the banks before but they seem unwilling to support the business."

"The problem with banks is that they need security against any form of loan. You don't own the premises and I guess that Fiona will not let you put up the bookshop and gallery freehold as collateral. There's virtually no value in the assets that you own: even the computers are on hire purchase. We have to find a bank manager who is sympathetic to the business and its community service."

"How are you going to find such a person?"

"We write a business plan with a convincing story of increasing the advertising income, maybe by producing special editions for high population areas. We need to think how we knock out the other competing freebies or even take them over."

"Huh. Easier said than done. That needs even more cash."

"Well, Raymond, you have to understand that your business is precariously poised – somewhere between success and failure. You have two sensible options; sell it and I'm sure that other

Tales From A Briefcase

freebies would buy it even just for its advertising income; the other is to expand using outside money. I'm happy to explore the bank route for a few more weeks."

We wrote the business plan with a good case for expansion, proposed bank borrowing of £100,000 and trailed it around the high street branches in North Hampshire and Reading. It was perhaps not surprising that the manager of the little branch in Hartley Wintney itself was alone in his interest in the business. After several weeks of persuasion and nail-biting delay, he obtained approval from within the higher echelons of his bank.

Fiona had the last word, "I can tell you Robert, if the money hadn't come this month, I'd have divorced the bugger, taken the shop and gallery and left him to play editor on his own!"

The business was successful in expanding according to the plan. I had the side benefit of it's printer in Worthing asking if I could help them also. They wished to offer a four-colour high-speed printing service to their newspaper clients across southern England. The two new presses, each worth £100,000, came from Czechoslovakia and would need to be leased. Another business plan had to be written and circulated around leasing companies. The funding was approved and before long the printer had won a contract to produce a colour supplement for a national newspaper.

CHEMICALS FOR CONCRETE

"We've been given seven weeks to raise six hundred thousand pounds to buy the company, or the group will sell it or close it. Friends say you are the only person who can help us in the time available."

I looked at the young man sitting opposite me in the lounge of a posh London hotel and took a large gulp of hot coffee while I tried to think through the problem.

"Your friends are very kind but you should understand that we are trying to create a miracle. Most fundings of this size take six months. You know, the published reason why your group is disposing of the subsidiary will have great influence on you raising the purchase monies or not. The best reason is 'disposal of a non-core business and management buy-out' and the worst 'disposal of non-profitable activity'. Can you get the group to push the first idea or say nothing?"

"I think I can do that but what about the seven-week time limit?"

"This size of funding will have to come from local agencies, some government backed. We're trying to save jobs in an area of high unemployment. We should go to the local authority and ask if they can help out; it would be in their interest not to lose the business rate and a hundred jobs from the area. We could go to the coal and steel industries, both of whom invest in companies who provide jobs to take up their redundancies. Then we have the local bank and the enterprise agency, making in all five possible investing parties."

"You haven't answered my question – how long?"

"And you don't know how the game is played. We need to go through some 'maybe' stages before we get to straight proposals and hard decisions. Starting now, two weeks to write a business plan and a further week for the parties to consider and respond. Another week to get round-the-table approval in principle. Thus, four weeks to reveal to the group our potential funders. Then at least another month to get through the legalities. We can't do it all in seven weeks but we will have sufficient ammunition in four weeks to convince the group we mean business!"

"What's our deal with you?"

"One more thing before that. Management will need to raise sixty thousand pounds equity as their commitment to the project before the other investors are likely to come in. Can you do it?"

"We'll have to. Four of us have houses that can be re-mortgaged and some of us have other sources of cash."

"My deal assumes that you will have no cash to pay my fees if I'm successful in raising the funding. I need twenty per cent of the company's equity which you will progressively purchase off me during the three years after funding. OK? I'll put it into a contract. Book me into a local hotel for four weeks and I'll come to Doncaster tomorrow."

On the following day I checked into a little Doncaster hotel which occupied three houses set around a Georgian square in the centre of town. The room was small but comfortable with a shared lavatory down the corridor. The hotel served substantial evening meals and breakfasts. Most of my funding contacts were in Leeds, Wakefield and Doncaster. I managed to produce the business plan in one week by working very long days and, in three weeks, all the parties sat around a conference table in a bank in Leeds, discussing possibilities.

In the following week we made our presentation to the group headquarters in Rickmansworth, extracted the commitment of preferred acquirer status for a period of a further six weeks, and finalized the purchase price and other conditions.

There was no time for entertainment or socializing and I spent every evening after dinner at the hotel falling asleep over a large scotch. Working from an agreement in principle, each investor appeared with his financial and legal advisers and the details were thrashed out. The final purchase agreement from the group was then finalised. The day of signing, involving all the parties, was arranged just eight weeks and two days from the start of the project. Bottles of champagne were opened for the occasion – my clients now owned the company and had saved their jobs.

Tales From A Briefcase

CHAPTER 36

WELSH MATTERS

GAS FIRES IN FLINT

I met John Poland in a London hotel where we found a quiet corner of the lounge and ordered coffee. He came over as a tough Liverpudlian who, over years of hard graft, had built up a company making and marketing modern 'living flame' gas fires in his modern factory on a Flint industrial estate. Thinning fair hair topped a round cheery face, perched on top of a clearly overweight body.

"I'm looking for more cash to invest in more factory facilities," he stated, coming straightaway to the point of the meeting, "I have no problem in selling. My problem is increasing the manufacturing capacity to keep up with the orders."

I sipped my coffee and looked at him more closely. "Your wife also works in the business?" I asked, wondering about heart attacks.

"Yes. Joyce is the administration director. I run production and sales and she runs the rest. She has a big job and I totally rely on her to keep things moving, especially when I'm away. You'll meet her when you come up to Flint."

"Can I see the accounts?"

"Sure. Here are copies of the accounts for the last three years. You'll see a pattern of increasing sales and profits."

Scanning the accounts quickly, I could see that the company had been funded by government grants and bank borrowings. "Your equity to debt ratio is a little low," I told him. "Most lenders would feel that you've borrowed enough already. You are asking them to back your future growth purely on your reading of the market. The national economy could change with unexpected events in the fuel supply market: North Sea gas running down, a war in the Middle East affecting oil prices, imported coal prices rising dramatically. How much do you want?"

"About a million pounds, half for a new factory block and half for equipment. We'll keep going with sales invoice discounting."

I reflected on this for a moment as I thought about low cost European loans and alternative sources of funding. "You've put external equity investment out of your mind – taking on shareholders?"

"Joyce and I have children from our first marriages. The business will eventually support their needs. Anyway I couldn't live with shareholders looking over my shoulder – so no external investors."

We discussed and agreed terms for my assignment

"OK. We're looking for debt finance of a million pounds. The next step is to produce a business plan and present it to the banking world starting with your present bankers, who, incidentally, handle European loans. I'll drive up to North Wales next week and you can get me into a local hotel."

"There's a nice seaside hotel at Colwyn Bay near where we live – I'll get you in there."

On the following Monday, I made the long drive from London to North Wales and, after a busy first day, checked into my hotel, had a meal and went to bed, exhausted.

The Flint factory produced several versions of three basic models of gas fire, each version geared to a major customer's specification, for example the Gas Board showrooms. The fires were decorative and could be purchased with a range of mantle pieces and flame effects. Apart from major customers like B&Q, the company owned a chain of high street retail shops throughout the UK, but the growth of the business came from the DIY chains as they opened new sites across the country.

John spent a high proportion of his time away in the market place, leaving Joyce to deal with the day-to-day problems in Flint. Every penny of borrowed funds was utilised, and the company often ran into cash flow problems involving negotiating and even haggling with the bank or invoice discounters.

Tales From A Briefcase

Further crisis arrived when the telephone in my hotel room rang in the middle of the night: it was Joyce.

"John has had a heart attack in his hotel in London and has been taken to the Westminster and Chelsea hospital. He's in intensive care and I'm leaving to drive down right now."

"Don't drive yourself. I'll organise a private car to take you down – say in half an hour. John's in the best place to deal with the problem. Call me later when you've got a picture. I'll stay with the factory for the time being."

Later in the day, Joyce telephoned to say that John was resting comfortably, would be in intensive care for another day and kept in hospital for some days after that. I advised her to stay in London until John was released – left to his own devices he would discharge himself as soon as he felt better.

From my point of view, John's illness might make the new funding impossible to raise without a management re-organisation. Other key managers had to be found on whom the funders could rely to take on and achieve the business plan.

A week later, John arrived at the factory by private ambulance and was taken to his office by wheelchair. He sat in his executive chair behind the big desk, his eyes gleaming – he had made it back!

"Welcome back," I enthused. "Aren't you supposed to be having a quiet time at home?"

"I just thought I'd turn up to prove to the troops that I'm still alive and kicking."

He went home with a box of files to read, having extracted from me a promise to report to him daily with the latest factory statistics.

I needed to urgently address the question of management. As in most companies with strong entrepreneurs at their head, the quality of second line management was weak, the managers rarely being allowed to make important decisions and learn from their mistakes. John, Joyce and I chatted about this with John getting very excited and red in the face.

"Look," I said, "my proposal is this. Joyce becomes deputy managing director and runs the company on a day-to-day basis. We recruit a financial director from outside and this will put in

Tales From A Briefcase

strength where the lenders believe you are weakest. You appoint your strongest production manager to factory manager. You headhunt the best sales manager from a competitor as your understudy; this will also weaken the opposition. Finally, you sell off the retail shops – they are the least profitable area of your business and absorb a disproportionate amount of management time. The sale of the freehold properties alone will fund your future cash needs."

I sat waiting for an explosive responsive to my proposals. John's jaw was working overtime as he mulled over the ideas, but he held back.

Eventually, I said "Don't give me a reaction now. Talk about it together over the next few days whilst I look at the costs and we can review the proposed plan again. This way you can fund your expansion; we'll take a small loan anyway so there's plenty of money in the kitty, you don't need to appoint new shareholders or even directors. However, I think a family trust might serve your purpose. John, you have a brother who is a successful businessman; I recommend you bring him onto your board."

We met to discuss my proposals a few days later, and John's brother attended the meeting. With few exceptions, the plan was approved and I was given the job to put it into action. The management team was supported by the addition of excellent executives, the retail chain was sold, and funding was arranged for future expansion. Of course John did not slow up and continued working and travelling at a furious pace. I later heard that he had died and that Joyce was doing a marvellous job as chief executive.

COMPLACENCY AND THREATS

"We want you to survey two of our subsidiaries, one in Newtown, Mid-Wales, and the other in Llay in North Wales, near Wrexham."

I was attending a meeting with a director of a Welsh development department at its headquarters in the centre of Cardiff. Previously, I had with some success undertaken

Tales From A Briefcase

assignments for this organisation as an independent business consultant.

"The company in Newtown is in bare, printed circuit board manufacture and employs about eighty in a factory unit on a small industrial estate. Jim MacDonald has been the MD since we funded it three years ago. The company has a poor financial performance and if it can't be improved we will sell it. It's your job to establish its potential and advise on retention or sale. I'll notify Jim about your visit when we have your programme settled. OK?"

"It sounds straightforward enough. There's plenty of competition in the marketplace and from larger producers. As a small producer they need to make profit on short-run work. How long can you give me to evaluate the business?"

"About a month. I thought you could assess the Llay subsidiary at the same time. That is a different story. The company is a hardware/software house manufacturing vertical systems for specific industries. Currently, they are developing a system for small builders – accounts, payroll, sub-contractor records and contract costing. Here we are, a year after funding and nothing to show for our investment. We have our suspicions that the managing director is using some of the company funds for his own purposes. We haven't anything specific on him nor have we time to investigate the situation. He's a difficult customer; he gets angry and foul-mouthed when put under pressure; you'd better watch your step or he'll give you one on the nose."

"Charming! I'll take judo lessons before I go there. What happens if there's substance to the misappropriation of funds?"

"Well, we'll be seeking a new managing director. When can you make a start on these two assignments?"

"I think the week after next. Say the first half week at Newtown and the second at Llay."

"Good. I'll notify both the managing directors of the timing and give them a written copy of your assignment instructions. Please send me a weekly report and come and see me if there's a real problem."

I started my journey to Wales on a Monday, crossing the Avon Bridge in thick fog, and leaving the M4 motorway to head

Tales From A Briefcase

north to Raglan and west on the A40 to Abergavenny and Crickhowell. Turning north up the Wye valley and the beautiful countryside between Builth Wells and Llandrindod Wells, I motored on to Newtown. I found a sleepy little market town set astride a tributary of the River Severn. Having checked into a local hotel in the centre of town, I made my way up to the factory estate.

Clearly, the managing director and his management had soaked up the sleepy and comfortable ambience of Mid-Wales and would never succeed in the competitive world of printed circuit boards. The company was sold 'lock stock and barrel' to another PCB company in Telford.

On Wednesday afternoon I continued my journey from Newtown to Llay in North Wales, following the A483 via Welshpool and Oswestry. The road follows the Severn for some of the way, and then from time to time I caught glimpses of the River Dee and the Llangollen canal. Soon, I was passing Wrexham and on the minor road to Llay, a small coal-mining village.

The mine was no longer worked, but the mine's office building had been developed to house the computer company. I entered and found an administration office where I introduced myself to the accountant, Stephen Williams, who knew nothing of my visit. Stephen was a short, slight man with an open face and a mop of black hair. He questioned me about my purpose and became quite agitated when I decline to reveal it; I came to the conclusion that he would spill the beans if there were any beans to be spilt. Apparently, Mr Vincent, the managing director was out on a business appointment and the office manageress was also away until tomorrow. I booked a meeting with the managing director for eight the next morning on the assumption that he would not start with the rest of the staff.

Next morning I arrived at the offices, where the staff had already started their day's work. Having sat in the waiting room until 8.30, I called Stephen Williams. "Did you advise Terry Vincent that I'd be here at eight?"

"Yes. I called him at his home last night and explained your need for a meeting."

Tales From A Briefcase

I could tell by the way Stephen was shuffling his feet that Terry Vincent had said a few strong words and most likely had decided to keep me waiting.

"Thank you. Here is a letter written by the chairman explaining my role. I wish to meet your technical manager at nine to learn about your computers."

At about ten o'clock, the door of the technical manager's office burst open and there stood one very angry man. His face was bright red and his fists were clenched.

"What the bloody hell do you think you're doing?" he yelled. "Get off these premises immediately."

I replied, "I think we should continue this discussion in your office, where I will give you a copy of my written instructions from the chairman. For the purposes of this visit, I carry the authority of a director of the board and should be accorded assistance and civility as a shareholder's representative."

When we reached his office I quietly asked him if he had received advance notice of my visit.

"Not a bloody dickie bird. I don't know why you're here. I'll not have spies in my company. I will personally throw you off the premises," he threatened, advancing towards me with his fists up.

Clearly he was a bully, but I judged that when someone stood up to him he would back down. "You have refused to comply with a lawful order of the company's owners and threatened me with violence. There are two possible consequences: I telephone the chairman and get the board to evict you, or I will telephone the police and make a complaint of threatened assault, and you'll end up in prison. Or do we talk sensibly about my assignment?"

After a few minutes' thought, he appeared to have quietened. "What do you want?"

"The board is dissatisfied with the company's performance. I am commissioned by the board to undertake a detailed review of the company's operations. I need access to all the company's records and to question staff – without your interference. If you get in the way, I'll have you suspended. I need my own office to work in. Finally, any more threats and you're out."

"I think I'd better stay out of your way. I'll be at home if you need me."

Tales From A Briefcase

"That's alright by me. You'll remain on the payroll while you're at home but you must attend the company when I need you. By the way, where is the office manageress – er, Judy Philips?"

"She's taken a few days leave and will be back next Monday."

He left and I took stock of his office. Large, wood-panelled, drinks cabinet and several doors to other places. The nearest door led to a toilet, nicely furnished; the next to a fully-equipped bathroom leading to a bedroom with double bed and strategically placed mirrors. Good God, what had he been up to!

Over the next few days my researches revealed that he had four company cars; apart from his own, there was one for his wife, two for his teenage children and one for his live-in housemaid who was also on the company's payroll.

Amongst the purchase invoices, I found some from a local flying club for flying lessons and hire of a plane and pilot to the Isle of Man. An analysis of his expenses revealed outrageous claims for entertaining, travel and the best hotels. Clearly Terry Vincent was using company monies to elevate his lifestyle.

I reported all this to the chairman, who gave me authority to deal with the situation in a low-key manner without the press getting hold of it. After all, if the company was a mess, they had some responsibility for letting it happen.

Judy Philips returned to work on the following Monday and it became immediately obvious what her relationship was with Terry Vincent. Surprisingly, she was not good-looking but rather plain and mousy. Faced with direct questioning it became obvious that she was Terry's accomplice in the misuse of funds. She signed a resignation letter without quibbling.

I found out that the board had invested three hundred thousand pounds for a majority shareholding, leaving Terry Vincent with a thirty-five per cent ownership. Asking him to come into the office, I told him of my findings and demanded his resignation and return of his shares. He was speechless and stamped out of the office. At my hotel that night he telephoned me, threatening violence and using incredibly bad language. The next day I contacted the local police and explained the situation; they promised to 'have a word'.

Tales From A Briefcase

The company's solicitor framed a letter asking for his resignation and his shares returned. The alternative offered was criminal proceedings. He complied, but he tracked me for long after I'd left the company and threatened dire consequences on the telephone and in writing.

My report on the company's future was not encouraging and the board thought a disposal by sale would be the best route. I was given the job of interim director and of selling the company. Quite by chance, I met a Californian with a computer company in Silicon Valley who was seeking to purchase a British computer company which could make his Arabic computer for European distribution. I introduced him to the chairman, and persuaded him to buy the company and its building in Llay. I even flew to New York to help him persuade the local stock market to float his stock.

Tales From A Briefcase

CHAPTER 37

VIDEOS, DATA PROCESSING AND JUMBO JETS

VIDEOS AT SHEPPERTON

The road barrier was down as I approached the film studios, just outside the village of Shepperton. A uniformed security man stepped out of the hut at the end of the barrier and came up to the car window.

"Good morning, sir. Which company are you visiting and who are you meeting?"

He was, as most security people are, quite civil and I was happy to provide him with the information: "Kaytec Vision and my 10.30 appointment is with Denis Mitchell and Lucian Bundy."

"Thank you, sir. I'll just telephone to tell them you're here."

He returned to his hut as my eyes swept over several huge buildings in the background, which I surmised must be the film stages.

The security man returned. "Would you please drive up that road for about three hundred yards and park outside Kaytec, which you will find on the left."

I thanked him and drove up to a two-storey building with several cars parked around it and two large boxed-in vans, sign-written with: Kaytec Vision, Field Operations. Entering by the ground-floor door, I approached the reception desk and announced myself to the receptionist, a cheery, round-faced and buxom blonde.

"Good morning, Mr. James. We're expecting you. My junior, Jilly, will take you up to the directors' office. Please sign the visitors' book."

Tales From A Briefcase

I followed Jilly, a rather smart and chatty teenager, up the stairs and into a spacious and comfortably furnished office. A grey-haired man of medium height, wearing dark, horn-rimmed spectacles, stood up from a desk at which he had been seated and approached me.

"I'm Dennis Mitchell, the MD of this outfit. Thank you for coming. I'll order some coffee. Lucian will join us in a minute; he's a talented young man and has the title 'Marketing Director'. I'll explain our management structure in a minute. Please sit down." He extended his arm to indicate a low-slung easy chair behind a coffee table.

He continued, "This is known as a facilities house, which programme makers, normally production companies, can book film and video facilities such as studios, camera and sound equipment and operators, and editing suites. If required, we also hire props and wardrobe and have make-up rooms adjacent to the studios. These are large enough to carry a stage set or a seated audience. Our outside operations unit can take these facilities into the field and transmit the shoots back to the studios here. We can also connect our studios to television channels for recorded or live broadcasts. OK so far?"

"OK. I guess you make money from hiring out these facilities?"

"Yes. We offer a menu of priced facilities and producers select what they need and ask us to quote. We are normally in competition with other facility houses and, if our quote is accepted, we present the client with a contract to sign."

"Does being here on the site of major film studios bring you extra business?"

"Yes. Some features are still shot on film but there is an increasing tendency to shoot digitally onto tape. Producers have preferences; some say that film gives you better image quality and others that digital tape makes for simpler editing. The digital camera crew is usually much smaller than a film crew because the unions are more flexible for that medium. It's down to image and sound quality, speed of recording and editing, and cost. Sometimes we're hired to shoot small sections of a feature to be spliced into that shot with a film camera, and sometimes to shoot

Tales From A Briefcase

in parallel to film cameras to produce a documentary about the making of a film."

"Tell me about your management team."

"Yes, I'll do that now and then later we can tour the studios and you can meet them in the flesh. As I've said, Lucian is young, about thirty, and has a degree in media studies. He's had about five years experience of this industry in various minor roles and has been with me for three of them, in which he's supported me in my work as a film producer. In film production, we normally have a producer whose job is to plan the production and organize all the component parts which come together to make the film. The director does just that, directs all the resources of people and equipment to make the feature. He is responsible for the finished product, image and sound. The producer could be working on a project years ahead of the production date whereas the director is shooting and editing the film rarely longer than a year. Until we took over managing this facility about three months ago, my career was focused in film production and Lucian was my assistant. I'll call him in now."

He dialled a number on his desk telephone and asked Lucian to join him.

I was rather surprised by Lucian's looks as he entered the office. He did not wear executive clothes as Denis had, but was dressed casually in corduroy trousers, a hand printed silk shirt and a scarf knotted around his neck. He was tall and his youthful face was dominated by large round glasses and a shock of blond hair. His handshake was limp and sweaty and he was reluctant to sustain eye contact.

Lucian opened up the conversation. "I'm interested to know what experience you are offering in our industry," he asked without preliminaries and, I thought, with some aggression.

I gave him details of my time with Irish Television and in funding several film and video projects.

"You understand that the board has not yet agreed to engage a consultant to assist them with the bid to the present owners of the studios and with raising the necessary money to acquire them?" His eyes switched to Denis, reflecting both a challenge and a question.

Tales From A Briefcase

Denis stepped quickly in. "This is Robert's first visit. Nothing has been decided or agreed and in any case, proposals will be put before the board. He'll have a quick look round and be invited to submit proposals and terms of engagement. He has already signed a confidentiality agreement. We should speak openly in front of him and tell him of our plans."

Lucian sat back in his chair and shrugged his shoulders; it was clear that a power struggle had already started between older and younger man. I decided to explore this further.

"How many directors and shareholders have you got?"

Denis responded fast, "Lucian and I have eighty per cent of the shares; one external investor has ten percent and two employees each have five per cent - our financial director and technical director."

"So essentially you, Denis and Lucian, control operating policy on a day-by-day basis. Are you unanimous on matters such as service to be provided, marketing and customer selection?"

I could see from the glances exchanged between them that I had hit the nail on its head. Lucian seized the initiative.

"We have two key markets: the pop video sector and that representing current affairs and training. We have business in both. For example, in the first we make videos for the top pop-stars. In the second category we have regular work with several auspicious clients: television presenters, political parties and the like. We've built a sound reputation in the pop market and we could get sufficient work to absorb all our facilities at good prices. In current affairs and training, we're always fighting competitors and our clients demand ever-increasing standards. I feel that we should concentrate on pop videos and Denis feels that we should share our facilities between the two markets."

I registered the trench lines and turned to the other key issue. "What about a bid for the business? Has the seller a leaning towards one or other of the markets? If you are going for a deferred terms deal, the seller will want you to be in a business that he understands and which he believes is more secure. That may be one that the directors may feel takes second place. If you pay outright for it, you will need to bring in more investors from outside, venture capital funders, and I doubt if either or both of you can present a strong enough management case; that route may not be open to you."

Denis jumped in. "Well it's worse than that; the seller wishes the purchaser to take over his video production needs for another three years. If we bought it, we would have to allocate at least a quarter of our facilities to his needs and then at a discounted price."

"Well gentlemen, that settles it. Unless you have a wealthy patron or are prepared to lose the majority of your shares to outside investors you are almost certainly going to have to deal with the disposer on his terms, which may include his retaining a minority stake until you've paid the whole purchase price. We can alter the balance a little in your favour by writing in some of your own protection into the contract."

"What do you propose to do for us?" asked Lucian.

"Only what you can't do for yourselves: publish a realistic four-year business plan, prepare a bid document using outside lawyers, negotiating the purchase deal and raising bank funding."

"What will you want for that?"

"Ten percent of the shares and a thousand pounds a week if the deal proceeds. Nothing if the deal fails due to the bidder not accepting our terms. If the directors abort the project, fifty thousand pounds abort fee for me."

"Bloody hell!" exploded Lucian.

"Look gentlemen, I have plenty of work as a consultant to companies who are prepared to pay me over a thousand pounds a week without risk. To me you represent inexperienced businessmen who have never run an independent business before; you have specialist skills but no track record of running a business profitably. I have. You will need me on board to see this through successfully. Take it or leave it. You can let me know your answer before Friday of this week. Good morning."

I shook hands with them and took my leave, thinking that I may have played my cards too strongly. On the other hand, I had a clear understanding of the risks involved.

I received a telephone call from Denis later in the week, "We want you to take on the consultancy assignment. Will you do it?"

"Well, I need to sort out in my mind how far you and Lucian are apart and decide how we are going to solve the problem.

Tales From A Briefcase

He's a novice at the management game and could turn out to be a real liability. I have to say that I also think he is a bumptious prick! You will need a written contract between you on how you would separate, if things became unbearable – a sort of divorce contract in advance. Also I would like to meet your other two directors before I go any further."

"OK. Send me your proposed contract which I'll get through the board. I'll get the other directors to contact you for an appointment. When can you start?"

"Full time in three weeks and a few days before then."

The telephone rang a few days later, "It's Michael Thompson, the technical director of Kaytec Vision. I hear that we should meet up?"

"Thanks for telephoning, Michael. I suggest that we meet at a pub for a meal any evening this week. What's convenient?"

"Thursday, the Hilton at Slough, seven thirty?"

I agreed, thinking that he was a typical engineer, positive and precise. A little later the telephone rang again. "This is Barbara Eccles, the financial director of Kaytec Vision." I couldn't tell if the low and purring voice was natural or put on for the occasion. "Lucian asked me to contact you about meeting up." I registered the Lucian.

"Oh yes, Barbara, fine. What do you suggest?"

"Well, Robert, I have a riverside flat at Shepperton and we could meet there – and eat there, if you wish? I'll fax you my address."

The alarm bells started ringing in my head – a seduction scene, but to what end and to whose advantage? "When do you suggest," I asked.

"Friday evening at nine?"

"Yes, fine."

Had Lucian got her to play his agenda to me? Did she need my support for her own scheme? I decided to telephone Denis. He answered my call quickly.

"Oh, hello Robert. Your contract will be in the post to you tomorrow. What can I do for you now?"

"Really, just one question. Are there any personal allegiances by the other directors to Lucian and yourself?"

"I've known Michael Thompson for some years. We're friends and I respect his technical ability. He'd vote my way under pressure. Barbara I'm not sure about. She appears on the surface to be her own person but I've heard from others that Lucian has been paying her a lot of attention recently. Why do you ask?"

I reported on the arrangements to meet Michael and Barbara.

"I wouldn't think she would set you up at this stage of the assignment. Nobody has played any cards yet. I can't see any advantage to revealing support for Lucian at this point."

Agreeing with him, I rang off. However, I resolved to check directors' contracts and shareholders' agreements at the earliest opportunity to assess who could get rid of whom and under what circumstances.

The meeting with Michael Thompson went very amiably. He was a very competent engineer and had introduced many technical innovations which had saved money for the company or generated more business. Under my further questioning he disclosed his concern for the relationship between Denis and Lucian.

Friday evening came and I prepared myself for the meeting with Barbara. A suit and a briefcase seemed appropriate props for a business meeting in social circumstances. The apartments, right at the water's edge, were newly built. I pondered on the cost and how a single junior accountant was able to afford the luxury. Pressing the appropriate button on the communication system, I was invited by a tinny voice to push open the door and go upstairs to a numbered flat.

The door opened. "Good evening, Robert. Welcome."

She was bare-footed, accentuating her shortness and her casual dress emphasised a shapely figure. A music system was quietly playing a romantic tune and the lights were low, low enough to make me feel uncomfortable.

"Please sit there." She indicated a deep sofa with large cushions and turned to remove a bottle of champagne from an ice bucket. "Be a sweetie and open it for me."

Feeling even more uncomfortable, I removed the cork expertly and poured champagne into two long-stemmed glasses.

Tales From A Briefcase

Taking a glass, she asked, "To what shall we drink?"

"A successful acquisition of the studios. What is your toast?" I replied, trying to keep the meeting on a formal track.

She lifted her glass and sipped. "That's not very exciting. Mine would be new adventures, new friends, more of the unexpected."

I looked at her, thinking this is where I nip these games in the bud.

"You know Barbara, I've been in business a very long time, travelled the world extensively, met quite a few friendly ladies and avoided some tricky honey-traps. I feel that you are setting me up. I'm intrigued to find out if you are doing all this for yourself, or for someone else. I think it would be interesting to discuss your take on life and where you're going."

She took another sip of her drink. "O.K. I'll tell you about me. You can hear that I'm a Mancunian. Mum and Dad were poor but they got me into a grammar school and I went to UMIST to study Business Economics. I was a swat and got a first. My first job was with the Accounts Department at Ferranti and I studied for an accountancy qualification part-time. When I qualified as a chartered accountant, I was promoted to be an accounts manager in Ferranti.

"When I was twenty-six, I met a young trainee accountant. We became lovers and lived together. I became pregnant and he and I decided that I should have an abortion and we should separate. I lost my job and returned to the foot of the accountancy ladder doing the accounts for a number of small firms, first in the Manchester area and then in London. Over a year ago, I met Lucian in a local wine-bar. He introduced me to Denis and I was appointed finance director of Kaytec. I negotiated a good salary, some shares and a directorship."

"That's quite a story. Do you have a relationship with Lucian?"

"We're not a regular item but we get together from time to time"

"And Denis? What do you think of him?"

"He's old fashioned, hasn't got Lucian's spark and is not hard enough to be a businessman."

"Lucian's spark is refreshing but he hasn't got the business experience to manage the company. I'm sure that many business professionals would agree with my opinion."

"Ah. That's where I come in. With me behind him controlling the company, he would measure up as a marketing director."

"I've heard that he's a big spender on entertainment – in fact, he buys the orders. Is that true and how would you deal with it?"

"I would be managing director and he would have an expenditure budget. If he overstepped the mark he'd be sacked."

"So there we have it. Your personal aim is to control the company and you seem prepared to do almost anything to achieve it, including buttering me up. However, being honest, I don't think you are qualified to be chief executive of this company. I don't think anyone on the board is. In my book it would be an outside recruitment."

She went quiet, her face becoming immobile and unreadable. I looked at the decorative gas fire and sipped my drink. "Shall we break off this meeting right now?" I asked.

She perked up immediately. "Not bloody likely. I've cooked a meal for you and you're going to eat it. I'll put it on." And she headed for the kitchen.

She served a casserole of pork loin with perfectly cooked vegetables. It was delightful.

"You've been married or lived with a man, haven't you?" I queried.

"Yes," she said, "I was married for three years. He wanted babies but my abortion had apparently disturbed my reproductive processes. We agreed a divorce so that he could find a mother for his future children."

"You've had a tough life and you appeared to have built a wall around yourself. The real you is buried deep inside, and the 'you' on show is a tough business manager with shallow emotions and a lively libido. Let's talk about how you continue towards the top job. What age are you now?"

"I'm thirty-two."

"There's plenty of examples of women making it to the top of large organisations. You should use this one to cut your teeth

Tales From A Briefcase

as a director and prepare yourself for the next step up. Neither Denis nor Lucian is going to help you much towards your ambition, and they could positively block your progress by their non-performance. If you stay, you must take an active part in controlling the business towards growth in sales and profits, making them appear successful. You won't get much of the glory, but you will be learning the job of a chief executive in preparation for the day when you become one. Right now, I need you in the team to achieve some tricky business deals."

"That sounds good and I appreciate your interest in my career. I'll think over what you say."

"Good. But my final advice to you is, don't show your hand and don't take sides with either of the principle directors. You'll be meeting top finance people in the near future and they will be asking you for your opinion. Give it to them as your own and be honest."

"Would you like to stay over?" she asked rather coyly.

I was still not really sure of her allegiances. "Barbara, we both have rather complicated issues on our hands. Let's keep our relationship simple and professional."

I left feeling that, underneath it all, she was a little lost girl who had experienced a rough deal in life but had plenty of guts to achieve her business ambitions as long as she didn't get distracted from them by men.

* * *

I sat in the conference room with the company's four directors. Denis spoke, "We would like you to be chairman for the foreseeable future. We have signed your contract and are now eager to get down to the business of funding and acquisition."

I looked at each director in turn, and they nodded their agreement, even Lucian.

"Right. The main items on the agenda are – business plan, acquisition bid document, negotiation with the vendor, arranging funds. We'll now allocate people to jobs and review progress every day."

It was a few days later when I found myself in the office of the financial director of the vendor, a large group in the construction sector. They had originally bought the studios to make promotional films but found that other work had to be brought in to absorb the capacity and make them economical. The director was a Greek Cypriot, and the fact that my mother was of the same nationality helped the discussions along.

The acquisition price, although important, was not to be the main consideration; continued support in production of their promotional films was paramount. I negotiated a four-year buy-out of the contract price of £600,000 with an annual level of corporate film output at fixed, discounted prices. The deposit was to be delivery of films currently in production at no cost. If Kaytec collapsed or failed to meet the acquisition terms they would re-acquire the studios. If the vendor failed to meet the acquisition terms, ownership passed to Kaytec. On the face of it, it was an easy deal.

A local bank, provided with a copy of the draft contract, agreed to provide a four-year bank loan of £100,000. New agreements were prepared for shareholders and directors. As long as the company could find £175,000 a year to pay off its commitments, the shareholders would own a company worth several millions.

About six months after acquisition, the company's marketing expenditure was on the agenda for the board meeting. A fierce argument broke out between Denis and Lucian on budgets for each market. I decided to close the meeting and see them individually.

"What the hell is going on between you two?" I asked Denis.

"He's going round the staff saying that he's going to depose me and those that back him will be viewed in a favourable light. He's polarised the staff into two camps and we are both giving them conflicting orders. Staff morale is down and the clients are getting to hear about the problem; when they ask, they're getting two versions, his and mine. We've even had a few booking cancellations."

"But you are the managing director and what you say goes. He has no authority to make statements about the company, internally or externally. We'll soon be faced with reviewing the situation against the separation agreement; this says that in a case of dispute between the major shareholders, one may make a bid to acquire the other's shares, the price to be mutually negotiated or fixed by an external professional body. There are, however, other controlling circumstances – the acquisition agreement and the bank loan agreement. In either case, an un-resolvable dispute between shareholders will invalidate the acquisition terms and the company returns to the vendor.

"On the board we have four executive directors and me as chairman with a casting vote. I will not take sides, but will feel obliged to notify the vendor and the bank without delay to protect my own professional standing. I intend to see Lucian now and call a board meeting in an hour. The agenda is board harmony and insolvency."

Lucian's reaction to my statement of the situation was petulant and almost childish. He confirmed he could not raise the money to buy out Denis. I warned him against making derogatory statements to the staff and clients and threatened him with suspension in the coming board meeting unless he agreed to desist.

The board assembled and I explained the company law position and the implications of a split board vote. Denis and Lucian confirmed that neither could mount a buy-out. They also agreed that clients and potential clients had got wind of the dispute and that orders had been cancelled. I forced through a restraint order on Lucian by using my casting vote – Barbara had voted in support of Lucian's position. Finally, I gave the board three days to present a resolved position or I would tell the vendor and the bank that the company could not continue to operate.

Three days later, the board was unable to propose a resolution of the conflict and I notified the vendor. At a meeting with the vendor's finance director I was advised that they would immediately invoke their take-back option, appoint me as executive chairman and gave me authority to suspend Kaytec's directors, if I wished. They also agreed to meet the bank and provide a guarantee to cover the loan.

I returned to Kaytec, called a board meeting to announce the vendor's decision, and advised the directors of their new responsibilities under the new arrangements. The staff were assembled and I announced the vendor's take back and the intention to continue to operate the company, including paying their salaries. Those wishing to resign could do so at their own will, but would forfeit all accrued employee benefits. This seemed to calm the atmosphere and everyone return to normal working.

We brought in valuation specialists to assess the net worth of the company, and a shock result was announced. All the main equipment was mostly non-digital for which selling prices were dropping rapidly as new digital equipment came onto the market. The studio building itself belonged to the owners of Shepperton Studios. On the open market, on a distress sale, Kaytec was virtually valueless.

The vendor advised the bank and it was agreed that the company should be declared insolvent and all the staff made redundant. Receivers were appointed, dealt with the staff redundancy arrangements and auctioned all the equipment and furniture. I was the last to leave, locking the doors and returning the keys to the site office.

Later I met Barbara in the village.

"What came over you?" I asked her. "You could have avoided taking sides and maybe opened up a new opportunity for yourself."

"I discussed the possible outcome with Lucian; he proposed marriage and I've accepted. We're both looking for jobs. Can you help?"

"No, I won't have anything more to do with Lucian. You'll both soon realise how the cold, outside world values your limited expertise and come to understand what an opportunity you have thrown away."

DATA PROCESSING IN CARDIFF

I had been commissioned by a South Wales company to get them some bank funding. Now, on my first visit, I was making a tour of the premises.

The clatter of forty tape-punching machines made it impossible to hear speech and one could barely hear the pop

Tales From A Briefcase

music blasting out from a radio playing at maximum volume. Each operator pounded the keys of a machine at somewhere between two and four keys a second and kept at it for two hours at a time before taking a ten-minute break.

The tapes were for use with mainframe computers. A typical application was for the gas or electricity boards, whose metermen visited customers' houses and recorded the readings on to a ticket. The punch operators recorded the readings on to tapes and the computers calculated the usage and costs for the accounts departments, which sent out the bills.

It was an extremely monotonous job requiring sustained attention. Young women were best at the job, particularly those single mothers who were the sole household earner. They were paid by the number of key-stokes and, by working up their speeds and working longer hours, could earn a living wage. They bonded well together and often had girlie nights out, got drunk at nightclubs and picked up men.

The offices of the company were on the Treforest Industrial Estate just north of Cardiff, and most of the operators came from within a five-mile radius by car or bus.

The owner of the business was Don Hebden, a Mancunian by birth, who had very early on seen the opportunities afforded by computerization and by the processing contracts which would be placed by the utility suppliers. He had built up a reputation for accuracy and timely delivery, and his South Wales business had expanded rapidly. He had also established a similar operation in central Manchester.

Don, of medium height and about fifty years old, was a dapper man, well dressed and conscious of his looks. Aftershave and other gentlemen's toiletries featured strongly in his ablutions; you could smell him across the room. He was a fair boss and the ladies loved him but he always gave the impression that he was made uncomfortable by their close presence; they sensed this and stood close to him with blouse buttons opened. He would return to his offices after such an encounter, very flustered indeed.

"Robert, did you see that Mary in the punch room. Her blouse was opened right down to her waist. She leant forward and I could see her nipples," he would complain with a straight face, but obviously pleasantly stimulated.

"You two-faced lecher," I responded, "you'd have them wearing topless uniforms, if you could!"

He blushed and straightened his tie. "No, I wouldn't. That's going too far."

He employed a manageress to supervise the punch operators, a tall thin blonde named Lesley, with good legs and small breasts. Regularly, after a meeting with her, he would return to his office in a highly excited state saying, "I could do things to her!"

Later on in my consultancy assignment, he brought his wife to meet me for dinner at my hotel. She turned out be a shapeless person of shallow intellect and I could understand how all these beauties at the office affected him so much.

He had another problem which tainted an otherwise pleasant man; he was miserly. Every company bill was scrutinized intensively and argued out with the supplier. To save money he decided not to use a lawyer to sell a Manchester property but prepared his own contract of sale. The deal was never concluded and resulted in him in having to dispose of the property at a lower price and sell his Manchester business at a knock-down rate. Unfortunately, this was accompanied by his South Wales business losing some major customers and he soon had troubles with the bank.

By working hard to get new accounts and reducing his own lifestyle, he managed to keep his data punching business alive and become involved in website design, which at that time was an up-and-coming activity. He became more focused on the business and aware of his limitations. I left him with the business stable and expanding, and headed back to the gentler environment of the Southeast.

LIVERPOOL AND JUMBO JETS

As the millennium approached, the early versions of the Boeing 747 jumbo jet had been flying for thirty years, some years beyond their design life. During that period the plane had proved

Tales From A Briefcase

itself a strong, safe passenger carrier and about nine hundred were flying in three versions of the original model. Ownership of these planes had changed hands several times over this period, with the larger international airlines selling off their older versions to the developing nations or for use as freighters.

When the planes were withdrawn from service for longer maintenance schedules, it was noticed that stress cracks were becoming prominent in the front fuselage, involving the first class section and the cockpit.

My clients, aviation consultants in Sussex, were given the task of designing a large repair facility which would replace nose sections on the older aircraft to extend their lives. The UK, Australia, Nevada and Hong Kong were earmarked for the new repair facilities. For the UK, the old fighter aerodrome near Liverpool Airport was selected as a possibility. The facility would be designed to house three jumbo jets, wing-tip to wing-tip.

I was asked by the aviation consultants to be the funding specialist for the project with a view to raising funds from central government, the local authority, and private enterprise.

The commercial airport and its nearby disused airfield were owned by a large national aerospace company. In talks with them, it was established that they had no interest themselves in servicing wide-bodied jets and they were reluctant to dispose of the old aerodrome. There was also political posturing taking place between the parties involved in the future development of Liverpool Airport as a transatlantic facility in competition with Manchester. The government was very much in favour of the repair project, which would create over a thousand jobs on a Merseyside now suffering from high unemployment.

My clients and I made our first presentation to the chief executive of the local authority, which at the time had its own internal political problems. Although the labour government at the time made a serious attempt to support the project, there were too many privately owned interests to meld into a common cause. The project foundered on the drawing board and the facility was later established in the Far East.

Tales From A Briefcase

CHAPTER 38

BUSINESS ADVENTURES WITH PETER

We sat drinking coffee in a London hotel. He was a charming man of medium height, thin of stature, well dressed, with grey hair and a captivating voice.

"I keep seeing all those advertisements of interesting businesses for sale and I would like to bid for some."

"Have you got any money to buy them?" I asked, rather naively.

"Well, no but you're the fund-raising expert. If there are any good buys, you should be able to raise the money for me."

I could see that he thought I could walk on water. "Well, it's not that simple. Some will be broke with owners trying to make money by selling the ashes. Others will have developed the companies to respectable sizes and earnings and are trying to make a killing. It's rare that one can borrow money to make a purchase; the thing to do is to find an investor who sees an opportunity to double his money in four of five years."

"Well look at this one," he said, waving a Financial Times advertisement under my nose. It was for an Essex company specialising in rubber technology products with a factory of about eighty people and selling in several markets. "I telephoned the accountants handling the sale and have arranged an appointment to view. Can you come along? I'll buy you lunch." It was for next Friday and I felt that I could lose a day.

The factory was on an estate that had probably been built just after the war. They made bouncy castles, large advertising balloons, decoy tanks and targets for the army and navy. Long rolls of coloured, treated rubber were pulled out on to long tables, cut to a pattern and fed into heavy-duty sewing machines. Products like bouncy castles could leak air slowly because, in

291

use, they were coupled to air pumps to keep them inflated. Other products, such as balloons, had to be manufactured air-tight and therefore needed more precise construction. In fact, the company had started its life in the war as a barrage balloon manufacturer.

The accountants provided us with the financial results and it soon became clear that sales had fallen away and the company was loss-making. Acquiring the workforce, the designs and the factory would not lead to a proposition attractive to an outside investor. We had a good lunch in a local pub and decided not to pursue it any further.

The next advertisement we followed up concerned a factory that made flags, flagpoles and marquees. They had branches all over the country which rented out marquees for outside events, such as the Farnborough Air Show. We were shown around by the company secretary, a pleasant old gentleman long past retirement age. The company was owned by the three widows of its founders, who wanted to sell. The company itself was controlled, rather haphazardly, by long-serving managers with little knowledge of modern management techniques, computers and accountancy; they were totally opposed to the sale. Looking at the accounts, I could detected that the customers paid their invoices very slowly and the debtors were extremely high in vale; factoring the debtors would achieve a lump sum which would more than pay for the company's acquisition. Peter was very excited as we, the only bidders, put in our bid. Later, it was declined and the sale was withdrawn.

Next we headed for Stoke on Trent. A large chinaware group was disposing of its factory producing low-cost mugs to concentrate on higher quality products. The factory was over a hundred years old and the production methods were from the post-war period. It was obvious from our tour that considerable investment was needed in automated or semi-automated machines and that many hard-working and skilled staff would lose their jobs. It was not an opportunity in which we could interest a funder. We had another good pub lunch and headed for home.

It was a long drive to Spalding in Lincolnshire where we inspected a plant company which sold its wares direct to the

Tales From A Briefcase

general public via a catalogue. The plants were grown in both Lincolnshire and Holland and the main factory was given over to receiving orders, packaging and posting. It was owned by a shifty-eyed Dutchman who appeared not to want to sell but was just testing the market price of his company. We had another superb pub lunch and headed home.

In case you are beginning to think that our relationship was founded on wasting time and eating pub lunches, I should mention that Peter had started a successful business in high quality shirts. They were made by contractors in Britain and Turkey and sold to customers in America and Japan. He decided to search for an English shirt-maker in decline due to lack of sales, of which there were several. Many of the English shirt manufacturers were being knocked out of business by the cheaper prices of Far Eastern producers.

We listed possibilities and targeted our first approach – a company in Kent. It was a family business run by an aged man and his sister. The multi-storied building, an old mill, was much in need of repair. There was no lift and materials had to be carried from floor to floor. The equipment was very old, thus involving a labour-intensive operation. The quality was, however, of the highest standard.

The company was short of work and short of cash and would soon be out of business. Peter fed them some orders to sustain them until we had assessed the possibility of raising funds to modernize the business. Again the owners declined to sell and mortgaged their private houses to stay in business.

I introduced Peter to southern France and now he and his wife are property developers and gite owners in Bergerac. Their children go to French schools and are fluent in French. He has lost the lust for acquiring companies and is enjoying his new French lifestyle, relaxed and just basking in the sunshine.

Tales From A Briefcase

EPILOGUE

Robert James decided to pack it all in. Business consultancy no longer gave him the buzz that it used to. Although he had been in consultancy for more than twenty years, he had to admit to himself that he had been a better industrial manager than an advisor. His knowledge was rapidly growing out of date, and his experience had been overtaken by changes in management styles and by rapidly advancing technology. Unions were no longer present as a strong force of opposition, to be fought and subdued by a skilful management.

Companies were getting smaller in terms of numbers of employees, and no single chief executive today would be allowed the scope of authority and responsibility that he had enjoyed in the sixties and seventies. Industrial society had become 'buttoned down', and jobs were now limited and confined by tightly-drawn job descriptions.

Even in the smaller companies, which represented Robert's consultancy clients, the harsh world of survival and the more distasteful relics of Thatcherism had turned decent people into monsters of greed and lack of human decency. Workers had responded to their employers' disregard for their well-being – poor contracts of employment, changing working hours to accommodate Sunday working, using outside workers from agencies, not managing their pension funds properly – by reducing their commitment and loyalty to their companies. Many now worked for themselves and from home.

Yes, he would pack it in. But a person active in body and mind couldn't just stop everything, retire to watch television in the sitting room and sleep long hours. Nor was it wise to moan about how the world had changed for the worse – and was that really so, anyway? So he became an author, initially writing stories remembered from a long and busy life and, later, developing new creative skills as a novelist.

Tales From A Briefcase

Printed in the United Kingdom
by Lightning Source UK Ltd.
107763UKS00002B/49-255